Acting with Technology

Acting with Technology
Bonnie Nardi, Victor Kaptelinin, and Kirsten Foot, editors

Acting with Technology

Activity Theory and Interaction Design

Victor Kaptelinin and Bonnie A. Nardi

The MIT Press
Cambridge, Massachusetts
London, England

MIT Press books may be purchased at special quantity discounts for business or sales promotional use. For information, please email special_sales@mitpress.mit .edu or write to Special Sales Department, The MIT Press, 55 Hayward Street, Cambridge, MA 02142.

This book was set in Sabon on 3B2 by Asco Typesetters, Hong Kong, and was printed and bound in the United States of America.

Library of Congress Cataloging-in-Publication Data

Kaptelinin, Victor.
Acting with technology : activity theory and interaction design / Victor Kaptelinin and Bonnie A. Nardi.
    p.   cm.
ISBN-13: 978-0-262-11298-7 (hc : alk. paper)
ISBN-10: 0-262-11298-1 (hc : alk. paper)
1. Human–computer interaction. 2. Design—Human factors. 3. User interfaces (Computer systems). 4. Action theory. I. Nardi, Bonnie A. II. Title.

QA76.9.H85K45   2006
004.01′9—dc22   2006042040

10 9 8 7 6 5 4 3 2 1

Contents

List of Figures

List of Tables

Acknowledgments

We would like to thank the following people for helpful comments on earlier drafts of chapters and for discussions about activity theory: Michael Cole, Paul Dourish, Yrjö Engeström, Martha Feldman, Kirsten Foot, Victor González, Jonny Holmström, Kristo Ivanov, Gloria Mark, Kenneth Nilsson, David Shaffer, Clay Spinuzzi, Kaushik Sunder Rajan, and Phillip White. We profited from the thoughtful comments of three anonymous reviewers and appreciate their input. Bob Prior and Valerie Geary at MIT Press provided excellent advice and support. The fall 2004 ICS 230 course at the University of California, Irvine, offered useful advice on an early version of chapter 3. Victor Kaptelinin is indebted to Aleksey Nikolaevich Leontiev and Vladimir Petrovich Zinchenko for introducing him to activity theory. He would like to thank the Department of Informatics at Umeå University for constant support. During work on the book Victor Kaptelinin was partly supported by VIN-NOVA, Swedish Governmental Agency for Innovation Systems. Bonnie Nardi would like to thank her employer, the University of California, Irvine, for valued colleagues and a hospitable environment in which to write. We would both like to thank our families for their patience as significant mindshare was at times taken up by the book.

I

Activity Theory in Interaction Design

1

Introduction

This book is about developing activity theory as an approach to the investigation of information technologies in the context of human practice. *Acting with technology* is a phrase to position our relationship to technology as one in which people act intentionally in specific ways with technology—ways that we can study and for which we can produce effective designs.

Activity theory was introduced to an international audience in the late 1970s and early 1980s through two publications: the English translation of Leontiev's *Activity, Consciousness, and Personality* (1978), and a collection of papers by Leontiev and other activity theorists edited by James Wertsch with an excellent introduction by Wertsch (1981).

But until the 1990s, activity theory was effectively standing in Vygotsky's shadow. Vygotsky's approach had become popular in the West, having a substantial impact on a wide range of research in psychology and cognitive science (Cole and Scribner 1974; Wertsch 1985; Hutchins 1995), education (Lave and Wenger 1991), and computer support for collaborative learning (O'Malley 1995; Koschmann 1996a). International interest in activity theory increased dramatically during the 1990s, judging from the frequency of citation of key works in activity theory (Roth 2004). A number of papers and books published during that time (e.g., Engeström 1990; Bødker 1991; Nardi 1996a; Wertsch 1998; Engeström, Miettinen, and Punamäki 1999) contributed to the increased awareness of the ideas and potential of the approach. According to Roth (2004), part of the credit for the uptake of activity theory should be given to Yrjö Engeström, who "through his publications and presentations in a variety of disciplines spread the word...."

The aim of *Acting with Technology* is to provide a thorough understanding of activity theory through a systematic presentation of its principles, history, relationship to other approaches, and application in interaction design. A decade ago, *Context and Consciousness: Activity Theory and Human–Computer Interaction*, a volume edited by one of us, and to which both of us contributed chapters, was published by the MIT Press (Nardi 1996a). *Context and Consciousness* presented a variety of positions and arguments unified by the common objective of making the case for activity theory as a potential theoretical foundation for human–computer interaction. *Context and Consciousness* contributed to the turn to contextual approaches in HCI, foregrounding an understanding of activity as central to the concerns of specialists in human–computer interaction.

The present book has different ambitions. *Acting with Technology* addresses three questions:

1. What impact has activity theory had on interaction design? We present and discuss key results of interaction design research based on activity theory.

2. How does activity theory relate to other theoretical approaches in the field? We contextualize activity theory in the ever-changing theoretical landscape of interaction design by way of a comparative analysis of current approaches.

3. What does "activity theory" really mean? Activity theory is sometimes considered an "esoteric" approach (Engeström 1999a) because systematic introductions to its main principles, intended for general audiences, rather than enthusiasts, are nonexistent. In this book we make an attempt to put together a primer in activity theory, to deliver activity theory "in a nutshell."

The domain of the book is *interaction design*, understood in a broad sense. The term has been used in the human–computer interaction (HCI) and computer-supported collaborative work (CSCW) communities (Winograd 1996; Preece, Rogers, and Sharp 2002; Bannon 2005; Pirhonen et al. 2005), and by those in the field of digital design who see their work as related to but distinct from human–computer interaction (Wroblewski 1991; Gaver, Beaver, and Benford 2003; Löwgren and Stolterman 2004). Löwgren and Stolterman (2004) defined interaction design as "the process that is arranged within existing resource constraints to create, shape, and decide all use-oriented qualities (structural, functional, ethical, and aesthetic) of a digital artifact for one or many clients." This definition reveals some reasons for the shift to the term "interaction design": it is not only computers, but digital artifacts of all kinds that interest us, and not only the computational abilities of such artifacts, but the totality of their potentials.

Winograd (1996) defined interaction design as "the design of spaces for human communication and interaction." This definition is similar in spirit to that of Löwgren and Stolterman, but more general. While Löwgren and Stolterman suggested a context of design in workaday settings, invoking clients and resource constraints, Winograd's definition can be construed as covering a wide range of issues, from empirical studies with design implications to work in hands-on design settings.

Interaction design is a broad term inflected in different ways in different communities. To us, interaction design comprises all efforts to understand human engagement with digital technology and all efforts to use that knowledge to design more useful and pleasing artifacts. Within this arena, the main audiences for this book are those who conduct work in the fields of human–computer interaction, computer-supported collaborative work, computer-supported collaborative learning, digital design, cognitive ergonomics, informatics, information systems, and human factors.[1]

Activity theory fits the general trend in interaction design toward moving out from the computer as the focus of interest to understanding technology as part of the larger scope of human activities. HCI began with the notion of a "user." Researchers developed a set of core concepts that advanced the field, such as "user-centered design," "the user experience," "usability," "usefulness," and "user empowerment" (Norman and Draper 1986; Thomas and Kellogg 1989; Cooper and Bowers 1995). Expanding these notions, Bannon (1991) coined the memorable phrase "from human factors to human actors" to emphasize actors in social contexts, consonant with the concerns of CSCW. More recently, attempts to incorporate human activity in interaction design have led to ideas of "activity-based," "activity-centered," or "activity-centric" computing (Norman 1998; Christensen and Bardram 2002; Geyer, Cheng and Muller 2003; Harrison 2004; Muller et al. 2004; Millen et al. 2005) and "activity management" (Moran 2003). These efforts seek to provide a richer framing for interaction design that more closely matches how people actually use technology at work and play.

While it is helpful that such notions of activity-based computing acknowledge the general importance of the meaningful context of interaction between subjects and the world, it is crucial to move to concrete understanding of what activities are. Activity theory can help bridge the gap between insights about the need for broader perspectives and the need for specific tools for thought. As we attempt to study human activities "in the world" (Bannon 2005), we will encounter issues long of interest to activity theory. We believe that activity theory fits a niche opened by the emerging sensibility that studying interaction and activity is essential to the development of interaction design. The basic principles of activity theory underwrite the emphasis in interaction design on the social, emotional, cultural, and creative dimensions of human actors in shared contexts.

Today activity theory is an approach that has transcended both international and disciplinary borders. It is used not only in Russia, where it originated, but also in Australia, Belgium, Brazil, Canada, Denmark, Finland, France, Germany, Italy, Japan, Norway, South Africa, Sweden, Switzerland, the UK, the United States, and other countries. It is applied in psychology, education, work research, and other fields. In this book, we discuss activity theory in the context of interaction design, but in appendix B the interested reader can find information and web links to international conferences, journals, and discussion forums devoted to research based on activity theory from a variety of perspectives.

The book consists of three parts. In part I we give an overview of the basic concepts of activity theory and how they have been used in interaction design research. We discuss the need for theory in interaction design in chapter 2. We explicate the fundamentals of activity theory in chapter 3. We describe applications of activity theory to practical problems of interaction design in chapter 4. We provide a detailed example of an application developed with activity theory in chapter 5.

In part II we turn to more advanced issues. We discuss the notion of the object of activity in chapter 6, describe the use of this notion in an empirical study in chapter 7, and review the history of activity theory, with a focus on key debates that shaped the development of the approach, in chapter 8.

In part III we draw on the discussions in parts I and II to outline current issues and future theoretical development in activity theory. In chapter 9, we compare activity theory with its leading contenders in interaction design—distributed cognition, actor-network theory, and phenomenologically inspired approaches. In chapter 10, we delve more deeply into issues regarding agency and asymmetry raised in chapter 9. We conclude in chapter 11 with some reflections on the future of activity theory.

If we have any advice to our readers, it is to be alert to the coherent whole that is activity theory. As we have explored other theories and empirical research, we sometimes have the sense of seeing a piece of activity theory developed independently. For example, early in his career, Herb Simon discussed the way people conserve "mental effort by withdrawing from the area of conscious thought those aspects of the situation that are repetitive" (Simon 1945). This sounds very much like the operational level of the activity hierarchy in activity theory. Without in any way critiquing Simon (who was not developing a psychological theory but rather describing organizational behavior), we can point to the way such insights crop up as "one-offs" across the theoretical landscape. In activity theory, the operational level is one of three linked levels in the activity hierarchy, not an isolated insight. Another example closer to home is that of GOMS models, which resemble the activity hierarchy but lack an activity level and the possibility of dynamic changes between levels that are part of activity theory. We hope to encourage a holistic reading of activity theory and a cognizance of the way concepts weave together into a patterned whole. Some of the power of activity theory lies in the way it ties insights into larger wholes to provide a clarifying framework for the bigger picture.

In this book we advocate and evaluate the continued development of activity theory as a basis for understanding how people act with technology. We hope to use theory to stimulate great design—the design of digital technologies that address the needs and desires of specific individuals and groups. We also want to understand the fundamentals of our human relationship with technology. These designs and understandings will include the usual activities that we know as the practice of interaction design, but may also stretch to less familiar projects involving how we act with technology, such as analyzing the impact of technologies on the environment or understanding the role of technology in viewing our spiritual relation to the cosmos. Though such projects may appear beyond the scope of interaction design, the technologies we design inevitably have major impacts in these arenas. If we are to continue to deepen our understanding of what it means to act with technology, such concerns will impinge on, and sometimes become central to, our labors.

Activity theory seeks to understand the unity of consciousness and activity. It is a social theory of human consciousness, construing consciousness as the product of an individual's interactions with *people* and *artifacts* in the context of everyday practical activity. Consciousness is constituted as the enactment of our capacity for attention, intention, memory, learning, reasoning, speech, reflection, and imagination. It is through the exercise of these capacities in everyday activities that we develop; indeed this is the basis of our very existence.

This social approach rooted in practical activity contrasts with, for example, biological explanations of consciousness that focus on genetically coded capabilities, or neuroscientific views that situate explanation at the level of nerve tissue, or the Jungian view positing universal archetypes accessible through dreams. Traditional cognitive science attends to representations, casting them as entities that can be modeled equally well for computers as humans. Freudian explanations focus on a small set of early social relations with parents and family. Activity theory proposes that consciousness is realized by *what we do* in everyday practical activity.

To take a simple example, let's consider how an activity theorist might analyze a young child learning arithmetic. Activity theory looks for key people in the child's universe and useful artifacts. In many cultures, children learn math from their teacher who explains numbers and arithmetic operations to them, and encourages and motivates them. The children may also consult more experienced peers. Children initially perform calculations on their own bodies, counting on their fingers silently until they have internalized addition and subtraction. The fingers come into play as a useful "artifact," appropriated by the child as a marking device to aid in counting. Once the child has mastered the facts of arithmetic, the calculation shifts to what activity theorists call the internal plane of actions, and the math is done in the head.

Part of what is distinctive about this formulation is that it goes beyond the representation of the arithmetic problem, beyond the bare bones of the arithmetical processes, out to the environment where the teacher, the friends, and the fingers are. These aspects of the child's universe are essential to our understanding of how the child learns arithmetic. Most theories miss these aspects, or see only one—perhaps the teacher, or the way the problem is represented on paper. In activity theory it is the *doing* of the activity in a rich social matrix of *people and artifacts* that grounds analysis.

This insight was expressed thousands of years ago in Eastern thought. In speaking to Vasettha, Buddha described the primacy of activity in human life:

> One is not a brahmin by birth,
> Nor by birth a non-brahmin.
> By action is one a brahmin,
> By action is one a non-brahmin.
> So that is how the truly wise
> See action as it really is.
> Seers of dependent origination,
> Skilled in actions and its results.
> Action makes the world go round
> Action makes this generation turn.
> Living beings are bound by action
> Like the chariot wheel by the pin.[2]

It is striking that the central image of this poem is a technical one, the chariot wheel with its pin. Here the poet intimates the close link between human action and the technologies that support it. Activity theory has developed the insights of the poets in a scientific idiom, delineating a set of core principles that frame the study of all human activity (see Zinchenko 1996).

We have found the principles of activity theory to be of help as we consider our own chariot wheels and how we design and use them. For several years we have advocated activity theory as a framework for thinking about human activity as it is expressed in the use of technology (Nardi 1992, 1993, 1996a; Kaptelinin 1992; Kaptelinin, Nardi, and Macaulay 1999; Bannon and Kaptelinin 2002). We have observed a steady and growing uptake in the adoption of activity theory among those who find a theoretical framework useful for negotiating the thickets of users and their needs, and technologies and their possibilities. We have been drawn to activity theory because of certain of its tenets that are encapsulated in the notion of people acting with technology. These tenets are:

- an emphasis on human intentionality;
- the asymmetry of people and things;
- the importance of human development; and
- the idea of culture and society as shaping human activity.

Let us first consider intentionality. We live in an ever increasingly designed world, furnished with technologies at every turn. Despite the clearly intentional nature of the act of design—behind every design there is an intention—many of our theories lack a concept of intentionality. In acting with technology, people deliberately commit certain acts with certain technologies. Such a mild statement, seemingly devoid of theoretical freight, is in fact at odds with theories such as actor-network theory and distributed cognition. These approaches posit a sociotechnical network whose generalized nodes are actors that can be either human or artifact. Such actors represent states that move through a system—whether the actor be a pencil or a person. Intentionality is not a property of these generalized nodes. Activity theory distinguishes between people and things, allowing for a discussion of human intentionality.

More broadly speaking, activity theory posits an asymmetry between humans and things—our special abilities to cognize through interactions with people and artifacts are distinctive from any sort of agency we could sensibly ascribe to artifacts. In activity theory, it is essential to be able to theorize intention, imagination, and reflection as core human cognitive processes. Accounts in which people and artifacts are the same deflect such theorizing.

In activity theory *people* act *with* technology; technologies are both designed and used in the context of people with intentions and desires. People act as *subjects* in the world, constructing and instantiating their intentions and desires as *objects*. Activity theory casts the relationship between people and tools as one of *mediation*; tools mediate between people and the world.

Another principle of activity theory is the notion of *development*. Activity theory shares the commitment of the cultural-historical school of psychology because of its commitment to understanding how human activity unfolds over time in a historical frame. Activity theory takes the long view: we cannot understand activity if we do not watch it cycle, grow, change. It would be desirable to establish a practice of design in which the development of users—their ability to grow and change with technology—is of paramount importance. In activity theory, development is a sociocultural process, but the individual is not reduced to society or culture. The dialogical nature of processes of internalization–externalization makes it possible for individuals to transform culture through their activity. As a psychological theory, activity theory has always had a strong notion of the individual, while at the same time understanding and emphasizing the importance of the sociocultural matrix within which individuals develop. As we will discuss in chapter 9, the individual is an important theoretical concept because of the need to account for the interrelated processes of creativity, resistance, and reflexivity. These processes take place in part within individuals as people have the capacity to radically restructure cultural conceptions, transcending culture in unpredictable ways.

Technological creativity is rooted in our primate past. Nonhuman primates can "think out of the box," developing and sharing simple tools to transform their activity. For example, capuchin monkeys have been observed using sticks to reach food (Beck 1980). The great apes, especially chimpanzees, have more sophisticated tool capabilities. In the wild, chimps may use assemblages of anvils and hammers to crack tough nuts (Mercader, Panger, and Boesch 2002). An individual animal in its own well-known environment can suddenly recognize a solution to a problem, and come to see an object as a tool for some useful purpose. As with humans, nonhuman primate development is cultural; tool use among higher primates is specific to distinct animal locales, with local tools and cultural practices providing knowledge of how to use the tools.

How does grounding our theory in a concept of intentionality and the asymmetry of people and things, as well as a strong notion of development, help us as interaction designers? We believe there are several benefits. First, such a theory can provide a matrix in which to reflect on our own practice, to arrange what seem to be disparate threads into a coherent framework. For example, the adoption of approaches such as participatory design and contextual design are responses to the larger problem of addressing the gap between the intentions of designers and the intentions of users. The continuing search for techniques of end user programming (Lieberman 2000) speaks to an unfilled need to increase end users' abilities to realize their own intentions so they can grow and develop over time, becoming increasingly adept with their technologies. The design of agent-based user interfaces, which seek to enact high-level intentions while sparing users the details, is one approach to bringing intentions into the user interface. The current state of designing and using information technologies in education also clearly indicates the importance of taking intentionality into consideration. There has been a growing realization that to have a positive impact on education, technologies should be designed to support purposeful actions of the human actors involved in everyday educational practices (Gifford and Enyedy 1999).

A second benefit of a theory grounded in intentionality, asymmetry, and development is that it can frame discussions of users' continuing frustrations. We do not have to go far to find users who are stymied in realizing their intentions because the technologies offered them are neither usable nor useful. And users often feel daunted by the rapid pace of technological change, which makes it ever more difficult to become skilled with a given technology. Only a decade ago, it was possible to write optimistically about "gardeners and gurus" (Gantt and Nardi 1992), those office experts who became especially proficient with the technologies in use in their local settings and could help their less technically inclined colleagues. Today, because technologies change more rapidly and work groups are less stable, we cannot be as sanguine about the role of local experts in the ecology of a given work setting. Activity theory's attention to issues of development commits us to taking such issues seriously.

The third benefit is that of reckoning with the long-term impact of the technologies we design. If a historical developmental perspective frames our view, we cannot merely hope for the adoption of the technologies we intentionally design; we must consider wider impacts. For example, the batteries and components of wireless devices contain arsenic, antimony, beryllium, cadmium, copper, zinc, nickel, lead, and brominated flame retardants—all toxic. Wireless devices, including cell phones, pagers, PDAs, pocket PCs, portable email readers, and mp3 music players, are being manufactured by the billions. Yet we have not designed or implemented adequate means of handling the wastes they release. Toxins leach into groundwater when wireless devices are discarded in landfills, and dioxins are created when they are incinerated. Used cell phones (and computers) are often donated to Third World countries, so the waste reaches its final resting place in the air and water of the poorest countries (see *Waste in the Wireless World: The Challenges of Cell Phones*, 2002). As designers, how do we respond to these realities?

Activity theory is self-reflexive, and we are encouraged to find ways to inform our own development. To mitigate the harmful effects of, say, the wireless devices we design, we might look to the fields of architecture and manufacturing which are working with techniques of "green design," "lifetime design," and life cycle assessment. While such a move might seem an unmanageable increase in the scope of our efforts, other disciplines have adopted these concerns as part of their practice. When our theories reveal intentionality and historical development as visible theoretical constructs, we are more likely to entertain conversations about long-term effects than if our theories conceal them. Miettinen (1999) noted that understanding the historical development of human consciousness is needed to make sense of the relations between humans and their environment. Such an understanding is critical when the aim is to analyze the work of constructing associations between heterogeneous entities and the work of creating "new assemblies of materials and humans" (Miettinen 1999).

Activity theory opens up avenues of discussion concerning human interaction with technology and potentially can be fruitful in encouraging participation in conversations about the larger global concerns that the deployment of our technologies unquestionably affects. If we are *acting with technology*, both possibilities and responsibilities expand. The object of this book is to stimulate further discussion of the theoretical basis for understanding how people act with technology.

2

Do We Need Theory in Interaction Design?

In this chapter we analyze the need for theory by discussing the impact of cognitive theory on interaction design and the challenge mounted against the cognitivist approach by the situated action perspective growing out of ethnomethodology. We suggest practical reasons for developing and using theory in interaction design. Following the distinction between "first-wave HCI" and "second-wave HCI" introduced by Cooper and Bowers (1995), we position activity theory as a second-wave theory, a representative of a group of interaction design theories that encompasses postcognitivist approaches.

2.1 CHALLENGING THE COGNITIVIST PARADIGM

A coupling of cognitive psychology and computer science brought forth the field of human–computer interaction in the early 1980s (Carroll 2003). HCI adopted the information-processing paradigm of computer science as the model for human cognition. Researchers created user models, conducted experiments to study factors underlying efficient use of the user interface, and emphasized usability. A burst of immense creativity, much of it at Xerox PARC, delivered the graphical user interface, a novel, usable framework for user interaction. The methods of experimental cognitive science were applied to improving graphical user interfaces (Johnson et al. 1989) and they are now in use by millions.

Despite this success, challenges to the cognitive paradigm began to appear as early as the mid-1980s. The limitations of the traditional information-processing paradigm were demonstrated in seminal books by Winograd and Flores (1986) and Suchman (1987). By the early

1990s, these limitations were acknowledged in the mainstream HCI community (see Kuutti 1996). Some expressed a "generally pessimistic view" of the power of cognitive theory to affect the development of HCI (Tetzlaff and Mack 1991). The trend toward the need for a broader focus in HCI research and development was identified by leading researchers such as Grudin (1990) and Bannon (1991).

Suchman's book *Plans and Situated Actions* (1987) provided a cogent critique of cognitivist thinking, arguing against the idea that the enactment of algorithmic plans underlies human action. While the critique was aimed at artificial intelligence research, it called into question the more general assumption that human cognition can be modeled as a computer program. Artificial intelligence researchers believed that their programs, which searched "problem spaces" according to preset goals in order to arrive at decisions or other outcomes, were descriptive of both human cognition and intelligent computational performance (Newell, Rosenbloom, and Laird 1989). Suchman proposed instead that the resources of the immediate situation shape human action. Human action is "situated," or ad hoc, she argued, responding opportunistically and flexibly to those resources. People are improvisatory. Computer programs may follow algorithms, but people do not.

This refreshing view imparted much-needed critical reflection on the cognitivist approach. In a deft stroke of Popperian falsification, Suchman undermined key cognitivist assumptions by way of a carefully developed counterexample involving experiments with copy-machine users who were shown *not* to be following algorithmic plans as they struggled to make copies (Suchman 1987).

A major clearing of the air had taken place. However, this significant critical moment did not lead to the development of a new theoretical foundation for interaction design. The work in situated action had developed from an unusually rebellious antitheoretical branch of sociology known as ethnomethodology.

Ethnomethodology, a small but influential subfield of sociology founded by Harold Garfinkel (1967), took as its project the description of how people produce orderly social conduct. Ethnomethodologists argue that orderliness is enacted as people draw on resources in their environments, resources with which to improvise meaningful action. Action is not preordered by anything that can be reduced to theoretical princi-ples; rather, the analyst considers specific instances of organized action, and describes those. An ethnomethodological account is often a sequen-tial depiction of moment-by-moment actions analyzed as responses to events in a "local scene of action" (Lynch 1999). Ethnomethodology is a serious attempt to discover and document the "methods" or "common-sense knowledge of everyday activities" of members of some natural language group (Garfinkel and Sacks 1970). A key task for ethnometh-odologists is to study

> members' methods for assessing, producing, recognizing, insuring and enforcing consistency, coherence, effectiveness, efficiency, planfulness, and other rational properties of individual and concerted actions. (Garfinkel and Sacks 1970)

This undertaking was a response to an overly formalized, sterile soci-ology that paid little attention to subjects' own rich understandings of their experience. Ethnomethodology took a respectful attitude toward subjects, acknowledging their deep expertise, much like anthropology's approach to attaining comprehensive knowledge of subjects' understand-ings of their cultures (Lynch 1999).

Despite an innovative research program, ethnomethodology was a completely renegade activity within academic sociology. Garfinkel and Sacks felt that what was necessary was not a compromise with tradi-tional formal theories, but a complete rejection of the whole idea of so-ciological theorizing. They even discouraged students from reading such theorizing (see Lynch 1999). This rejection pushed ethnomethodology into a radical antitheory position, where much of it remains today. Such-man (2000) explained that ethnomethodology "refuses the call to engage in theory-building" in order to "recover" practical activity in "its endless detail." The ethnomethodological view prescribes that we avoid general-ization and abstraction. Lynch (1999) noted that "Garfinkel and Sacks explicitly reject general theory and turn to 'naturally occurring,' 'actual,' 'real-worldly' sources of insight and inference."

Is an atheoretical focus on the recovery of endless detail a good idea? One answer comes from anthropology. Anthropology went down the atheoretical path early in the twentieth century, when squabbles erupted between "historical particularists" who believed anthropology's mission was to document human cultures in intensive, atheoretical detail, and generalists who were looking for theoretical principles such as cultural evolution. Historical particularism is little practiced now; it became increasingly difficult to justify simply collecting more and more detail about various cultures. Anthropology has turned to distinctly theoretical pursuits. Though new squabbles have been launched, they are played out within sophisticated theoretical arenas.

Mainstream sociology also rejected description as an end in itself. For example, Brint (2001), evaluating the study of community in sociology, observed that purely descriptive work is no longer conducted and "must be judged a failure." Descriptive work on community "failed to yield a cumulative set of generalizations about human social organization ... and has largely disappeared from contemporary sociology." Hollan, Hutchins, and Kirsch (2000) advocated that HCI develop theory to "free research from the particulars of specific cases," as we move to identify and understand the "important constituents" of interaction among people and artifacts.

Thus atheoretical accounts that substitute description for theory face the same obstacles that positivism created for itself. Lacking a theoretical compass, there is no way to know where to begin. And it is impossible to cover, or recover, all the details; a descriptive infinite regress sets in immediately upon trying.

Antitheory such as ethnomethodology struggles with its own contradictions. The very idea of the orderliness of human conduct is itself an abstraction. The work of studying orderly conduct through the empirical investigation of specific instances amounts to the development of a theoretical principle, much as investigating instances of species diversity is part of the work of developing a theory of biological evolution. That human conduct is "orderly" is not itself a foregone conclusion. Human conduct might be studied as chaotic, or as swinging between order and disorder, or as order within chaos. The assumption that specific instances of organized action can be studied theory-free is without ground. All observation is a view from somewhere.

The difficulty of atheoretical social science is illustrated by the development of ethnomethodology itself. Its most studied area, conversation analysis, is notable not for vivid descriptions of talk grounded in specific instances, but for the revelation of the existence of general rules of conversation. The ethnomethodological theory of conversation has produced a set of well-documented rules characterizing orderly conversations, such as turn-taking, repair, and back-channeling. As it is actually practiced, then, an important area of ethnomethodology has embraced just that which it set out to reject—accounts of general rules and principles of action. These accounts have, over the years, become more and more technical, documenting in minute quantitative detail the techniques by which conversations are managed. And the accounts are patently theoretical: conversation is explained as being orderly because people follow specific well-established rules (see Pollner 1991).

Perhaps the technicalization of ethnomethodology is understandable because of the difficulty of producing arresting accounts, again and again, of specific instances of organized action. Looking once more to anthropology, we find only a few practitioners, such as Clifford Geertz, who are noted for riveting "thick descriptions." Geertz is a superb writer, rendering a Balinese cockfight, a Moroccan souk, even Javanese rice paddy farming, with the skill of a novelist (which he at one time planned to be). Not many can carry it off.

Beyond the struggle to write well, what can we say about the status of accounts from the situated action perspective? Dourish (2001a) observed:

> [Situated action] rejects abstract depictions of action and argues instead that we must see the orderliness of action as derived "bottom-up" from the local, situated activities of actors. This model places the real-time, real-space activities of social actors—embodied actions—before abstractions or theoretical accounts of them. (Dourish 2001a)

Dourish pointed out that there is a *model* here, and as such, it must be selective, artifactual—a *rendering* of "bottom-up" activities. A model must not, however, be confused with the embodied actions themselves. We have only the menu and do not want to suppose it is the meal. The call to place embodied actions before abstractions summons precisely this confusion, a confusion that dwells uneasily beneath the surface of ethnomethodological accounts. Lynch, himself a respected ethnomethodologist, acknowledged the precariousness of employing terms such as "naturally occurring" and "actual." It is not possible to reproduce events in such a way that accounts would be "actual" in any sense (Lynch 1999).

Suchman (2000) observed that ethnomethodology resists "turn[ing] lived experience and embodied practice into general lexicons and associated models." While such resistance has a place in challenging overly formal sociological accounts, it is problematic when pushed even a little. If lived experience is not "turned into" models, what is the nature of the account? The account cannot be coterminous with the lived experience. The actions and practices have come and gone with the passage of time. We have only representations, which of necessity are abstractions. We fashion these representations to the best of our ability, but inescapably shape them with our viewpoints, perspectives, constructs, and theories in doing so. We use lexicons and models to explicate what we think we have understood. We do not "recover" practice, which, as a lived thing, passes beyond us as time advances.[1] The word cannot, at least within the scope of science, be made flesh. To represent our accounts as "natural" or "actual" is to obscure the culturally specific application of theory that shapes all accounts.

Ethnomethodologists themselves do not get by without lexicons and models. For example, Goodwin (1994) developed notions of professional practice such as "highlighting for perception" and "professional vision," notions invoked by Suchman (2000) to investigate the practice of civil engineering. While these concepts seem innocuous compared to gorillas like "cultural evolution" or "the unity of consciousness and activity," they initiate a slide down the slippery slope of theorizing, moving beyond description of specific instances of organized action.[2]

Sacks et al. suggested that ethnomethodological work is "context free, yet context sensitive" (quoted in Button and Dourish 1996). This statement expresses the contradictions of ethnomethodology but does little to clarify matters. Lynch commented on Garfinkel's own theorizing:

> Despite his disclaimers about theorizing, Garfinkel again and again enunciates a comprehensive vision of how "the ordinary society" organizes itself ... through its members' use of methods of all kinds ...: formal and informal, tacit and explicit, expert and ordinary, efficient and inefficient, rational and non-rational, methods for analyzing other methods, etc. and etc. (Lynch 1999)

The final words of this long sentence point to a key tension in ethnomethodology. At the beginning of the sentence it is made clear that ethnomethodology is about order in society. By the end, ethnomethodology's yearning to break free of theory sets in motion a most disorderly "etc. and etc." So devout was the attachment to the details that Lynch recalled that Garfinkel demanded that his students *master* the practices they studied. This extreme participant-observation left some struggling to become adepts in such fascinating but difficult endeavors as truck driving and Tibetan argumentation (Lynch 1999).

Ethnomethodologists themselves have suggested that ethnomethodology has had a limited practical impact on interaction design because of what Button and Dourish called the paradox of technomethodology:

> Given the concern with the particular, with detail, and with the moment-to-moment organization of action, how can ethnomethodology be applied to the design of new technology? Certainly, ethnomethodologists have urged that designers take into account the methods and actions through which social action, interaction, and categories of work are organized; but in the face of the unavoidable transformational nature of technology and system design in working settings, it would seem that ethnomethodology becomes relatively powerless. (Button and Dourish 1996)

Lynch (1999) observed that in ethnomethodology "the vision projects a picture, but it does not deliver a foundational theory that sets up a coherent program of ... research." Ethnomethodology, he suggested, can be thought of as an "attitude" of "indifference" in which what is "*not take[n] up*" (emphasis in original) is "a social science model, method or scheme of rationality for observing, analyzing, and evaluating what members already can see and describe as a matter of course."[3]

Our critical analysis of ethnomethodology does not, of course, question the fact that key developments in interaction design can be credited to ethnomethodology. The critique of the cognitivist paradigm was fruitful in encouraging new lines of investigation and in helping interaction design move toward a wider range of accepted pursuits such as the inclusion of social and organizational factors in human–computer interaction and computer-supported collaborative work (Grudin 1990; Bannon 1991; Carroll 1991, 2003). Ethnomethodologically inspired research helped to extend the scope of interaction design and chart new territories of inquiry with thoughtful empirical studies. Button and Dourish (1996) suggested that designers can learn from ethnomethodology by developing system "accounts" that "continuously offer [representations] of their own behaviour and activity, as a resource for improvised and contextualized action." Such an approach could open up computer systems by allowing them to provide more of their own detail to users. This seems an innovative and potentially useful application of ethnomethodology.

Ethnomethodology is "indifferent" toward theory, but its attitude of respect toward subjects in their own practice—those for whom we design—is important. This commitment to respecting those we study and their deep understandings of their own practice is critical as we develop technologies that often dramatically alter those practices. Button and Dourish (1996) remarked that as designers we might profit by ethnomethodology's "respectfulness for the notion of improvised design, or for the social production and use of representations."

2.2   THE NEED FOR THEORY

The situated action approach growing out of ethnomethodology shook up the cognitivist paradigm. But ethnomethodology's attitude of indifference toward theory left interaction design without a means of theorizing what situated action claimed to be missing—the social and contextual aspects of human activity. Might we get along without theory, as Garfinkel and Sacks proposed? Why exactly are we searching for a postcognitivist theory for interaction design? In this section we discuss some practical reasons for theory in interaction design.

Most broadly speaking, theory forms community through shared concepts. While we will never achieve perfect communal unity in vocabulary and concepts (and would not want to), without some theoretical connective tissue we cannot speak to one another (Carroll 2003). We cannot merely relate accounts of endless detail with no summarizing, shaping, transforming tools at hand. We need the power to compare, abstract, and generalize.

Theory also helps us make strategic choices about how to proceed (Halverson 2002). The results of comparing, abstracting, and generalizing will always be provisional and mutable, but they will attain enough recognizable form that we can take stock and prepare for the next step.

An absence of theory is an absence of "dialogicity," that is, the opportunity to juxtapose different points of view so that each may illumine the other (Mannheim 1936; Bakhtin 1981; Miettinen 1999). Theory encourages multivocality by its very nature: theories are exactly testable, dynamic, contingent things, designed to be subjected to critique, revision, or complete reformulation. Theory gives voice to multiple points of view by inviting—or rather demanding—critiques, revisions, and reformulations. To eschew theory is to endorse a unitary point of view in which a single activity becomes a closed endgame.

To move forward, to know where to invest our energies, we have need of theory. Otherwise we will always be going back to the square one of detailed renderings of particular cases. As interesting as the cases might be, we have no way of assessing whether they are typical, whether they are important exceptions to which we should pay particular attention, or if they are corner cases we do not have time for at the moment (see Kaptelinin 2002). We cannot discuss trends or look for commonalities across cases that could help us determine where to place our bets. Miettinen (1999) observed that positivistic empiricism was hobbled by a lack of theory. He asked, "How is it possible to decide what is important and essential and what is not without theoretical preconceptions?" Whittaker, Terveen, and Nardi (2000) argued that interaction design will advance more quickly when we develop means of utilizing reference tasks, an approach that has been successful in other related fields such as speech processing. Reference tasks demand intensive comparative work and a willingness to follow standard scientific methodologies of generalizing and seeking principles applicable across cases.

We believe that theoretical frameworks will facilitate productive cooperation between social scientists and software designers. Not only can such approaches help formulate generalizations related to the social aspects of the use of technology and make them more accessible to designers, they can support reflection on how to bring social scientists and software designers closer together, much as cognitive science and computer science found common ground in a shared model. The adoption of activity theory approaches by software designers is evident in work such as that of Barthelmess and Anderson (2002), Collins, Shukla, and Redmiles (2002), Fjeld et al. (2002), Zager (2002), and de Souza and Redmiles (2003), as well as researchers collaborating with software designers such as Bellamy (1996), DeCortis, Rizzo, and Saudelli (2003), and Gay and Hembrooke (2004).

Richard Rorty (1991), a philosopher of pragmatism, asked why the enterprise of science, with its theories, has been so successful. He concluded that science produces results that many people find valuable; in other words, science works because it delivers things people want. Scientific theories are not perfect representations of reality, noted Rorty, but they are good enough for important human purposes. Rorty observed that knowledge "[is not] a matter of getting reality right, but rather ... a matter of acquiring habits of action for coping with reality." There is no single correct vocabulary of knowledge; different vocabularies suit different human purposes (Rorty 1991). Writing about activity theory, Barthelmess and Anderson (2002) echoed this view, saying,

> The value of any theory is not "whether the theory or framework provides an objective representation of reality" (Bardram 1998), but rather how well a theory can shape an object of study, highlighting relevant issues.

Science and theory succeed because they attain desired objects often enough to keep the activity moving forward. Despite uneven progress, mistakes, and miscalculations, science has steadily expanded human knowledge in ways that people find worthwhile.

2.3   CHALLENGES IN INTERACTION DESIGN

The two approaches that have been dominant in interaction design at different times in its history are, in a way, mirror images. The cognitivist approach is based on a well-developed and highly structured conceptual framework that allows for generalizable models. These models are relatively easy to convert to design. However, the scope of the approach is too narrow; as discussed earlier, it ignores many issues critically important to interaction design. By contrast, ethnomethodological accounts often succeed in providing rich depictions of practice, but the accounts are not generalizable and are difficult to relate to designers' concerns (Button and Dourish 1996).

In our view, the history of conceptual developments in interaction design suggests that the search for an adequate theoretical foundation should be carried out somewhere in the middle of the territory marked by these extremes of cognitive science and ethnomethodology. The theory must meet two criteria: it should be (a) rich enough to capture

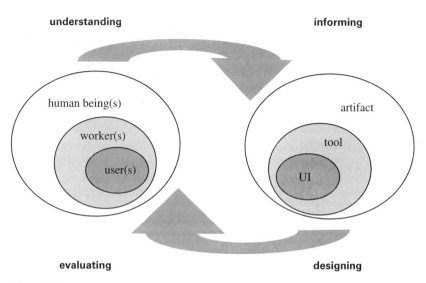

Figure 2.1
The expanding scope of interaction design.

the most important aspects of the actual use of technology and (b) descriptive and generalizable enough to be a practical, useful tool in interaction design, as suggested in figure 2.1. Figure 2.1 sketches a post-cognitivist perspective that incorporates the complexity of real practice, widening analysis to include a cycle of evaluation and design in which people and artifacts influence one another.

The arenas in which we believe we will get the most leverage from theory are those involving complex systems with multiple actors and objects. The focus in design is changing from a knowledge worker using a desktop computer to: (a) collaborative uses of technology by groups and the larger society, (b) varied virtual and physical contexts, (c) an expanded set of activities (including those conducted at home), and (d) human experience in general, not just cognition. Of particular interest are the ways individual and collective activities are linked, negotiated, and managed over time.

Recent trends in interaction design include emotion in design, extending usability to include the "pleasurability" of interactive products (Norman 2004), technology as experience (McCarthy and Wright 2004), the technology of connected presence (Licoppe 2004), persuasive technologies (Fogg 2000), affective computing (Picard 1997), affective design (Aboulafia and Bannon 2004), autonomous characters (Tomlinson 2005), performative design (Kuutti, Iacucci, and Iacucci 2002), context-aware computing (Dourish 2001b), cultural probes (Gaver, Dunne, and Pacenti 1999), and intelligent buildings and workspace integration (MacIntyre et al. 2001; Nardi et al. 2002; Kaptelinin 2003; Fisher and Nardi in press).

Let us consider some examples of the trends mentioned above. Systems designed to promote e-democracy may involve thousands or millions of users collaborating to elect a candidate or influence a legislative body (Foot et al. 2003; Robertson 2005). New forms of disseminating publications online, such as full-service digital portals, require negotiating what it means to be published, finding the best ways for digital materials to be widely disseminated and retrieved, and integrating documents and services for communities served by portals. New modes of publication such as blogs and wikis may penetrate beyond small groups to larger arenas such as political conventions and campaigns, or loop back to print publication as authors gain devoted audiences. Scientific collaboration is growing in scale in disciplines such as molecular biology and ecology, creating the need for better digital tools (Baker, Bowker, and Karasti 2002; Zimmerman 2003).

New technologies such as robotics and nanotechnology pose interesting user interface challenges. We have some science fiction scenarios to help us imagine interacting with advanced robots, but what about invisible machines small enough to clean our teeth or deliver medication intravenously?

Work itself is changing. Work is more distributed, more contingent, less stable. How do we understand social forms such as networks and virtual teams that partially replace standard organizational hierarchies (Mortensen and Hinds 2001)? Many workers experience constant interruptions (Kirsh 2001; Czerwinski, Horvitz, and Wilhite 2004; Fussell et al. 2004; González and Mark 2004). This reality needs to be taken into account as we design. Knowledge work usually involves multitasking and working with diverse groups and individuals. Efforts to design technologies to meet these conditions benefit from careful theoretical analysis of workers' activities (Kaptelinin 2003; dePaula 2004; Morteo et al.

2004; Fisher and Nardi in press). Work is not accomplished simply with mental representations but involves complex, flexible assemblages of diverse tools arranged by workers to meet their particular needs (Spinuzzi 2003).

Interaction design is not all work and no play. Online games with thousands of participants playing in persistent worlds herald new forms of global collaboration. We are just beginning to see the formation of ways of interacting that involve little if any face-to-face interaction. MMOGs or massively multiplayer online games, are less than a decade old but engage millions of players worldwide. Several million copies of Lineage 2 have been sold in Korea, and references to the game permeate Korean pop culture (Whang and Kim 2005). MMOG characters are bought and sold on eBay. Friendships are formed in the games, and players collaborate to kill enemies, heal the wounded, and engage in all the other high fantasy actions of the games. Experience in these games may translate to other arenas such as work and school. The social networks formed online in games and other venues may shape social interaction in unexpected ways (Wellman 2001).

Education is also changing. The information transfer model is being supplanted by constructivist approaches influenced by Vygotsky. Digital educational tools in this emerging tradition are gaining ground (Cole 1996; Koschmann 1996a; Pea 1999; Sharples 2000; Haythornwaite 2002; Roschelle and Pea 2002; DeCortis, Rizzo, and Saudelli 2003; dePaula 2004; Gay and Hembrooke 2004; Stahl 2006). And design itself is evolving. New digital environments for more collaborative design are the result of careful theoretical analysis (dePaula 2004; Fischer 2004).

A theory offering a set of basic concepts to guide systematic exploration of the ever-expanding universe of complex and often confusing issues could be of enormous help in modern interaction design. Such a theory could support researchers and designers by structuring ways to approach the object of study, breaking down problems into smaller, more manageable subproblems, setting priorities, and establishing the relative importance of research issues.

We believe that activity theory could be useful for such efforts. The focus of activity theory is on *purposeful, mediated, human social activities*. A fundamental insight of the approach is that the understanding and design of technology should be based on analysis of its role and place in activity. The concerns of interaction design can include moral and ethical issues (Friedman 1997), cultural diversity, social implications, critical analysis (Muller 1999), emotions, feelings, and spirituality (Muller et al. 2001). With its developmental perspective on purposeful mediated actions in a social context, activity theory plausibly addresses the widening purview of interaction design.

Shneiderman (2002) identified five types of roles and uses of theories (which are not mutually exclusive): (1) descriptive theories identify key concepts or variables and make basic conceptual distinctions; (2) explanatory theories reveal relationships and processes; (3) predictive theories, such as Fitts' Law or GOMS, make it possible to make predictions about performance in a range of potential contexts; (4) prescriptive theories provide guidelines based on best practice; and (5) generative theories facilitate creativity, invention, and discovery.

Activity theory can play at least three of these roles. First, it is a descriptive theory that identifies a number of fundamentally important concepts such as mediation. Second, it is an explanatory theory that suggests mechanisms explaining why and how certain phenomena take place (e.g., internalization and externalization). And, it is a generative theory, with application to problems of interaction design (discussed in chapters 4 and 5) as well continuing theoretical development (discussed in chapters 6, 7, and 10).

The search for theory in interaction design also includes the postcognitivist approaches of distributed cognition, phenomenology, and actor-network theory. These approaches are discussed in chapter 9 and compared to activity theory. In the next chapter we introduce the fundamentals of activity theory, presenting them in the historical context in which they were developed.

3

Activity Theory in a Nutshell

3.1 INTRODUCTION

The inspiration for this chapter comes from Aleksey Leontiev's *Activity, Consciousness, and Personality* (1978), the most authoritative exposition of activity theory. This "small theoretical book," as Leontiev himself described it, is not an introduction to activity theory, but a collection of essays, each focusing on a limited set of fundamental theoretical concepts. Leontiev specifically emphasized that many issues were mentioned only in passing and not clearly articulated in the book. Currently there is no standard systematic, entry-level introduction to activity theory. There is a clear need for such an introduction, especially in interdisciplinary fields such as interaction design where not everyone may have encountered original works by Leontiev, Vygotsky, and other key contributors.

This chapter is intended as a primer in activity theory. It introduces the reader to key ideas, concepts, and principles of activity theory. The chapter is different from most other short introductions to activity theory (e.g., Wertsch 1981; Davydov 1990a; Bødker 1991; Kuutti 1992; Nardi 1992, 1996a, 1998; Blackler 1995; Kaptelinin, Kuutti, and Bannon 1995; Kaptelinin 1996a; Kaptelinin and Nardi 1997; Verenikina and Gould 1998; Bertelsen and Bødker 2003). These works typically summarize the basic ideas of the theory, while giving the historical development of the ideas much less attention. Such summaries appear to be the only feasible approach, given the space limitations of a journal article or a conference paper. We ourselves have used this approach on more than one occasion. However, according to our experience, this way of introducing activity theory is not always effective. The underlying ideas of the theory are difficult to grasp without an understanding of where the ideas come from. In this chapter we use a different approach. The main focus here is on the historical development of activity theory which is followed by a summary of its basic concepts and principles.

The chapter deals primarily with the version of activity theory developed by Aleksey Leontiev within the general framework of what is known as "Vygotsky's cultural-historical tradition," understood in a broad sense. A diversity of theoretical approaches influenced by Leontiev's activity theory has emerged in recent decades (e.g., Engeström 1987; Greif 1991; Rabardel and Bourmaud 2003). Some of them are discussed later in the book. In particular, an influential approach developed by Engeström (1987; 1990) is described in chapter 4 and compared with Leontiev's framework in chapter 6.

This chapter puts together and organizes into a coherent structure materials and ideas taken from a variety of diverse sources. Inevitably, we used our judgment, so our way of structuring the main concepts and principles of activity theory reflects our own preferences and views. Our interpretation of what constitutes the core of activity theory may differ from other interpretations.

This overview of activity theory is oriented toward interaction design. Issues that are currently, in our view, less closely related to this domain, such as the development of personality or the structure of consciousness, are discussed in less depth than other issues we think are more relevant to interaction design.

The chapter is structured as follows. We begin with a discussion of the concept of activity in general and its implications for interaction design. We then present a historical overview of the development of the main ideas underlying activity theory, from its roots in Vygotsky's cultural-historical psychology to the conceptual framework formulated by Leontiev, to current theoretical developments. We conclude with a summary of the basic principles of activity theory.

Figure 3.1
A basic representation of activity (S, subject; O, object).

3.2 THE CONCEPT OF ACTIVITY: BRIDGING THE GAP BETWEEN THE SUBJECTIVE AND THE OBJECTIVE

3.2.1 The Basic Notion of Activity

Activity theory is an approach in psychology and other social sciences that aims to understand individual human beings, as well as the social entities they compose, in their natural everyday life circumstances, through an analysis of the genesis, structure, and processes of their activities. The concept of *activity* is therefore the most fundamental concept in activity theory. Activity in general, not only human activity, but activity of any *subject*, is understood as a purposeful interaction of the subject with the world, a process in which mutual transformations between the poles of "subject–object" are accomplished (Leontiev 1978). The most basic representation of activity is shown in figure 3.1.

When defined in such a general way, activity appears to be the object of study within a variety of other conceptual frameworks as well. What sets activity theory apart is its fundamental insight about the primacy of activity over the subject and the object. Activity is considered the most basic category; analysis of activities opens up a possibility to properly understand both subjects and objects. This idea may appear counterintuitive. Traditional analytical thinking, typical, for instance, of natural sciences, would assume that to understand an activity it is necessary to understand the subject and the object separately and then make an inference about their interaction. Activity theory challenges this assumption. It claims that this apparently flawless logic can be misleading.

First, activity theory maintains that no properties of the subject and the object exist before and beyond activities (e.g., Leontiev 1978). These properties do not just manifest themselves in various circumstances; they truly exist only in activities, when being enacted. Of course, one can make generalizations and assume that subjects possess abstract attributes not limited to specific situations, such as "John is not good at math." To a certain degree such generalizations are useful and even inevitable. However, the accuracy of predictions based on such generalizations can be limited. The way an abstract attribute is manifested can depend critically on the situation at hand. For instance, the same arithmetic operation can be performed successfully on familiar objects in common situations but not necessarily in the case of abstract or artificial tasks (Cole 1996).

Second, activity is considered the key source of *development* of both the object and the subject. In particular, developmental changes in the subject, which result from participating in activities and are determined by the nature of these activities, may cause substantial changes in the subject's properties. Let us consider a person lifting weights in a fitness room. One can argue that the process of weightlifting is determined by the physical strength of the person. If the person is strong enough, the weight will be lifted; if not, the attempt will not be successful. This causal explanation appears to be the only possible one. However, let us put the event in a larger-scale historical perspective. We might well find that the cause–effect relation is the reverse. If the person has developed muscles over an extended period of time through determined and persistent efforts, then weightlifting is the cause of the physical strength, not vice versa.

Therefore, a straightforward, logical approach to defining activities through their components can be problematic. The problems can be avoided if the analysis begins with focusing on purposeful activities. In other words, activity is proposed as the basic *unit of analysis* providing a way to understand both subjects and objects, an understanding that cannot be achieved by focusing on the subject or the object separately.

3.2.2 Agency

The notion of activity cannot be extended to all types of interactions. In activity theory, any activity is an activity of a subject. Not any entity is a subject. Subjects live in the world; they have needs that can be met only by being and acting in the world. Information-processing units, for instance, do not have "needs" (except in a metaphorical sense) and cannot be considered subjects. Therefore, interaction between the subject and the object, shown in figure 3.1, is not a symmetrical relationship between two components of a larger-scale system. The interaction is initiated and carried out by the subject to fulfill its needs. The meaning of the word "interaction" as used throughout this book when referring to activities can be described as "acting-in-the-world." Agency, the ability to act in the sense of *producing effects*, is a fundamental attribute of both the subject and the object. The very notion of interaction implies mutual effects produced by both sides on each other. However, the agency manifested by the subject of activity is of a special character. It can be defined as *the ability and the need to act*. (Different meanings of "agency" are discussed further in chapter 10.)

The asymmetry between subjects and objects can be observed even in very early and simple forms of life. Living organisms have internal biological needs for survival and reproduction that cause them to interact with reality in specific, patterned ways. Nonliving things lack these internal needs for survival and reproduction. They have the ability to act but not the need to act. For living things, the combination of the ability and the need to act entails unique forms of agency. Living things have remarkable internal capabilities to struggle for their own survival (and subsequent reproduction). Part of this struggle involves the ability to orient to objects in the world. Even amoebas stretch out their pseudopods toward food, and pull it into their bodies. They swarm with other amoebas. In short, they act as subjects, however primitive, in the effort to live.

Nonliving things do not orient to reality in order to survive or reproduce in a self-generated way based on internal needs. A computer virus, for example, appears to struggle to survive and reproduce, but it follows a program from outside itself (written by a programmer). This program is not the same as a need. The computer virus's behavior is more analogous a human rolling a ball down an incline plane than it is to the activity of amoebas—which they generate internally from their own "programs" encoded in their RNA and DNA. These "programs" are far more flexible, mutable, and responsive to changing conditions than computer programs (a topic science is learning more about from the field of proteomics), giving "life," at least as we know it so far, a qualitatively different character than the mechanisms governing the behavior of nonliving things.

3.2.3   Implications for Interaction Design

Models of human–computer interaction popular within first-wave HCI, based primarily on information-processing psychology (e.g., Nielsen

1986), appear to focus on the same unit of analysis as activity theory, that is, on interaction between human beings (users) and objects (interactive systems). However, while the "user–system" interaction can be considered a component part of activity, the purposeful interaction with the world cannot be limited to interaction with the user interface of an interactive system. HCI models deal with lower-level interaction limited to "tasks." Tasks are typically described in terms of the functionality of a system rather than their meaning for the subject. However, using a system does not normally have its own purpose; its meaning is determined by a larger context of human activity carried out to accomplish things that are important regardless of the technology itself, such as writing a memo to a colleague or keeping in touch with a friend.

Activity theory requires that the scope of analysis be extended from tasks to a meaningful context of a subject's interaction with the world, including the social context. The boundary of the "objective world" is not limited by the user interface. People are interacting with the world "through the interface" (Bødker 1991). In other words, according to activity theory, "user–system" interaction is too narrow a phenomenon to count as a genuine activity. Making a meaningful activity the unit of analysis means that not only an interaction between people and technology is considered, but also the objects in the world with which subjects are interacting via technology.

Another difference between the activity theory perspective and traditional HCI is that while traditional HCI models focus on abstract, formal representations of individual component parts of interaction (the user and the system), activity theory emphasizes the importance of studying the real-life use of technology as a part of unfolding human interaction with the world.

Finally, traditional approaches and models in HCI pay limited attention to developmental changes, with some exceptions such as attempts to provide an account of the differences between novice and expert computer users (e.g., Allwood 1989; Mayer 1988).

Therefore, focusing on the activities of people using technology rather than on "user–system" interaction calls for going beyond the limits of traditional HCI and points to specific directions of such a development:

Table 3.1
From "user-system" interaction to activity.

	Unit of analysis	
	User-system interaction	Subject-object interaction
Context	Users and systems	Subjects in the social world
Level of analysis	System-specific tasks	Meaningful goal-directed actions
Methods	Formal models, lab studies	Studies of real-life use
Time span	Limited time span	Developmental transformations

• extending the scope of analysis to include higher-level, meaningful tasks that can be supported by diverse technologies;

• studying technology in use instead of focusing on users and systems separately; and

• taking into account long-term developmental changes in users, technology, their interaction, and the overall context.

These claims, summarized in table 3.1, represent a preliminary set of implications based on a very general notion of activity. More implications will be discussed later in the book as the notion is elaborated further.

3.3 THE ORIGINS OF ACTIVITY THEORY: CULTURAL-HISTORICAL PSYCHOLOGY

3.3.1 Russian Psychology of the 1920s and 1930s

Activity theory is not an esoteric teaching that claims to possess deep truths obtained from a mysterious source. In fact, it is a part of a time-honored worldwide intellectual tradition that can be traced back for hundreds, even thousands of years. In chapter 1 we quoted Buddha speaking of the primacy of activity in human life. Looking to the West, we find Goethe's Faust thinking the same thing:[1]

'Tis written: "In the beginning was the Word!"
Here now I'm balked! Who'll put me in accord?
It is impossible, the Word so high to prize,
I must translate it otherwise

If I am rightly by the Spirit taught.
'Tis written: In the beginning was the Thought!
Consider well that line, the first you see,
That your pen may not write too hastily!
Is it then Thought that works, creative, hour by hour?
Thus should it stand: In the beginning was the Power!
Yet even while I write this word, I falter,
For something warns me, this too I shall alter.
The Spirit's helping me! I see now what I need
And write assured: In the beginning was the Deed!

It has been, and continues to be, the project of activity theory to explain how it is that we are "bound by action" as Buddha said, how we begin not with word or thought, as Faust learned, but with activity.

In this chapter we begin with the immediate predecessor of activity theory, cultural-historical psychology, developed in Russia in the 1920s and 1930s by Lev Vygotsky and his colleagues. The founder of activity theory, Aleksey Leontiev, was a disciple of Vygotsky and conducted his first studies under the direct supervision of Vygotsky. Many ideas underlying cultural-historical psychology were directly and organically assimilated into activity theory. The line between cultural-historical psychology and activity theory is so fine that in recent years these two approaches are sometimes collectively referred to as *CHAT*, which stands for "cultural-historical activity theory" (Center for Activity Theory and Developmental Work Research, n.d.).

The time and place of the birth of cultural-historical psychology was not accidental. After the Bolshevik Revolution of 1917, there was a social demand in Russia to create a new Marxist psychology that would replace the old "bourgeois" one. A variety of conceptual frameworks were suggested during this time as candidates for the new psychology. Many of them were short-lived and are of purely historical interest. Fortunately, however, some of the ideas developed during that time proved to be important contributions and had a significant impact on the development of psychology in the twentieth century. These ideas included the notions of the unity of consciousness and activity and the social nature of the mind.

The unity of consciousness and activity   An idea shared by many Russian psychologists, including Vygotsky, was that the human mind is intrinsically related to the whole context of interaction between human beings and the world, that it is an organ of a special kind, emerging and developing in order to make interaction with the world more successful. Therefore, an analysis of mind should include an analysis of the interaction between human beings and the world, in which the mind is embedded.

The social nature of the human mind   Another fundamental idea that greatly influenced Russian psychology was that the human mind is social in its very nature. This idea was closely related to the principle of the unity of consciousness and activity. At a philosophical level, the notion of the embeddedness of the human mind in activity followed from dialectical materialism's maxim that "social being determines consciousness" (Marx and Engels 1976). Therefore, according to the Marxist philosophy adopted by Russian psychologists of the early Soviet era, the interaction between subjects and objects—that is, "being"—was understood as social.

This notion applies to both poles of the interaction. On the one hand, the subject is social. Human beings are shaped by culture, their minds are deeply influenced by language, and they are not alone when interacting with the world. Typically, they act with, or through, other people, for instance, as members of groups, organizations, communities, or cultures. A key factor of an individual's success is the success or failure of the social entity, a collective subject, to which the individual belongs. On the other hand, the world itself is fundamentally social. The entities people are dealing with are mainly other people and artifacts developed in culture.

These ideas signified a radical deviation from other psychological approaches of the time. Selecting social activities as the main object of psychological research contrasted with the exclusive focus on either subjective or objective phenomena, a focus typical of the leading theoretical frameworks of the early twentieth century including introspective psychology and behaviorism. Gestalt psychology (see, e.g., Köhler 1925) attempted to extend the scope of analysis to both subjective and objective phenomena by proposing the notion of an isomorphic relationship between the phenomenal world and the physical world. However, to explain this relationship, Gestalt psychologists employed the concepts of physics—more specifically, physical field theory—which set them apart from the underlying assumptions of Russian psychology. Nevertheless, Russian psychology of the 1920s and 1930s had a natural affinity with Gestalt psychology, especially with studies of child development (Koffka 1924) and environmental/social psychological studies (Lewin 1936).

Most closely related to Russian psychology of the 1920s and 1930s was the constructivist approach developed by the Swiss psychologist Jean Piaget (1952). Piaget's psychology was based on a biological view of organisms trying to reach equilibrium with their environments, rather than on the notion of culture. However, the fundamental idea of the human mind emerging as a component part of the interaction between individuals and the world was not that different from the principle of the unity of consciousness and activity. According to Piaget, the objective constraints and regularities of the interaction of an organism with the world determine the logics underlying human cognition. In other words, cognitive functions and abilities are *constructed* by individuals in their continuing attempts to strike an equilibrium with the environment. It is no coincidence that the notion of internalization, which played a key role in Piaget's constructivism, was also one of the basic concepts of Russian psychology.

However, despite the similarity between Piaget's constructivism and Russian psychology, the two approaches were fundamentally different with respect to the role of culture. For Piaget, culture was an important but secondary factor that contributed to cognitive development. In Russian psychology, culture played (and continues to play) a more prominent role. The very interaction between human beings and the world was defined in terms of culture and society.

3.3.2 Lev Vygotsky (1896–1934)

Lev Vygotsky is the most prominent, and even legendary, figure in Russian psychology. He is considered one of the greatest psychologists of the twentieth century (Toulmin 1978). Vygotsky's career in psychology lasted only ten years. It started, as the legend has it, in 1924, with an outstanding presentation at a national psychological congress after which the obscure teacher from the provincial town of Vitebsk was invited to Moscow to work at the Psychological Institute. Ten years later Vygotsky died of tuberculosis at the age of thirty-seven. During his brief career, Vygotsky undertook one of the most ambitious projects in the history of psychology. He considered contemporary psychology to be in crisis: empirical studies resulted in an accumulation of evidence in fragmented areas rather than in new fundamental insights about the nature of mind. Vygotsky's ambition was no less than to lay the foundation for a new approach that would allow integration and generalization of psychological knowledge.

3.3.3   The Cultural Determination of the Human Mind

The most fundamental issue for Vygotsky was the relationship between the mind, on the one hand, and culture and society, on the other. He believed that the notion of culture should not be limited to a set of external factors influencing the human mind. Vygotsky maintained that culture and society are not external factors influencing the mind but rather are generative forces directly involved in the very production of mind. It was critically important, according to Vygotsky, that this fundamental idea be assimilated by psychology.

At the same time, Vygotsky rejected a straightforward view of culture and society as directly determining or shaping the human mind. Vygotsky argued that the only way to reveal the impact of culture on the mind was to follow developmental, historical transformations of mental phenomena in the social and cultural context.

The idea of a nonstraightforward, dialectical cultural determination of mind was elaborated by Vygotsky into a set of principles, concepts, and research methods. He contributed to the advancement of a research methodology suitable for developmental research by introducing the notions of *molar units of analysis* and the *formative experiment*. This methodology was employed in studies of the mechanisms of the cultural determination of mind, studies that questioned traditional dichotomies of the external and the internal, the individual and the collective.

3.3.4   The General Methodology of Developmental Research

Psychological experiments typically aim at establishing, through observations or controlled studies, how certain variables are related to each other. Traditional experimental methods are difficult to apply in studies of human development. When analyzing developmental changes one cannot limit the analysis to isolated variables, because the relationship between the variables can change over the course of development.

An alternative approach, proposed by Vygotsky, is to identify "the germ" of the phenomenon under investigation, that is, the most basic, initial form, which already has the most important features of the analyzed phenomenon. Tracking down the moment when the germ emerges in the process of development and then following its transformations into more and more developed forms was considered by Vygotsky to be the basic strategy for developmental research.

Vygotsky asserted that analysis should be conducted by "units" rather than by "elements." This meant that the germ cannot be defined simply as a sum of its component parts. The parts can be the same, but if they are not related to each other in a certain way, they make up not the same germ but a different entity.

This idea was illustrated by Vygotsky with the example of water. A molecule of water consists of atoms of oxygen and hydrogen joined in a certain way. The molecule, but not its constituent parts, can be considered a germ of water. For instance, both oxygen and hydrogen are highly flammable substances when taken separately. However, the attributes of individual components are of little consequence when the components are integrated within a higher-level unit. It is the structure of the molecule of H_2O that makes water nonflammable.

Another feature of Vygotsky's methodology differentiating it from most other psychological research is its position regarding the effect of research on the object of study. Traditional psychological research methodology requires that researchers avoid any intentional intervention into the phenomena they study. However, in the context of developmental research, conducting a controlled experiment, that is, a comparative study of the impact of various factors on the process of development necessarily involves an intervention into the process. The ability to influence the process of development can be considered an indication that the underlying understanding of development is correct. On the other hand, if the outcome of development is different from what is expected, this can be crucial feedback indicating the need for further analysis. An intentional intervention into the process of development can be considered a legitimate and even necessary research strategy (see, e.g., the concept of "action research," Argyris and Schön 1996). Accordingly, the preferred method of empirical study within Vygotsky's cultural-historical psychology was the "formative experiment," an experimental intervention into the process of development aimed at facilitating the emergence of certain developmental outcomes.

These general methodological principles were applied by Vygotsky in studies of the relationship between the mind and society. The studies focused on two dimensions of the dialectical interaction between individuals and the world: (a) internal–external, and (b) individual–collective. These two dimensions were addressed with sets of different, if closely related, concepts and research methods. However, the general idea in both cases was the same: the border between the individual and the social world is not an absolute one. The human mind is intrinsically related to culture and society through processes and phenomena that transcend the borders between internal and external, individual and collective.

3.3.5 The Internal–External Dimension: Higher Psychological Functions, Mediation, and Internalization

One concept proposed by Vygotsky for analysis of the social determination of mind was the notion of higher psychological functions. Higher psychological functions can be contrasted with "natural" psychological functions, that is, mental abilities such as memory or perception with which every animal is born. Natural functions can develop as a result of maturation, practice, or imitation, but their structure does not change and these functions are basically the same in similar species. Human beings have natural psychological functions, too, which are similar to those of other primates. However, human beings also develop higher psychological functions. Higher psychological functions emerge as a result of a restructuring of natural psychological functions in a cultural environment. This restructuring can be described as an emerging mediation of natural psychological functions.

Human beings seldom interact with the world directly. An enormous number of artifacts has been developed by humankind to mediate our relationship with the world. Using these artifacts is the hallmark of living the life of a human being. Tools or instruments—physical artifacts mediating external activities—are easy to recognize, and their impact on the everyday life of every individual is obvious.

By way of analogy to conventional technical tools (like hammers), Vygotsky introduced the notion of psychological tools, such as an algebraic notation, a map, or a blueprint. Technical tools are intended to help people affect things, while psychological tools are signs intended to help people affect others or themselves (Vygotsky 1982a). Of course, "psychological tools" and tools in a more traditional sense are very different. Vygotsky warned against pushing the analogy too far (Vygotsky 1982a, 1983).[2] However, one thing is common to instruments and signs: their role in human activity. Both hammers and maps are mediators. The use of mediators, whether crushing a nutshell with a hammer or orienting oneself in an unfamiliar city using a map, changes the structure of activity. Psychological tools transform natural mental processes into *instrumental acts* (fig. 3.2), that is, mental processes mediated by culturally developed means. Vygotsky referred to mediated mental processes as

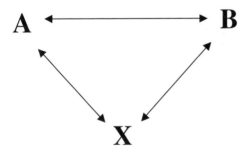

Figure 3.2
The structure of an instrumental act (Vygotsky 1982a). "A-B" represents a simple association between two stimuli, underlying a natural mnemonic act. When memory transforms into a high-level psychological function, this association is replaced with an instrumental act comprising "A-X" and "X-B."

higher mental functions, to separate them from unmediated *natural mental functions* that can be observed in other animals as well.

Initially, Vygotsky (1982a) made no distinction between psychological tools as physical artifacts (e.g., pieces of art, maps, diagrams, blueprints) and as symbolic systems (e.g., languages, numeric systems, algebraic notations) that in some cases can exist only "in the head." It did not take long, however, for him to realize the importance of whether or not psychological tools are physical, external artifacts. Empirical studies of higher psychological functions showed that in many cases, subjects who used external mediational artifacts to solve a task spontaneously stopped using these artifacts and improved their performance. Vygotsky (1983) explained this phenomenon in terms of internalization,[3] or the "transition of an external operation into an internal one" (Vygotsky 1983, our translation).

In the process of internalization, some of the previously external processes can take place in the internal plane, "in the head." The processes remain to be mediated, but mediated by internal rather than external signs. It should be emphasized that internalization is not a translation of initially external processes into a preexisting internal plane; the internal plane itself is created through internalization (Leontiev 1978). Internalization of mediated external processes results in mediated internal processes. Externally mediated functions become internally mediated.

Internalization is not just an elimination of external processes but rather *a redistribution* of internal and external components within a function as a whole. Such a redistribution may result in a substantial transformation of both external and internal components, such as an increased reliance on internal components at the expense of external ones, but both internal and external components are always present. The raison d'être for internal activities is their actual or potential impact on how the individual interacts with the world. The impact can be made only through external activities. For instance, after conducting calculations "in the head" a child may decide to buy fewer candies than she had originally planned because she realizes that their total cost would exceed the amount of cash she has.

Internalization was the object of study in an empirical investigation conducted by Leontiev (1931) under Vygotsky's supervision. The study employed a method called "double stimulation," created by Vygot-sky specifically for studies of the development of higher psychological functions. The main feature of this method is presenting the subject with two sets of stimuli. The first, primary set comprises stimuli used by the subject to solve an experimental task. The task could be—as it was in Leontiev's study—remembering a set of words (stimuli) for subsequent recall. The subjects are also provided with another, secondary set of stimuli as auxiliary means for performing the task. Stimuli of the second-ary set are *signs* referring to the stimuli of the primary set. The aim of using the method of double stimulation was to be able to compare prob-lem solving with and without secondary sets of stimuli. The design allowed for the analysis of the impact of mediation on subjects' perfor-mance in various cognitive tasks.

In the study conducted by Leontiev, the double stimulation method was employed as follows. Subjects of three age groups—preschool chil-dren, middle school children, and university students—were presented with lists of words with the instruction to remember the words. After the presentation the subjects were asked to recall as many words as pos-sible. The lists of words constituted the primary sets of stimuli. Each group of subjects was divided into two subgroups corresponding to two experimental conditions. In one condition the words were the only stimuli presented. In another condition the subjects were given a second-ary set of stimuli, a stack of picture cards, which they could use as mne-monic tools. For instance, to remember the word "dinner," a subject could select a picture of an onion and lay it away. Layaway cards could be used by the subjects during the recall phase of the experiment.

It was found that performance in each of these conditions improved with age and that using cards generally improved performance. How-ever, the difference between recalling words with or without cards was manifested differently in the three age groups (see fig. 3.3).

In preschool children, the performance was rather poor and approxi-mately at the same level in both conditions. In middle-school children the usage of cards resulted in a marked increase in performance level com-pared to the no-cards condition. University students showed a high level of performance under both conditions, and the difference between the conditions was small.

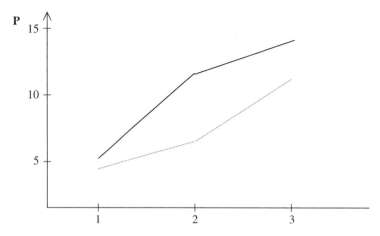

Figure 3.3
"Leontiev's parallelogram": memory task performance with and without second-ary stimuli in three age groups (P-performance, the number of correctly recalled words; solid line, memory recall with secondary stimuli; broken line, memory re-call without secondary stimuli; 1, preschool children; 2, middle school children; 3, university students) (adapted from Leontiev 1931).

The data were interpreted by Leontiev as an indication that children of the three age groups were at different levels in the development of medi-ated memory. Preschool children had not yet developed mediation capa-bilities, so they could not benefit from using the cards. That was why there was little difference between their performance under the two con-ditions. Middle-school children could successfully use the cards as exter-nal mediational tools and that was the reason they could substantially benefit from using the cards. Finally, the university students, according to Leontiev, reached similar levels of performance in both conditions be-cause their memory was mediated whether or not they used the cards. When they could use the cards, they relied on them as external media-tors. When no external mediators were provided, they used internal mediators, which were almost as effective as external mediators.

Empirical data from this and other studies employing the double stim-ulation technique (Vygotsky 1982b) supported the view of a restructuring of mental processes as a result of development in a cultural environment. The restructuring follows the stages of (a) no mediation, (b) external me-diation, and (c) internal mediation resulting from internalization.

Therefore, over the course of internalization, external processes can transform into internal ones and there is no firm boundary between the internal, the inner world of subjective phenomena, and the external, the objective world. Internalization is one of the main modes of cultural determination of the mind. Internalization enables external mediation by culturally developed tools to effect internal, mental processes, which become culturally mediated, as well.

The individual–collective dimension: The dynamics of the social distribution of the mind   Vygotsky's call for a revision of the traditional view of a border separating the mind from the physical world was paralleled by a call for a revision of another dichotomy, that between the individual and others. It was claimed that individuals and their social environments are not separated by an impenetrable border. Instead, they were to be understood as two poles of a single individual-collective dimension. Mental processes transform along this dimension of the dynamics of mental processes over the course of their development.

Sometimes this dimension is not clearly differentiated from the previous one: both the internal–external dimension and the individual–collective dimension are considered different aspects of the same phenomenon of internalization. In other words, internalization is considered a process during which phenomena external to the subject, both physical and social, become both individual and internal.

However, these two dimensions—internal–external and individual–social—should not be merged into a single dimension (see also Arievitch and Van der Veer 1995). The dynamics of the internal and external components of psychological functions can be relatively independent of the dynamics of individual and collective processes.

This can be illustrated with examples of internalization that are not paralleled by a transformation of collective activities into individual ones. For instance, consider a person driving a car who initially relies on a map but eventually learns the map and gets by without it. The means of carrying out the navigation task undergoes a significant transformation: from relying on an external artifact to relying on an internalized representation. However, over the course of this transformation the activity does not necessarily become less (or more) collective; it remains an individual activity. Or, consider a musician who plays in an orchestra and internalizes musical scores when participating in the collective activity. The degree to which the musician relies on external artifacts (music sheets) has little to do with participation in the collective activity of the orchestra.

These examples indicate that a decreased reliance on an external artifact does not necessarily imply a corresponding transformation of a collective activity into an individual one. But it does not mean that these two processes are completely independent. They may well be two aspects of the same phenomenon. Yet they are different issues and each deserves a special analysis.

The dynamics of the individual and the social was a key issue in cultural-historical psychology. This issue was addressed by Vygotsky with two concepts, closely related to each other: the law of psychological development and the zone of proximal development.

From interpsychological to intrapsychological   According to Vygotsky, the acquisition of psychological functions is subordinated to a universal law of psychological development: new psychological functions do not directly appear as functions of the individual (i.e., intrapsychological functions). First a function is distributed between the individual and other people; it emerges as an interpsychological function. Even though the individual may carry out some or even most components of a function, she cannot initially perform the function alone. Over time, the individual progressively masters the function and can reach the phase at which he can perform the function without help from others.

For instance, when new drivers start learning to drive a car in a specially equipped training car, they may appear responsible for the driving (performing basic operations such as pressing pedals and turning the steering wheel). But much of the driving may in fact be performed by the instructor, who sets the direction, monitors the overall situation, and makes most decisions. With time, the learner can assume responsibility for more and more tasks and eventually develop the ability to drive on his own. The same or similar phenomena can be observed in practically any other case of an individual acquiring a new function, including reading and writing. Even if an individual appears to learn alone, a closer look may reveal support provided by other people in the design of a textbook, the functionality of an interactive help system, or other artifacts and environments that embody the experience of other learners, helpers, and teachers.

Therefore, the "universal law of psychological development" states that new psychological functions first emerge as interpsychological ones and then as intrapsychological ones. An application of this law to the practical tasks of assessment and support of child development resulted in the formulation of the most well-known concept of cultural historical psychology, the concept of the *zone of proximal development*.

3.3.6   The Zone of Proximal Development

Traditionally, the way of assessing the level of development of a child has been (and still is) to measure the *achievement level* of the individual, that is, what the individual can accomplish at the moment of evaluation. The achievement level can be measured, for instance, by establishing the maximum level of difficulty of tasks that can be solved by the individual. Vygotsky observed that, paradoxically, achievement-based methods of developmental assessment do not assess how a child is going to develop. They are oriented toward the past. Indicators of current performance can only assess the outcomes of development that has already taken place. These indicators are not especially useful for assessing the future of development, of how the level of performance can be expected to change over time.

The idea of the zone of proximal development was proposed by Vygotsky as a solution to this problem with traditional methods of assessment of development. Vygotsky's original definition of the zone of proximal development was as follows:

> The distance between the actual level of development as determined by independent problem solving and the level of potential development as determined through problem solving under adult guidance or in collaboration with more capable peers. (Vygotsky 1978)

Vygotsky's suggestion was to measure the level of development not through the level of current performance, but through the difference ("the distance") between two performance indicators: (1) an indicator of independent problem solving, and (2) an indicator of problem solving in a situation in which the individual is provided with support from other people.

Imagine two eight-year-old children. The kinds of math problems the children can solve are approximately the same and correspond to what is considered "normal" for their age. However, if the same amount of help is provided to these two children in solving the test problems, the results may be very different. The first child reaches the level characteristic of twelve-year-olds, while the second child only reaches the level characteristic of nine-year-olds. Apparently, the developmental potential of the first child is higher than that of the second child. However, these differences cannot be captured by the traditional methods used to measure the level of development.

The notion of the zone of proximal development can be derived from the law of psychological development described in the previous section. According to this law, psychological functions develop through two phases: first they emerge in the interpsychological plane and then in the intrapsychological plane. The emergence of a function in the interpsychological plane can be the first phase of further development, for the function that emerges in the interpsychological plane is likely to appear in the intrapsychological plane as well. Even if the individual has not yet reached a certain level of psychological function according to indicators of actual development (e.g., independent problem solving), the fact that this function already exists as distributed between the individual and other people can be a powerful predictor of the next step in the individual's development.

At the same time, the notion of the zone of proximal development does not imply that the law of psychological development should be understood in a deterministic sense. The first interpsychological phase of development of a function creates conditions for the second phase, but it does not mean that this function will inevitably emerge as an intrapsychological one.

Once again, the emphasis of this discussion on two separate dimensions of the relation between human beings and the world—the internal –external dimension and the individual–collective dimension—does not mean that these dimensions are independent of each other. Even though these dimensions are distinct, they are still closely related. For instance, when an external component is internalized, it also affects the individual –collective dimension. Externally used tools and signs can be shared and thus facilitate communication, while internalization can make communication more problematic.

3.3.7 Pushing the Boundaries of the Individual

Taken together, Vygotsky's ideas defined a new perspective in psychology. This perspective attempted to find the origins of mind in culture and society. Instead of considering the social world an external context in which mind originates and develops according to its own immanent laws, cultural-historical psychology considered culture and society to be a generative force shaping the very nature of the human mind. Many other approaches took (and still are taking) for granted that the subjective processes of the individual constitute a separate world related to objective reality mostly through perception. It is up to the individual to decipher sensory inputs and transform them into a meaningful picture of reality (and, possibly, actions, understood as motor responses). Cultural-historical psychology takes a radically difference stance. It postulates that reality itself is filled with meanings and values. Human beings develop their own meanings and values not by processing sensory inputs but by appropriating the meaning and values objectively existing in the world. The most thorough perceptual analyses of the shape, color, and other visual attributes of religious symbols and texts do not guarantee that the perceiver understands the commandments of a religion, for example. Such an understanding requires an interaction with the world at a higher level than visual perception: the person needs to relate to meanings that are already there. The border between the mind and the physical world, between the individual and other people, is not closed. It is being dynamically redefined on a moment-to-moment basis depending on a variety of factors. Meaning and values can cross these borders— and of course, are creatively transformed along the way.

The ideas of cultural-historical psychology were carried further by Aleksey Leontiev, who elaborated them (or at least some of them) into a system of concepts and principles known as activity theory. Interestingly enough, the development of activity theory, as we discuss below, was in a sense a by-product of another project undertaken by Leontiev.

3.4 THE DEVELOPMENT OF THE MIND

3.4.1 Aleksey Leontiev (1904–1979)

As mentioned, during the first phase of his professional life as a psychologist, Leontiev studied phenomena of mediated memory within the framework of a large-scale research program initiated and coordinated by Vygotsky. Later in his career, Leontiev formulated his own agenda which directed his research for several decades. This agenda was one of the most ambitious in the history of psychology (after all, Leontiev was a student of Vygotsky). The objective was no less than to provide a historical account of the mind, from the emergence of basic forms of psyche early in biological evolution, all the way through to advanced forms of human consciousness. The study, reported in the book *Problems of the Development of Mind* (Leontiev 1981),[4] is one of the most well-known and influential studies in Russian psychology. However, no matter how fundamental and insightful, it is not Leontiev's exploration of the evolution of mind that is considered his main contribution, but the conceptual framework of activity theory which eventually grew out of the evolutionary exploration of mind.

3.4.2 The Concept of Activity and the Evolution of Psyche

The general idea of the human mind as a special kind of organ that emerged in evolution to help organisms survive has been part of Russian psychology since the 1920s. However, the idea remained an abstract statement, a philosophical claim rather than a theory. Leontiev's ambition was to translate this general statement into a concrete description of how the first phenomena that can be called "psyche" emerged in history, and how they developed into the current variety of mental phenomena. To accomplish this goal Leontiev needed a special kind of analytical tool, a concept more general than psyche, that would make it possible to define the context in which the psyche emerges and develops. An obvious candidate for such a concept is "life," since ultimately this is what undergoes evolutionary changes. However, this concept is too general and too vague. "Activity," as we will see below, was chosen by Leontiev as a concept that can provide a more concrete insight into what "life" is.

The concept of activity first played the role of an analytical tool helping to build a theory of the evolutionary development of the mind. However, over the course of the implementation of Leontiev's research program, the concept underwent substantial transformations. It was elaborated on, its meaning became more developed, and its relation to mind in general became more concrete. In effect, Leontiev's research program produced two results instead of one. Not only did it provide an account of the historical development of the mind, it also formulated a number of ideas and principles about the nature of activity. In the 1970s Leontiev summarized these ideas and principles into a coherent, if incomplete, framework comprising the foundations of activity theory (Leontiev 1978).

3.4.3   The Emergence of Psyche in Biological Evolution

The analysis of the evolution of the mind was conducted by Leontiev according to the main principles of the developmental research methodology described above. This methodology requires: (1) identifying the point in development when the initial, early instance of the developing system (the phenomenon under consideration), which already has the characteristic features of the system, emerges for the first time; (2) identifying the main contradictions existing at each phase of development; and (3) tracing the development of the system, unfolding as a result of resolving the contradictions. Contradictions in developmental research methodology are understood in a broad sense, as inconsistencies or discrepancies within the system or, more commonly, between the system and its environment.

For Leontiev, the phenomenon under consideration, the developing system he analyzed, was the mind, or psyche. Accordingly, the first challenge was to find the earliest, most elementary form of psyche as it emerged in evolution. The task was anything but trivial. There were a number of views regarding when exactly in biological evolution psyche appears for the first time. Is psyche a property of all living organisms?

Must the "evolutionary threshold" be raised to include only animals having central nervous system? Only humans? Since answers to these questions were, quite understandably, based on logical arguments and beliefs rather than empirical evidence, it was hardly possible to establish with certainty which of the answers, if any, was correct. Therefore, the problem remained open and a space was left for suggesting new possible solutions. Leontiev did just that by developing his own line of arguments and proposing his own hypothesis about the emergence of psyche in biological evolution. These arguments and hypothesis can be summarized as follows.

A characteristic feature of all biological organisms is their ability to actively respond to environmental factors, that is, their *responsiveness*. Organisms are not passively influenced by the environment; they develop their own internal and external responses using their own energy. This responsiveness, according to Leontiev, can be of two different types. First, organisms can respond to stimuli that produce direct biological effects. For instance, food may trigger digestive processes and can be actively assimilated by an organism, while changes in the ambient temperature may result in responses directed at maintaining an organism's own temperature within certain limits. Another type of responsiveness takes place when an organism responds to a stimulus that does not produce a direct biological effect. A smell of food or a sound signifying danger can elicit a strong response without immediately affecting the organism's biology. This second type of responsiveness, called *sensitivity*, that is, an ability to respond to *signals* carrying biologically significant information, was considered by Leontiev the most basic manifestation of psyche.

Since the inception of sensitivity there have been two main lines of development of organisms in biological evolution. The first line is the development of the ability to maintain basic life-support processes, such as digestion. The second line is development of the ability to interact with the environment which results in the acquisition of new perceptual, cognitive, and motor functions and organs, such as the senses, the nervous system, and limbs.

Having identified the most basic form of psyche, Leontiev went on to trace the development of progressively more advanced forms of psyche caused by dialectical contradictions between organisms and their environments. He considered changes in the environment, on the one hand, and the acquisition of more sophisticated forms of interaction with the environment, on the other, to be the driving forces behind development.

The emergence of psyche itself was, according to Leontiev, caused by a radical change in the life conditions of biological organisms: a transition from living in a homogeneous "primordial soup," in which life originally appeared, to living in an environment consisting of discrete things, or objects. Objects are characterized by relatively stable combinations of properties. Some of these properties, which are of direct biological importance, are systematically associated with other properties, which are not. The latter, therefore, can be used as signals of the former. As a result, organisms that develop sensitivity—the ability to respond to signals—have better chances of survival in an environment composed of distinct objects than do organisms without such an ability.

Leontiev discerned three stages of the development of psychological functions in animals: the sensory stage, the perceptual stage, and the intelligence stage. At the sensory stage, organisms recognize and respond to isolated attributes of the environment but cannot recognize whole objects and their relations. Imagine a fish that is placed in an aquarium where food, located very close to the fish, cannot be reached directly because of an obstacle, say, a glass wall separating the fish from the food. The fish eventually learns to reach the food by following the shape of the obstacle. When the obstacle is removed, the fish can get the food much more easily, but, as shown in some experimental studies (Leontiev 1981), it may continue to follow the shape of the obstacle for some time after the obstacle is removed. Most animals are at a more advanced perceptual stage of development. When they see that the obstacle between themselves and the food is removed, they go to the food directly.

Some animals, such as apes, reach the highest stage in Leontiev's hierarchy of animal psyche, the intelligence stage. These animals are able to develop sophisticated mental representations of problem situations in which they are immediately engaged. Such representations allow for problem-solving behavior characterized by effectiveness, fast learning, and high transfer. An example of intelligent animal problem solving is Köhler's famous chimpanzee trying to reach a banana without success and suddenly "realizing" that a stick could be used to get the banana (Köhler 1925). Such an insight can instantly change the chimpanzee's behavior and can be applied directly, without any trial-and-error, in a wide range of similar situations.

3.4.4   The Origins of the Concept of Activity

The concept of activity plays a crucial role in Leontiev's analysis of the evolution of psyche. The concept was introduced as fundamental as soon as Leontiev set out to discover the earliest manifestations of mind:

> I will call the processes of *activity* the specific processes through which a live, that is, active relation of the subject to reality is realized, as opposed to other types of processes. (Leontiev 1981)

Immediately after introducing the concept of activity Leontiev introduced the concept of the object of activity. He emphasized that activities cannot exist without their objects: "Any activity of an organism is directed at a certain object; an 'objectless' activity is impossible" (Leontiev 1981).

A distinction between mental and nonmental phenomena required that both be defined in terms of a general overarching concept and then differentiated within this frame of reference. Activity was chosen by Leontiev to play the role of such a basic, fundamental concept. He used this concept to describe the transition from "premental" life, that is, life processes prior to the emergence of psyche, to more advanced forms of life associated with mental phenomena, as

> a transition from a "pre-mental" activity, that is, activity, which is not mediated by a representation of objective reality, to activity, which is mediated by a representation of objective reality.... Therefore, psyche, mental activity, is not something that is added to life but a special form of life, inevitably emerging in the process of its development. (Leontiev 1981)

Thus, two historical threads can be discerned in Leontiev's analysis of the evolution of psyche. The first thread is a long-term project dealing with developmental transformations of the mind. The second thread is a development of the key analytical tool used by Leontiev in his historical analysis, the concept of activity. When the concept is first introduced, it is a basic and rather undeveloped seed, possessing the crucial attributes of the concept (an active relation of the subject to reality, always oriented

toward and determined by its object) but virtually nothing else. However, over the course of Leontiev's developmental analysis, as will be
shown in the next section, the meaning of the concept also develops,
especially when Leontiev goes on to discuss the development of the
human mind.

3.4.5   The Historical Development of the Human Mind

The development of the human mind was a radically new phase in the
evolution of the psyche. For animals, mind is an organ of survival; it
increases the organism's fitness regarding its natural environment, just
as claws or fur do. Through assuring the survival of the fittest, evolution
stimulates the development of mind in animals. But with the emergence
of human culture and society, biological evolution ceased to be the
main factor in the development of the mind. The survival of an individual living in society depends on economics, politics, and technologies,
rather than fitness understood as the body's ability to adapt to the natural environment. Accordingly, the nature of the human mind is determined not only by biological factors but also by culture and society.

   Leontiev specifically analyzed three aspects of culture that have a fundamental impact on the mind: tools, language, and the division of labor.

   In his analysis of the role of tools and language, Leontiev by and large
followed the approach established by Vygotsky. He considered tools to
be a vehicle for transmitting human experience from generation to generation. The structure of a tool itself, as well as learning how to use a tool,
changes the structure of human interaction with the world. By appropriating a tool, integrating it into activities, human beings also appropriate
the experience accumulated in the culture. Elaborate practices of creating, storing, and maintaining tools are the most basic features of human
beings, differentiating them from other animals.

   The use of tools is closely related to other factors influencing the development of the mind, namely, the use of language and the division of
labor. Continuing the cultural-historical tradition of using the tool metaphor for understanding the role of signs and symbols in the functioning
and development of the mind, Leontiev focused on the role of tools in
the development of concepts. Concepts have a general meaning applica-

ble to a variety of concrete situations and experiences. Over the course of their individual development (*ontogenesis*), human beings learn and appropriate concepts already existing in their cultures. The concepts, however, have not always been there. They are a result of the positive and negative experiences of people who contributed to the development of the culture. One might ask: How did the first concepts, the first generalizations emerge from individual human experience? Leontiev suggested a hypothesis that may provide an answer, at least a partial one, to this question.

Early tools, such as a stone axe, could be used for a variety of purposes. They could, for example, cut trees, kill animals, or dig soil. The objects to which an axe was applied could be soft or hard. Some objects were easy to cut, some required substantial time and effort, and some were so hard that it was impossible even to leave a dent on them. Despite these differences, all the objects could be compared against the axe, which was an invariant component of all encounters. Therefore, the axe could be considered an embodied standard of softness/hardness. Using the axe for practical purposes to do something with an object in the environment had the side effect of placing the object on a "scale" of softness/hardness. This scale emerged as a generalization of the individual experience of using the tool. Since people followed shared, culturally developed procedures of creating and using tools, the tools could serve as an embodiment of abstract concepts based on the generalization of both individual and collective experience.

Another implication of the use of tools for the historical development of the human mind is their role in the emergence of the division of labor. Even though the division of labor was the result of a variety of factors, it was tools that assured the development of the sophisticated forms of coordination typical of collaborative work and other socially distributed activities. On the one hand, the production of tools became a separate activity that required specialized skills. Individuals who possessed these skills were likely to make tools for other members of a social group, which was probably one of the first examples of the division of labor. On the other hand, tools and other artifacts (such as clothes) could facilitate the coordination of individual contributions to collective activities by signifying the social status and specific responsibilities of their owners.

The division of labor, according to Leontiev, had special significance for the development of the mind. When a person participates in a socially distributed work activity, his actions are typically motivated by one object but directed to another. Let us consider Leontiev's canonical example of activity, the collective activity of hunting. Individuals participating in a collective hunt may be divided into two groups: one group (the beaters) beats the bushes in order to scare the animals and make them move in a certain direction, and another group hides, waiting to ambush the animals directed toward them by the beaters. Both groups are motivated by food. However, for members of the first group, the immediate goal is not to get closer to the animals and kill them but, on the contrary, to scare them away. These hunters are motivated by their share of the whole catch which they expect to receive as a reward for their contribution to the hunt. But taken out of the context of the collective activity, the actions of these hunters appear to have no meaning.

A noncoincidence of objects that motivate an activity and objects at which that activity is directed is a characteristic feature of human activity. In animal activities, motivating objects and directing objects basically coincide. If the activity of an animal is directed toward an object, this object typically immediately corresponds to a certain need. In human activities, however, the link between what an individual is doing and what she is trying to attain through what she is doing is often difficult to establish. The structure of human activities, as opposed to the structure of the activities of other animals, can be extremely complex. The main reason behind this, according to Leontiev, is a transformation that individual activities undergo as a result of participation in the division of labor. When an individual takes part in a socially distributed activity, the difference between motivating and directing objects is forced on the individual by the organization of the activity. The division of labor makes dissociation between the motivation and the direction of activity an objective attribute of an individual's interaction with the world. Internalization of this dissociation changes the structure of individual activities. Individual activities can potentially develop a complex relationship between motivating and directing objects.

In a way, the historical evolution of mind illustrates the "universal law of psychological development" formulated by Vygotsky for individual development: new functions and attributes emerge first as distributed between the individual and his or her social environment (that is, as interpsychological ones) and then become appropriated by individuals (that is, become intrapsychological ones). The division of labor makes attaining a goal within a collective activity meaningful (or at least rewarded) even if the relation of the goal to the object of the activity as a whole is not straightforward. The ability to connect the current focus of one's efforts with their ultimate intended outcome and to integrate indirectly related actions first emerges in history as supported by the division of labor. At this stage of development, the ability to coordinate intermediate goals can exist only as distributed between people. For instance, the beaters in the hunt above could perform their roles without understanding the actual meaning of their actions. But it seems plausible that collective activities can be carried out much more successfully if contributing individuals understand the relationship between intermediate and ultimate outcomes. Therefore, the division of labor creates conditions for the dissociation between motives and goals. This dissociation first emerges in collective activities and then in individual activities and minds.

3.4.6   The Structure of Human Activity

Needs, motives, and the object of activity   So far we have discussed "activity" in a broad sense, as subject–object interaction in general. In this broad meaning, any process of a subject's interaction with the world can be qualified as an activity. However, in activity theory, the term also has a narrower meaning. According to this meaning, activity refers to a specific level of subject–object interaction, the level at which the object has the status of a *motive*. A motive is an object that meets a certain need of the subject. The reason the notion of motive plays a key role in the conceptual framework of activity theory will be evident from the discussion below.

Let us consider more closely the idea of subject–object interaction that takes place at several levels simultaneously. Obviously, at any given moment, we can discern a whole range of objects with which a subject is interacting. For instance, depending on the angle from which a person is viewed, he can be described as hitting a key on a computer keyboard, typing a word, or writing a novel. Accordingly, the objects the person is dealing with include the key, the word, and the novel, all at the same time. These objects constitute a hierarchy, where objects located higher in the hierarchy define larger-scale units of subject–object interaction. The top-level object in the hierarchy, according to activity theory, has a special status. The reason the subject is attempting to attain this object is the object itself. The object is perceived as something that can meet a need of the subject. In other words, the object motivates the subject—it is a motive.

Activity in the narrow sense is a unit of subject–object interaction defined by the subject's motive. It is a system of processes oriented toward the motive, where the meaning of any individual component of the system is determined by its role in attaining the motive.

Therefore, according to activity theory, the ultimate cause behind human activities is *needs*. Needs can be viewed, according to Leontiev, from either a biological or a psychological perspective. From a biological perspective, a need is an objective requirement of an organism. Having a need means that something should be present in the environment. Organisms may need food, water, air, or a certain temperature maintained in an appropriate range, in order to survive and reproduce. From a psychological perspective, a need is a directedness of activities toward the world, toward bringing about desirable changes in the environment. It is expressed in particular behavior and subjective experiences.

At the psychological level, needs can be represented in two different ways. Needs that are not "objectified," that is, not associated with a concrete object, cause general excitement which stimulates the search for an object to satisfy the need. The subject may experience discomfort ("a need state"). However, this discomfort cannot direct the subject and help satisfy the need, except in stimulating an exploratory behavior that is not directed at anything in particular. When a need meets its object, which, according to Leontiev, is "a moment of extraordinary importance" (1978), the need itself is transformed, that is, objectified. When a need becomes coupled with an object, an activity emerges. From that moment on, the object becomes a motive and the need not only stimulates but also directs the subject. An unobjectified need is a raw state of need looking for an object, while an objectified need is one with a defined object, where the subject knows what it is looking for.

Therefore, the most fundamental property of needs, according to Leontiev, is that they cannot be separated from objects. The defining feature of unobjectified needs is that they are seeking objects, while objectified needs manifest themselves through their objects. The very concept of activity includes its orientation toward an object, an object that both motivates and directs the activity. The object of activity, which is defined by Leontiev as the "true motive" of an activity (Leontiev 1978), is the most important attribute differentiating one activity from another.

Human needs are different from other animals' needs. Psychological needs of other animals are related to biological needs, and their activities are directed toward objects associated with biological needs. However, even in nonhuman animals, biological needs do not directly determine the objects of the needs. When selecting objects of their activities, animals can rely on a wide range of attributes that may be only indirectly related to biological properties. This ability provides obvious advantages. For instance, a lion that attacks only the slower antelopes might survive longer than a lion that attacks indiscriminately. The more developed an animal, the more its psychological needs are influenced by the structure and affordances of the environment, and the more difficult it is to trace the behavior of the animal to underlying biological needs.

In humans, some psychological needs are clearly based on biological needs. However, even these needs are transformed by culture and society which provide incentives, guidance, and constraints on selecting the objects of the needs and the means of satisfying them. More importantly, human psychological needs are not limited to needs based on biology. The relationship of human psychological needs to biology is difficult or impossible to trace, and sometimes this relationship appears to be negative rather than positive. Some cultural practices and many rituals do not seem to be healthy, sensible, or even pleasant.

Activity theory neither proposes a taxonomy of potentially effective needs (as do some psychological approaches, e.g., Maslow 1968) nor provides strict criteria to differentiate motives from nonmotives. Human needs are always in the process of developing, so it is impossible in principle to give a definitive description of all possible needs and motives.

What activity theory does propose is a conceptual framework to bridge the gap between motivation and action. Activity theory provides a coherent account for processes at various levels of acting in the world.

Activities, actions, and operations   Activity in a narrow sense is a unit of life, a subset of all possible processes related to the interaction of the subject with the world. The subset is defined by its orientation toward a specific motive. However, activities are not monolithic. Each activity, in its turn, can be represented as a hierarchical structure organized into three layers. The top layer is the activity itself, which is oriented toward a motive. The motive is the object, which stimulates, excites the subject. It is the object that the subject ultimately needs to attain.

However, human activities are typically not directed straight toward their motives. As in the hunters example, described above, socially distributed activities are characterized by a dissociation between their motivating and directing objects. Complex relations between these two types of objects are present in society and are a fact of life for people who live in society. Participation in social activities makes it necessary for individual subjects to reproduce within the structure of their individual activities the complex, mediated dissociation between (a) objects that attract them and (b) objects at which their activities are directed.

In other words, an activity may be composed of a sequence of steps, each of which is not immediately related to the motive even though the sequence as a whole may eventually result in attaining the motive. According to activity theory terminology, these components of activity are *actions*. The objects at which they are directed are called *goals*. Goals are conscious; we are typically aware of the goals we want to attain. In contrast, we may not be immediately aware of our motives. Leontiev observed that making motives conscious requires a special effort of making sense of "indirect evidence," that is, "motives are revealed to consciousness only objectively by means of analysis of activity and its dynamics. Subjectively, they appear only in their oblique expression, in the form of experiencing wishes, desires, or striving toward a goal" (Leontiev 1978).

Actions, in their turn, can also be decomposed into lower-level units of activity called *operations*. Operations are routine processes providing an adjustment of an action to the ongoing situation. They are oriented toward the conditions under which the subject is trying to attain a goal. People are typically not aware of operations. Operations may emerge as an "improvisation," as the result of a spontaneous adjustment of an action on the fly. For example, walking through a crowd, one can carry out elaborate maneuvering to avoid colliding with other people and physical obstacles without even realizing it. Another source of operations is the automatization of actions. Over the course of learning and frequent execution, a conscious action may transform into a routine operation. For instance, some skills that in experienced car drivers are apparently operations result from many hours of practice. When first learning to drive a car, a novice may need to focus consciously on the procedure of, for example, changing lanes. Changing lanes for inexperienced drivers can require total concentration, making it impossible to be engaged in any other activity (such as conversation). However, gradually this action may become more and more automatic. Eventually a driver reaches the phase at which changing lanes is done automatically and is hardly noticed. The driver can now also engage in other simultaneous activities.

The separation between actions and operations according to their orientation—respectively, toward the goal and toward the conditions in which the goal is "given" to the subject—is relative rather than absolute. Some actions are more directly related to the object of activity than others. For instance, adding a new section to a draft document is clearly related to the goal of writing a paper. However, accomplishing this goal may require a range of auxiliary actions more loosely related to the goal at hand. One may need to respond to other people's comments, learn new features of a word processor such as styles or "track changes," or find information in physical or electronic archives. Therefore, the main criterion separating actions from operations is that operations are automatized.

Levels of activity, shown in figure 3.4, can transform into one another. Automatization is an example of transformations between actions and operations. Over the course of practice actions can become automatic operations. The opposite process is "deautomatization," the transformation of routine operations into conscious actions. Such a transformation can take place, for instance, when an automatized operation fails to produce the desired outcome and the individual reflects on the reasons for

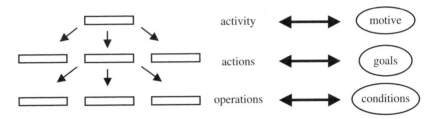

Figure 3.4
The hierarchical structure of activity. Activities are composed of actions, which are, in turn, composed of operations (left). These three levels correspond, respectively, to the motive, goals, and conditions, as indicated by bidirectional arrows.

the failure and on how the operation can be "fixed." Typically a new, more appropriate procedure is devised which first is carried out as a conscious action and then becomes an operation. Transformations can also take place between activities and actions. For instance, a goal subordinated to another higher-level goal can become a motive, so that a former action acquires the status of an activity.

Functional organs   A key concept of activity theory from the point of view of interaction design is the concept of *functional organs*. The origins of this concept can be traced to earlier works, for instance, those by the Russian physiologist Ukhtomsky, who defined a functional organ in a broad sense as "Any temporary combination of forces which is capable of attaining a definite end" (Ukhtomsky 1978, cited in Zinchenko 1996). Leontiev (1981) elaborated this concept by introducing the idea of functional organs as created by individuals through the combination of both internal and external resources. Functional organs combine natural human capabilities with artifacts to allow the individual to attain goals that could not be attained otherwise. For instance, human eyes in combination with eyeglasses, binoculars, microscopes, or night-vision devices, constitute functional organs of vision that may significantly extend human abilities.

To create and use functional organs, individuals need special kinds of competencies (Kaptelinin 1996b). *Tool-related competencies* include knowledge about the functionality of a tool, as well as skills necessary to operate it. *Task-related competencies* include knowledge about the higher-level goals attainable with the use of a tool, and skills of translating these goals into the tool's functionality.

One implication of the notion of functional organs is that the distribution of activities between mind and artifacts is always functional. It takes place only within subsystems that have specific functions, more or less clearly defined. Such subsystems, whether distributed or not, are integral parts of the subject, who makes ultimate decisions on when to use a functional organ and whether it has to be updated, modified, or even completely abandoned. Therefore, the subject must have competencies of a special type to create and use functional organs efficiently. These competencies, which can be tentatively labeled as *metafunctional*, integrate the functional organs into the system of human activities as a whole (Kaptelinin 1996b). In contrast with tool-related and task-related competencies, metafunctional competencies are not directly related to employing functional organs for reaching goals. Instead, they deal with the coordination of multiple goals that can be attained via one action, with the limitations of functional organs (for instance, which goals *cannot* be achieved with them), and with side effects, maintenance, and troubleshooting.

3.5 BASIC INSIGHTS AND PRINCIPLES OF ACTIVITY THEORY: AN OVERVIEW

The aim of this section is to summarize the concepts discussed earlier in the chapter. We identify two main ideas underlying activity theory and a set of basic principles that elaborate the ideas and jointly constitute the general conceptual system of activity theory. The structure we use to outline the approach builds on a set of the main features of activity theory identified by Wertsch (1981).

3.5.1 The Main Ideas of Activity Theory

The two main ideas underlying activity theory, originating from Russian psychology of the 1920s and 1930s, are

1. the unity of consciousness and activity, and
2. the social nature of the human mind.

The first idea asserts that the mind emerges, exists, and can be understood only in the context of the subject–object relationship. The second idea claims that society and culture are not external factors influencing the human mind but rather generative forces directly involved in the very production of the mind.

It is important to mention that Leontiev specifically emphasized that the individual is not a carbon copy of culture and society. In particular, he pointed out that meanings live a "double life" in the consciousness of the individual as both (a) meanings that objectively exist in a culture and are generally shared by individuals who belong to the culture and (b) "personal senses" that are different for each individual.

3.5.2   Basic Principles of Activity Theory

Object-orientedness   All human activities are directed toward their objects. When people design, learn, or sell, they design, learn, or sell *something*. Their dreams, emotions, and feelings are also directed toward something in the world. Analysis of objects is therefore a necessary requirement for understanding human beings, acting either individually or collectively. Objects of activities are prospective outcomes that motivate and direct activities, around which activities are coordinated, and in which activities are crystallized in a final form when the activities are complete. Objects separate one activity from another. The world provides resistance and affordances to our attempts to reach the objects of our activities; through resistance and affordances, objects constrain and direct what we do. We also develop internal, subjective counterparts of the objects, which may be no less effective in constraining and directing our activities than the resistance and affordances of the world. Therefore, objects can be considered as both external and internal.

A way to understand objects of activities is to think of them as *objectives* that give meaning to what people do. Concrete actions can be assessed as to whether or not they help (or otherwise) accomplish the objectives. But objects do not unilaterally determine activities: it is activity in its entirety, the subject–object relationship, that determines how both the subject and the object develop.

For example, a new family house can be the object of a person's activity (as well as an activity of a family as a whole). Over the course of the activity, the initial idea of the home could change many times, and the final outcome may look very different from what people envisioned initially. The subjects of the activity, the individuals and the entire family, may also change as a result. The house becomes a part of social reality—for instance, it is partly shaped by explicit and implicit rules, norms, and requirements (even, probably, conflicts) existing in the family and the wider community. Therefore, neither subject nor object alone is the determining factor; activity unfolds in a social context, transforming both the subject and the object. It is important that not only subjects but also objects are taken into account when understanding people and their activities.

Objects can be physical things (such as the bull's eye on a target) or ideal objects ("I want to become a brain surgeon."). Leontiev clearly understood that the concept of object in psychology could not be limited to the physical, chemical, and biological properties of things. Socially determined properties, including those of artifacts, and the very involvement of things in human activity, are also objective properties that can be studied with objective methods. So, the principle of object-orientedness states that human beings live in a reality that is objective in a broad sense: the things that constitute this reality have not only the properties that are considered objective according to natural sciences but socially and culturally defined properties as well.

The hierarchical structure of activity   An activity in its broad sense, such as the subject–object relationship, can be analyzed at different levels: *activities, actions*, and *operations* (Leontiev 1974). Actions are conscious goal-directed processes that must be undertaken to fulfill the object. Different actions may be undertaken to meet the same goal. Goals can have lower-level goals, which can have lower-level goals, and so forth (akin to the concept of goals/subgoals in artificial intelligence research and other traditions). For example, making a hunting weapon is an action that entails at a lower level, finding suitable materials and tools for the manufacture of the weapon. Therefore, the level of actions is itself hierarchically organized and can be decomposed into an arbitrary number of sublevels, from higher-level actions to lower-level actions.

Moving down the hierarchy of actions we cross the border between conscious and automatic processes. For instance, dialing a phone number can be a conscious action, but implementing this action by pressing phone buttons can be performed automatically. The automatic processes, according to activity theory terminology, are *operations*, which correspond to the way the action is actually carried out. Operations may emerge spontaneously, but a more common source of operations is the automatization of actions, which become routinized and unconscious with practice. Operations do not have their own goals; rather they provide an adjustment of actions to current situations. When one is learning to drive a car, the shifting of the gears is an action with an explicit goal that must be consciously attended to. Later, shifting gears becomes operational, and "can no longer be picked out as a special goal-directed process: its goal is not picked out and discerned by the driver" (Leontiev 1974).

Activity theory holds that the constituents of activity are not fixed but dynamic, and this can change as reality changes. This is an important distinction between activity theory and other constructs such as GOMS. In activity theory, all levels can move both up and down (Leontiev 1974). As we saw with gear-shifting, actions become operations as the driver habituates to them. An operation can become an action when "conditions impede an action's execution through previously formed operations" (Leontiev 1974). For example, if a user's email program ceases to work, the user continues to send mail by substituting another program, though now it is necessary to pay conscious attention to an unfamiliar set of commands. The object remains fixed, but goals, actions, and operations change as conditions change.

Internalization–Externalization   The human mind is not separated from culture and society. Internalization and externalization are processes that relate the human mind to its social and cultural environment. There are two dimensions of externalization–internalization. The first dimension corresponds to the distinction between mental processes and external behavior. The second dimension corresponds to the distinction between individual (intrapsychological) and collective (interpsychological) phenomena. These dimensions emphasize, respectively, the physical and the social aspects of internalization and externalization.

Mental processes vs. external behavior   Activity theory differentiates between internal and external activities. The traditional notion of mental processes (as in cognitive science) corresponds to internal activities. Activity theory maintains that internal activities cannot be understood if they are analyzed in isolation from external activities, because there are mutual transformations between the two kinds of activities. Internalization is the transformation of external activities into internal activities. For example, when first learning to type, the learner may look at the keys. Later, after much practice, "touch typing" is possible and the typist types without looking at the keyboard. The internal activity grows out of the external activity. But it is not a carbon copy of the external activity, that is, the typist does not see a keyboard in her mind. A transformation has taken place in which the external becomes internal, but also changes somewhat in form.[5]

Internalization provides a means for people to consider potential interactions with reality through mental simulations or imaginings without performing any actual manipulations with real objects. Internalization is not a simple transfer of previously external actions into an internal plane, "in the head"; even the most skilled typists and the most experienced drivers of manual transmission cars still need to press physical keys and change gears. Internalization causes a redistribution between external and internal components of activity, and in some cases, external components can be omitted in order to make an action more efficient, as in the case of the typist not needing to look at the keyboard.

Externalization transforms internal activities into external ones. Externalization is often necessary when an internalized action needs to be "repaired," or scaled. For example, if a suspect result is achieved when mentally adding numbers, or if a calculation is too large to do in the head, a calculator may be deployed. Externalization is also important when a collaboration between several people requires their activities to be performed externally so that the activities are coordinated. While the concept of internalization shares much with traditional cognitive science's notion of information processing, externalization is not emphasized in cognitive science. Activity theory emphasizes that it is the constant transformation between the external and the internal that is the basis of human activity.

Interpsychological vs. intrapsychological According to Vygotsky (1986), there are two stages in the development of mental abilities. First, these abilities emerge as *interpsychological* mental functions, distributed between the learner and other people, and after that they become *intrapsychological* functions, when social distribution is no longer necessary.

In many respects, the dimension of intrapsychological–interpsychological is similar to that of mental processes–external behavior. In both cases the dynamics of human activity include mutual transformations between two extremes. These transformations produce similar outcomes. Internalization as individual appropriation of socially distributed functions is a powrful source of development. Externalization as social redistribution of activities relates individuals to their social environments and can be a way to "repair" a process in case of a breakdown.

Mediation Activity theory's emphasis on social factors and on the interaction between people and their environments explains why the principle of tool *mediation* plays a central role within the approach. First, tools shape the way human beings interact with reality. And, according to the principle of internalization–externalization, the shaping of external activities eventually results in the shaping of internal ones. Second, tools usually reflect the experience of other people who tried to solve similar problems earlier and invented or modified the tool to make it more efficient and effective. Their experience is accumulated in the structural properties of tools, such as their shape or material, as well as in the knowledge of how the tool should be used. Tools are created and transformed during the development of the activity itself and carry with them a particular culture—the historical evidence of their development. So the use of tools is an accumulation and transmission of social knowledge. It influences the nature of external behavior and also the mental functioning of individuals.

Many relevant theoretical explorations were conducted either before the notion of mediation was developed within the Vygotskian tradition or in parallel with cultural-historical studies. For instance, the problem of identifying a border between an individual and the world was addressed by William James (1890) and Gregory Bateson (1972). From different perspectives, both James and Bateson came to the idea that some artifacts can be considered a part of the individual rather than the "outside" world. Crucial insights about the main types of artifacts and the ways they influence individual experience were provided by Marx Wartofsky (1979).

All these perspectives capture crucially important aspects of mediation. But they are different from the activity-theoretical view, which integrates the functional and the developmental aspects of mediation, placing artifacts in the context of purposeful interaction between the subject and the world, and, at the same time, in the context of the creation and transmission of social experience within a culture. In other words, activity theory recognizes a special status of culturally developed artifacts, considering them as fundamental mediators of purposeful human actions that relate human beings to the immediately present objective world and to human culture and history. This view identified the key components of mediation: subjects, objects, and mediational artifacts. In addition, this view suggested that the relationship between components can change over time, and that developmental, historical analysis is the only way to gain insight into the three-way interaction between these entities. It was this particular notion of mediation, developed within the cultural-historical approach, that was introduced to HCI by Bødker (1989, 1991), employed to develop the concepts of cognitive artifacts (Norman 1991) and "person plus" (Perkins 1993), and more recently used to revise the direct manipulation paradigm (Beaudouin-Lafon 2000). (Chapter 4 discusses such work in detail.)

Development   Finally, activity theory requires that human interaction with reality should be analyzed in the context of development. Of course, activity theory is not the only psychological theory that considers development as a major research topic. However, in activity theory development is not only an object of study, but also a general research methodology. Activity theory sees all practice as the result of certain historical developments under certain conditions. Development continuously reforms and develops practice. That is why the basic research method in activity theory is not that of traditional laboratory experiments but that of the formative experiment which combines active participation with monitoring of the developmental changes of the study participants. Ethnographic methods that track the history and development of a practice have also become important in recent work. Activity theory does not prescribe a single method of study. It only prescribes that a method be chosen based on the research question at hand. Unlike approaches wedded to a particular method, such as contextual inquiry, activity theory starts from the problem and then moves to the selection of a method.

3.5.3   Integration of the Principles

These basic principles of activity theory should be considered as an integrated system because they are associated with various aspects of the whole activity. That is, systematic application of any of the principles makes it eventually necessary to engage all the others. For instance, an analysis of the mechanisms underlying the social determination of the human mind should take into consideration tool mediation, internalization of social knowledge, and transformations of the structure of activity resulting from learning and development. Activity theory insists on the unity of these principles and does not abstract out any single process because the whole activity could not then be understood. It is sometimes the case that other theoretical traditions or approaches mirror aspects of activity theory (such as Haraway's [1991] concept of the cyborg; or mental representations in cognitive science—see e.g., Norman 1991), but the insights are not integrated into a larger theoretical framework as in activity theory.

Having provided a primer of the basic ideas, concepts, and principles of activity theory in this chapter, we now turn to a discussion of interaction design informed by activity theory.

4

Interaction Design Informed by Activity Theory

In this chapter we analyze the impact of activity theory on interaction design. We provide a brief history of the introduction of activity theory to interaction design and then discuss the ways in which it has helped reframe key concepts including transparency, affordance, and direct manipulation. We describe an activity-theoretical framework developed by Engeström (1987, 1990) and discuss the influence of both Leontiev's and Engeström's versions of activity theory on empirical studies of technology use, and their impact on research in computer-supported collaborative work and computer-supported collaborative learning. We discuss two hybrid approaches to design influenced by activity theory: instrumental genesis and genre tracing.

4.1 A HISTORICAL OVERVIEW

In Russia, activity theory has been one of the main theoretical foundations for research in ergonomics and human factors for over forty years (e.g., Zinchenko, Leontiev, and Panov 1964; Zinchenko and Munipov 1979; Munipov 1983; Bedny and Meister 1997). In the 1970s and '80s it also influenced the development of German work psychology (Greif 1991). However, activity theory became known to international research communities in human–computer interaction, computer-supported cooperative work, and information systems relatively recently, around the early 1990s. A combination of conceptual influences, backgrounds, and research agendas resulted in exposing these research communities to activity theory.

The first articulate and systematic attempt to introduce activity theory as a theoretical foundation for human–computer interaction was made by Susanne Bødker, a Danish computer scientist and a key figure in the participatory design community. In 1982–1983, when human–computer interaction was emerging as a new research field based on information-processing psychology (Card, Moran, and Newell 1983), Bødker was a visiting researcher at Xerox PARC. At a time when most researchers were still enthusiastic about the prospects for cognitive psychology as the foundation for HCI (Carroll 1987), Bødker's participatory design background made her aware of the limitations of focusing exclusively on the information-processing aspects of human–computer interaction. Several years later, in her Ph.D. thesis ("Through the Interface: A Human Activity Approach to User Interface Design"), she made the case for activity theory (Bødker 1987). The thesis was summarized in a journal paper (Bødker 1989) and later published as a book (Bødker 1991). Bødker proposed activity theory "as formulated by Leontiev and his followers" as a theoretical foundation for HCI (Bødker 1991). The main idea was the need to consider the human use of technology within a wider context of human interaction with the world: an interaction *mediated* by technology.

As a result of Bødker's publications, as well as papers by Bannon (1990) and Kuutti (1991), the activity theory perspective in interaction design soon became a recognized and respected voice in international theoretical discourse. One of the most influential interaction design books, an edited collection entitled *Designing Interaction: Psychology at the Human–Computer Interface* (Carroll 1991), featured chapters explicitly influenced by activity theory (Greif 1991; Norman 1991) and a chapter presenting the approach as a potential framework for HCI (Bannon and Bødker 1991). A seminal paper by Liam Bannon, "From human factors to human actors" (1991), which, according to Cooper and Bowers (1995), marked the turning point from "first-wave HCI" to "second-wave HCI," was influenced by activity theory. During the early 1990s, activity theory was proposed as a potential framework for the field of HCI in numerous presentations at international conferences, in journal papers, and books chapters (Kuutti 1991, 1992; Raethel 1992;

Kaptelinin 1992; Nardi 1992, 1993, 1994; Bødker 1993; Draper 1993; Kuutti and Bannon 1993).

In the early 1990s, a small community of researchers in HCI and CSCW who based their research at least partly on activity theory, had taken shape. The community comprised barely more than a half-dozen individuals working in as many countries (Denmark, Finland, Germany, Ireland, Russia, and the U.S.) and having diverse backgrounds, including anthropology, computer science, and psychology. The work at that time was mostly theoretical, more concerned with understanding the prospects for using activity theory as a foundation for HCI and related fields than with using it as a tool for the analysis and design of concrete technologies. It was concluded that activity theory could be used to inform a broader perspective on real-life uses of technology than the traditional cognitive approach (Bannon 1990; Bannon and Bødker 1991; Kuutti 1991, 1992; Bødker 1993; Kaptelinin 1992; Nardi 1992), that it provides an integrated account of processes taking place at various levels (Kuutti and Bannon 1993), and that it could help formulate new research questions for further studies in HCI and CSCW (Kaptelinin 1992; Kuutti 1992; Raeithel 1992). Other issues elaborated in early activity theory–based research in interaction design included a comparative analysis of activity theory and other theoretical approaches, such as situated-action models and distributed cognition (Nardi 1992, 1993), and revisions to some traditional HCI concepts such as affordances (Kaptelinin 1992).

A series of East–West HCI (EWHCI) conferences, which took place in Russia in 1992–1995, contributed to consolidating early interaction design research based on activity theory. The conferences provided a meeting place and a forum for researchers already interested in activity theory. They made the approach more visible for the HCI community in general and promoted its wider spread in international HCI research. The conferences stimulated new activity theory–based research initiatives in Australia (Bourke, Verenikina, and Gould 1993; Hasan, Gould, and Hyland 1998) and France (Linard and Zeiliger 1995).

To illustrate their conceptual claims, early activity-theoretical studies in HCI relied mostly on retrospective accounts of existing systems and reevaluation of empirical studies. For instance, Bødker (1991) revisited several design projects she was involved in including the development of Smalltalk 80 at Xerox PARC, the UTOPIA project, and the design of a mail-handling system at Aarhus Polytechnics. These cases were used as illustrations demonstrating that complex project activities could be described in terms of actions, operations, tools, and the coordination of individual activities within a collective activity. Nardi (1994, 1996b) reflected on a previous study of the use patterns of slide presentation programs. A surprising finding of the original study was the discovery that, contrary to researchers' expectations, there was no simple correlation between the complexity of software and user expertise. It was thought that simple tools would be used by relatively inexperienced users, while experts would progress to more advanced ones. However, it was found that even though expert users did employ advanced software more frequently, they regularly resorted to simple presentation programs. Applying activity theory, which moved the focus of analysis from technology to users' goals, provided a simple and natural explanation of the unexpected use pattern. Different types of software were more appropriate for different purposes, so users selected optimal tools depending on the context. Basic, easy-to-use tools were employed to create standard presentations while more sophisticated tools were selected for more demanding tasks.

Early activity theory–based studies in interaction design were described in the edited collection *Context and Consciousness: Activity Theory and Human–Computer Interaction* (Nardi 1996a). This book made the approach more visible to the international research community and presented it in more detail, and with more relevance to the concepts, concerns, and research agenda of contemporary HCI research. Apparently it stimulated more attempts to apply activity theory in analysis, evaluation, and design of information technologies.

During the decade that has passed since *Context and Consciousness* was published, activity theory has continued to contribute to the theoretical development of HCI, CSCW, and CSCL. Applications of activity theory have become more specific. Abstract conceptual analyses have been complemented by concrete contributions to design and evaluation methodologies, as well as contributions to the design of concrete applications and systems. And the activity theory perspective in interaction design has become more diverse. Several theoretical frameworks proposed during the last decade share the most basic assumptions of activity theory but at the same time were often shaped by other theoretical influences, such as experientialism (Imaz and Benyon 1996), participatory design (Bødker and Christiansen 1997), French ergonomics (Rabardel and Bourmaud 2003), and Bakhtinian concepts (Spinuzzi 2003).

In recent years, activity theory has become well established in the interaction design community. The number of papers, analytical tools, and systems based on the approach is constantly growing. Several international journals have published special issues devoted to studies based on activity theory, including the *Scandinavian Journal of Information Systems* (2000), *Computer Supported Cooperative Work* (1999, 2002), and *Interacting with Computers* (2003). This trend is part of a larger picture. Activity theory is becoming increasingly popular not only in interaction design but also in other fields, including education (Roth 2004), communication studies (Foot 2002b), and ergonomics (Bedny and Karwowski 2004).

In the next section we review activity theory–based research in HCI and CSCW, with a special focus on more recent studies, that is, those conducted in the decade since *Context and Consciousness* was published. The large volume of the research makes it impossible to cover all studies, and some important work is likely to be missing, but we have tried to include the most pertinent studies.

4.2   REFRAMING HUMAN–COMPUTER INTERACTION

4.2.1   Extending the Scope of HCI

A key theoretical contribution of activity theory to HCI was an extension of the field's scope of analysis and subject matter. In activity theory, the use of technology is

- embedded in meaningful context;
- not limited to information processing; and
- operative at several levels, which have to be integrated.

Along with other postcognitivist approaches, activity theory was instrumental in reformulating the general objective of HCI. Instead of being predominantly concerned with conducting laboratory studies aimed at revealing the underlying mechanisms of human information processing—which are basically the same regardless of who is interacting with technology—and then employing these mechanisms in user interface design, the field of HCI was understood as dealing with specific meanings and contexts of uses of technology in everyday life. By considering technology as a mediator between human beings and the world, rather than a pole of interaction, activity theory brought to light important new issues. Bødker (1989, 1991) identified three aspects of the user interface that should be taken into account in design:

- physical aspects (operating with a device as a physical object);
- handling aspects (the logical structure of interaction with the interface); and
- subject–object-directed aspects (how objects "in the computer" are related to objects in the world).

While the first two aspects were studied within mainstream HCI, the third aspect was largely ignored in HCI research at the time of Bødker's studies.

The emphasis on the role of technology within the entirety of meaningful, purposeful human interaction with the world revealed limitations of purely cognitive analyses. Computer users are not just information-processing devices but individuals striving to achieve their goals. Their interests, emotions, hopes, passions, fears, and frustrations are important and powerful factors in choosing, learning, and using a technology. Many studies that raised these issues in relation to interaction design have been based on, or influenced by, activity theory (Christiansen 1996; Engeström and Escalante 1996; Agre 1997; Nardi and O'Day 1999).

Activity theory provides a coordinated description of the use of technology at several hierarchical levels at the same time, and thus opens up a possibility to combine, or at least coordinate, analyses of different aspects of the use of technology, such as physical interaction, conceptual interaction, and social "contextual" interaction (Kuutti and Bannon 1993). These aspects, considered to be different levels of analysis, are traditionally studied by different disciplines (respectively, psychophysiology, cognitive psychology, and sociology or sociocultural psychology). To guide design effectively, requirements and considerations originating from different levels of analysis should be integrated into a coherent set of system requirements. Activity theory offers a conceptual framework that allows a vertical integration of different levels of analysis.

4.2.2   Rethinking HCI Concepts

The underlying principles of activity theory were used to reconsider some of the most central concepts of traditional HCI, including concepts of transparency, affordance, and direct manipulation.

Transparency   *Transparency* has traditionally been considered a key aspect of user interface quality (see, e.g., Hutchins, Hollan, and Norman 1986; Bødker 1991; Shneiderman 1998). The exact meaning of this concept is rather elusive and rarely clarified. Typically, its meaning is indicated by describing what it is *not*, as a lack of distractions caused by the user interface itself (Bardram and Bertelsen 1995). Transparent interaction is an interaction in which the user can focus on his work, while the system—the mediating artifact—remains "invisible." Therefore, user interfaces can be called "transparent" in a metaphorical sense, which is related to attention rather than perception: the notion of transparency implies that users are not aware of the system, not that they do not actually see it.

According to activity theory, individuals are aware of their *actions*, while routine operations are carried out automatically without interfering with conscious processes. Therefore, transparency can be accomplished through skill automatization (Kaptelinin 1991), that is, the transformation of actions into operations (Bardram and Bertelsen 1995). Transparency is not a fixed property of a system; almost any user interface, provided that sufficient time and effort is invested by the user, can become transparent (Kaptelinin 1991; Bardram and Bertelsen 1995). In other words, transparency cannot be "built" into a system. Designers can only create preconditions for development of operations, but transparency itself is an emerging property of interaction as a whole, which may or may not be present in each individual case of using a system. Of course, there are a number of ways in which designers can facilitate skill automatization, for instance, by mapping user interface components to unvarying spatial locations (Kaptelinin 1993). However, the outcome—whether or not an interface is transparent—depends critically on concrete users in concrete contexts of use. Even the best designs under certain conditions will not result in transparent interaction. And even the "worst," such as UNIX (a welter of terse algebra-like text commands), can reach the highest levels of transparency in the hands of proficient users.

Affordance   *Affordance* is a concept that has sparked much debate in HCI. Originally the concept was proposed by Gibson (1979) within the framework of his ecological approach to visual perception. According to Gibson, "the affordances of the environment are what it offers to the animal ..." (1979). Gibson maintained that animals (including *Homo sapiens*) *perceive directly*, rather than infer through step-by-step processing of sensory inputs, the most important aspects of their environments— the possible ways of acting in an environment.

The concept was introduced to HCI by Norman (1988) and became especially popular with practitioners who widely believed that a key to good interface design was to implement affordances that "provide strong visual clues to the operations of things" (Norman 1988). More recently, Gibson's and Norman's interpretations of the concept have been widely discussed (Norman 1999; McGrenere and Ho 2000; Torenvliet 2003), but the discussions appear to generate new conceptual contradictions rather than resolve old ones.

Despite a variety of perspectives on affordances, there is a common understanding that affordances are the possibilities for action provided by the environment, and that they "exist relative to the action capabilities of a particular actor" (McGrenere and Ho 2000). Discrepancies between individual interpretations of "affordances" emerge when different theorists, often implicitly, assign different meanings to terms such as "actor," "action," and "action capabilities."

There have been several attempts to address the issue of affordances from an activity theory perspective (Kaptelinin 1996c; Albrechtsen et al.

2001; Baerentsen and Trettvik 2002). These analyses articulated a few ideas that may help avoid a narrow understanding of "action" and "action capabilities" when developing a conceptually consistent view on affordances.

The meaning of "action" in activity theory includes much more than motor responses dissociated from perception. Perception is an integral part of human interaction with the world. It plays a key role in both carrying out actions and determining what the action capabilities of a particular individual are. Since affordances are a property of interaction between an animal and the world, an animal cannot engage an affordance without perception. In this respect, the activity theory position is consistent with Gibson's (1979) view and inconsistent with separating affordances and perception as suggested, for instance, by McGrenere and Ho (2000) and Torenvliet (2003).

McGrenere and Ho (2000) made a strong claim: "Let us be clear, the existence of the affordance is independent of the actor's experiences and culture...." Separating affordances, experiences, and culture is in conflict with the underlying ideas of both Gibson and activity theory. Gibson's examples of affordances include those taking place in complex types of activities such as business and politics. The possibilities for action in these contexts are apparently determined by culture. Therefore, conceptual similarities between activity theory and Gibson's ecological psychology (Logvinenko 1988; Baerentsen and Trettvik 2002) help contextualize the concept of affordances in interaction design.

Another way activity theory–based analyses contributed to a conceptual exploration of affordances was through exploring the differences between Gibson's approach and activity theory. In particular, activity theory's emphasis on mediation and learning and its view of human activity as hierarchically organized have no parallel in ecological psychology (Albrechtsen et al. 2001; Baerentsen and Trettvik 2002). Affordances are typically interpreted in terms of low-level manipulation with physical artifacts. Therefore, the concept is limited to the level of operations. According to Baerentsen and Trettvik (2002), these affordances can be called "operational affordances." Operational affordances indicate which operations can be carried out with the objects at hand. However, as Baerentsen and Trettvik (2002) pointed out, the concept can be extended to levels of actions and activities, as well. From an activity theory standpoint, the notion of affordances needs to be extended to human activity as a whole, not just the level of operations.

Direct manipulation (Shneiderman 1983; Hutchins, Hollan, and Norman 1986) is another fundamental concept of traditional HCI that was revised within the framework of activity theory. The concept of direct manipulation was introduced by Shneiderman (1983) in the early 1980s as an attempt both to describe the main features of a new type of user interface emerging at the time and to formulate criteria for designing successful interfaces of the new type.

The transition to a new interaction paradigm was truly remarkable. To utilize the resources of the previous generation of personal computers, users had to type in text commands that required extensive learning and effectively prevented computers from becoming part of the everyday lives of most people. The new type of interfaces allowed a range of operations, such as moving or deleting computer files through "physically" manipulating graphical objects on the screen. The resounding success of WIMP (windows, icons, menus, and pointing) interfaces can be considered one of the most astonishing technological successes in history. According to Shneiderman, this success capitalized on human abilities to act with objects in the physical world, perfected through millions of years of evolution. He suggested that the new user interfaces reified the principles of direct manipulation, namely: (a) continuous representation of the objects of interest, (b) physical actions instead of complex syntax, (c) rapid incremental reversible operations with immediate feedback, and (d) spiral learning.

For many years, these principles, and the underlying vision of direct manipulation as the ideal user interface, were rarely challenged in HCI research. However, a recent activity theory–informed analysis of how these principles are implemented in actual user interfaces revealed that users seldom operate on their objects of interest, such as documents, directly (Beaudouin-Lafon 2000). In both physical and virtual environments people employ "instruments," such as hammers and screwdrivers, or scroll bars and toolbars, when performing operations on things. Driving a screw into a piece of wood is typically accomplished not by pressing and turning the screw with bare hands, but by applying an effort to a screwdriver, which, in turn, produces the desired effect. Similarly, scrolling a document is accomplished by controlling a scroll bar, which, in turn, makes the document scroll. According to Beaudouin-Lafon (2000), user interface designers should differentiate between *domain objects* and *interaction instruments*. Domain objects are potential objects of interest for the user. For instance, a text is an object of interest for a user composing the text, while a text style may be an object of interest for a user formatting a text. Interaction instruments are user interface components that transform user actions into commands for domain objects. An example of an interaction instrument is a scroll bar. When the user clicks on a scroll arrow, the scroll bar transforms this action into a small incremental movement of the text (the domain object) in a window. The concept of instrumental interaction was proposed by Beaudouin-Lafon as a revision and extension of direct interaction in guiding the design of both WIMP and post-WIMP interfaces. According to the proposed approach, the aim of design should be to provide an optimal integration of domain objects and interaction instruments, rather than to make interaction as direct as possible.

4.3 EMPIRICAL WORKPLACE STUDIES

While ethnomethodological perspectives have inspired a number of detailed empirical studies of collaboration and collaborative workplaces (e.g., Heath and Luff 1992; Bowers, Button, and Sharrock 1995), relatively little attention has been paid to the most common uses of computers, that is, the everyday work of office and knowledge workers. This is paradoxical, since the virtual work environment is a habitat, as Ducheneaut and Bellotti (2001) called it, where people spend most of their working time. In contrast to physical work environments, where failures to adequately and efficiently organize tools and resources are immediately obvious and may be recognized as problems (Malone 1983), managing virtual work environments is mostly an individual activity, often invisible to other people and rarely shared with others. Perhaps that is one of the reasons why problems of the virtual desktop are seldom recognized as issues that need to be addressed by further empirical research. Users are provided with building blocks, such as files and folders, but they are offered little help on how to use them to create efficient and comfortable environments. Basically, each user has to construct his environment from scratch. Different people come up with different solutions. An indicator of the underlying diversity is the variety of the appearance of individual desktops, which is really just the tip of the iceberg. Invisible to external observers are numerous, often unreflected, and ad hoc design decisions about the structure of individual desktop environments.

It seems that an underlying assumption shared by most designers and researchers is that creating a virtual work environment by using the facilities of current operating systems is a simple task that users are well equipped to carry out. However, empirical studies of how people use conventional desktop operating systems indicate that making information technology a part of everyday work is far from trivial (Cypher 1986; Barreau and Nardi 1995; Nardi, Anderson, and Erickson 1995; Erickson 1996; Kaptelinin 1996d; Ravasio, Guttormsen-Schär, and Krueger 2004).

Nardi, Anderson, and Erickson (1995) found that users employed three types of information objects in their digital work environments: working information, archived information, and ephemeral information. Typically, the design of virtual environments reflects a formal logical view of the organization of information rather than users' needs and requirements. In particular, the environments do not take into account the need to manage ephemeral information, which plays a number of roles, including reminding people about things to be done. Nardi and her colleague found that users creatively employed facilities provided by existing operating systems to manage ephemeral information. For instance, ephemeral items were often placed on the desktop, where they could be noticed easily and, if necessary, moved to the trash bin. However, this use is not intentionally supported by designers and may even be in conflict with the underlying metaphor. The source object of the desktop metaphor—the surface of a regular desk—is typically reserved for documents in use, and is seldom employed as an intermediate storage for low-value items on their way to the waste basket.

Another study of approaches and strategies used for creating digital workspaces for everyday work (Kaptelinin 1996d) found that many users of a popular operating system had common problems, including organizing various types of information around individual projects, cleaning up their workspaces, and keeping private and public information separate. The study revealed a variety of approaches developed and employed by the users to cope with these problems. It was also found that none of the standard system features intended to help users with these problems, such as "labels" or "aliases," was actually used.

New types of hybrid "physical–virtual" work environments present challenges that need to be understood and dealt with adequately. In a study of a technician at a wastewater plant (Bertelsen and Bødker 2002) it was shown that the work activities were mediated by "clusters of artifacts," that is, compound entities comprising both information-processing and more traditional technologies. It appears that this conclusion regarding clusters of artifacts can be generalized to all types of work environments. Office environments have long been dominated by a general-purpose desktop computer as the main tool. However, combinations of tools have always been used, and a recent trend toward distributed and mobile work supported by a coordinated use of several information devices (such as desktop computers, laptop computers, PDAs, and mobile phones) makes this especially obvious.

Empirical studies informed by activity theory, described above, comprise a substantial part of all empirical research of the use of information technologies in work tasks performed in typical work settings. Even though important research in this area has been also undertaken from other theoretical standpoints (e.g., Kidd 1994; Ravasio, Guttormsen-Schär, and Krueger 2003), it is hardly surprising that activity theory has had a significant impact in this area given its interest in tool mediation and integrated, multilevel accounts of purposeful human activities.

4.4   UNDERSTANDING AND SUPPORTING COLLABORATION

4.4.1   Activity Theory and Computer-Supported Cooperative Work

HCI was originally established as a discipline dealing with the user interface. It took several years of development to extend its reach and include a broader context of meaningful social human activity. However, in areas that from the outset were predominantly concerned with social interactions, namely, computer-supported cooperative work and computer support for collaborative learning, there was no need to advocate the crucial importance of understanding the social context. In these areas, activity theory was immediately recognized as a promising conceptual framework.

In papers presented at CSCW conferences in the early 1990s, Kuutti (1991) proposed activity as the basic unit of analysis for CSCW research, and Kuutti and Arvonen (1992) presented one of the first analytical tools based on activity theory (described in detail in section 4.5.2). Despite a marked interest in activity theory in CSCW, the most influential approach in CSCW has traditionally been ethnomethodology which emphasizes the importance of paying attention to every detail and avoiding theoretical presuppositions when studying the complex reality of everyday collaboration. As discussed in chapter 2, there are substantial differences between activity theory and ethnomethodology. In contrast to ethnomethodology, activity theory does apply theoretical presuppositions. However, within CSCW, there is a certain affinity between these approaches. Both maintain that the reality of everyday work, rather than its abstract rational model, should be taken as the point of departure when understanding collaboration, and that this understanding should be used to inform design. It is not uncommon among system developers to believe that an appropriate way to understand work is to interview managers, analyze formal job descriptions, and ask systems analysts about the optimal logical structure of work that should be supported, and even enforced, by a new system (Sachs 1995). Both activity theory and ethnomethodology oppose the idea that it is sufficient to base system design on formal, normative descriptions of work. Both theories point out that actual work practices are much more complex than their formal descriptions.

Sachs (1995) contrasted two views on work which she called an "organizational, explicit" view, and an "activity-oriented, tacit" view. The former is represented by descriptions of work tasks, methods, and procedures, while the latter deals with the activities, communication practices, relationships, and coordination through which the work is actually being done. The organizational, explicit view and the activity-oriented, tacit view emphasize different aspects of work, respectively: training versus learning; tasks versus "know how"; organizational hierarchy versus informal networks; procedures and techniques versus conceptual understanding and rules of thumb; work flow versus work practices; and teams versus communities. According to Sachs, design for workplaces needs to take into account both views but is often influenced only by the organizational view. The distinction between the two views is illustrated with the example of a system referred to as the Trouble Ticketing System (TTS). TTS was intended to optimize the work of a telephone company by issuing and monitoring individual assignments. The system was not successful because workers had fewer possibilities to learn from each other and tried to redirect tasks to other workers as quickly as possible in order to minimize their individual time spent on a task.

The CSCW literature of the 1990s reported several ethnomethodological analyses of why workflow systems fail. The systems were intended to optimize the efficiency and effectiveness of organizational activities, but they did not take into account how people actually go about their work (e.g., Bowers, Button, and Sharrock 1995). These studies indicated some directions for designing more successful systems. In particular, they emphasized the importance of articulation and awareness in traditional cooperative work, and maintained that articulation and awareness need to be supported in computer-based environments, as well (e.g., Heath and Luff 1992).

However, in general, ethnomethodological research on workflow systems was not easily applicable to design (Lancaster University and Manchester University 1994). In addition to the divide between social science research and systems design (Bowker et al. 1997), there was another reason for these difficulties. Even though ethnomethodological criticisms of workflow systems were not unfounded, the analyses adopted a generally negative attitude toward the systems and rejected them altogether rather than suggest how they could be improved. This attitude can be partly explained by the influence of Suchman's view of human actions (Suchman 1987). Since human actions, according to Suchman, typically emerge in a concrete situation rather than follow a predefined plan, workflow systems were viewed as attempts to fit situated work into the Procrustean bed of predetermined procedures.

Activity theory seeks to strike a balance between relatively stable higher-level goals of the subject and highly situated processes of attaining these goals (Nardi 1994, 1996c). This viewpoint is evident in a different perspective on workflow systems. Bardram (1997, 1998) conducted an activity theory–based study of workflow systems in a hospital setting within the framework of the SAIK[1] project which aimed to develop computer support for clinical work. The study dealt with the role of plans in setting up and carrying out work activities in the setting. It was found that plans served a number of coordinating functions in collective activities; they were used as means for dividing work, providing work status overviews, and making records.

Bardram concluded that, from an activity-theoretical standpoint, "a plan can be defined as *a cognitive or material artifact which supports the anticipatory reflection for future goals for actions, based on experience about recurrent structures in life*" (Bardram 1998, italics in the original). In other words, the need to adjust collective activities to specific contexts requires plans as a special type of coordination artifact. Therefore, if properly designed, workflow systems as "embodiments" of plans can support the situated nature of work rather than defy it. The approach proposed by Bardram, called "situated planning," leveraged the benefits of flexible plans as coordination artifacts supporting collaboration.

The concept of collective activity has been employed by CSCW researchers as a useful analytical tool helping to understand cooperative work as a continuous attempt to resolve the contradiction between the common object of a joint endeavor and the potentially conflicting perspectives of the participants. Such an account helps to identify specific types of contradictions and the ways information technologies can be designed to take these contradictions into account. The concepts of "the collective object" and "the collective subject" were employed in order to face the challenge of understanding modern forms of collaboration, often induced by the use of information and communication technologies that do not fall into traditional categories of "teams," "organizations," and "communities of practice" (see, e.g., Clases and Wehner 2002; Nardi et al. 2002; Zager 2002).

Nardi et al. (2002) presented empirical evidence and a theoretical analysis arguing that more and more work is being done in "intensional networks," that is, personal social networks emerging across organizational boundaries. A key phenomenon in intensional networks is the development of collective subjects, which are constituted through remembering and communicating. These understandings were used to develop a system "ContactMap" which organized the desktop according to users' personal social networks (Nardi et al. 2002; Fisher and Nardi in press).

Zager (2002) proposed the design of "virtual worlds" to support coordination within loosely organized collaboration processes, such as the management of computer networks in large organizations. This approach has been implemented in a system Zager designed called Trinity.

The notion of collective activity also provides a lens for understanding the processes of knowledge production and management in organizations. Since the generation of knowledge, from an activity theory perspective, is a process that can be embedded in different types of interaction between participants in a collective activity, technological support for knowledge generation and management needs to take into account the diversity of contexts, potentially conflicting perspectives, the ways coordination and cooperation are regulated in collective activity, and the fact that collective activities more often than not have to deal with unexpected events (Clases and Wehner 2002).

4.4.2   Activity Theory and Computer Support for Collaborative Learning

In 1996, Koschmann described computer support for collaborative learning (CSCL) as an emerging paradigm in instructional technology: "I argue ... that we are currently witnessing the emergence of a new paradigm in IT (instructional technology) research; one that is based on different assumptions about the nature of learning and one that incorporates a new set of research practices" (Koschmann 1996b). Koschmann identified cultural-historical psychology and activity theory as key sources of insight underlying the paradigm shift. From the very emergence of the field, activity theory was one of the main frameworks employed in CSCL research.

Activity theory influenced CSCL in a variety of ways. In addition to a general emphasis on the need to consider learning activity as a meaningful context for understanding the design and use of technology, activity theory made a number of specific contributions to the field. A variety of empirical studies that explored new ways of supporting collaborative learning with information technologies were based on activity theory. The theory supported conceptualization of the distinction between individual and group learning, modeling the context of collaborative learning, and development of analytical tools for designing CSCL systems.

One of the first CSCL projects, the Fifth Dimension project, was an attempt to create a computer-based learning environment as a mixed-activity setting. The aim of creating the setting was to facilitate learning and development in the zone of proximal development. The Fifth Dimension project was initiated by Michael Cole and his colleagues at the University of California in San Diego in the mid-1980s (Cole 1996).

The research attempted to deal with two key issues: sustainability and the social context of educational computer use. Promising educational innovations often die away when researchers are no longer involved in running the projects. The Fifth Dimension was intended to be a sustainable setting that could survive as a regular part of an educational institution. At the time the project was initiated there was a tendency to overestimate the importance of technology, to see it as a silver bullet for solving all of education's problems. By placing the main focus on the social context of learning with computers, the Fifth Dimension became one of the first research initiatives to explore the social context of learning with information technologies, rather than technologies per se.

To deal with these issues, the Fifth Dimension, which is an ongoing project,[2] was designed as follows. Children and undergraduate students play and learn together in a fantasy world organized around computer-based activities. The setting is sustainable because it is based on the long-term interests of the main stakeholders, that is, (a) the children's interest in computers and in communicating with other people, (b) the undergraduate students' interest in learning a university subject (e.g., psychology, child development, or education) that includes visiting a Fifth Dimension site, and (c) the community's interest in providing children with new opportunities for learning. A low child–adult ratio in the setting creates favorable conditions for the implementation of ideas underlying cultural-historical psychology, especially the notion of the zone of proximal development.

Fifth Dimension sites are typically set up as after-school settings where collaborative learning is organized around playing computer games. They are designed as "model cultures," that is, they have their own rules, norms, artifacts, and even mythology. Collaborative computer game playing is the central type of activity in the setting. This activity is regulated by a set of specially created rules and norms. Computer tools— more specifically, educational computer games—are just one component of the whole system.

A key issue addressed within the Fifth Dimension project, as well as in CSCL research informed by activity theory in general (see Stahl 2006), has been the relationship between learning as an individual phenomenon and as a collective phenomenon. This issue was addressed in a seminal paper by Cole and Engeström (1993), one of the most-often cited references in CSCL. Cole and Engeström extended Vygotsky's unidirectional view of development (from the interpsychological to the intrapsychological) to understanding learning and development as bidirectional phenomena. This understanding provided an account for both internalization and externalization, the impact of collective learning on individual learning, and vice versa.

The line of CSCL research established by Cole and Engeström was continued in more recent studies such as those by Bellamy (1996) and Kaptelinin and Cole (2002). Bellamy (1996) addressed fundamental questions regarding how and why technology can promote change in school education. Bellamy concluded that the potential of technology to promote change is related directly to the role of technology as a mediator of human activity. She formulated three criteria a technology should meet to be appropriate for school education: support for communities of learners, support for constructing artifacts, and support for authentic activities.

Empirical evidence obtained during the Fifth Dimension project was analyzed by Kaptelinin and Cole (2002) from the point of view of mutual transformations between individual and collective activities. They found that learning in the setting was characterized by both appropriation of rules and norms of the Fifth Dimension by individual participants (internalization) and enacting the rules and norms in interactions with other participants, which ensured cultural continuity of the setting (externalization).

Activity theory was employed as a guiding theoretical framework in a series of studies of teaching and learning in videoconference-based learning environments conducted by Hedestig and Kaptelinin (2002, 2005). The first of these studies focused on *technological remediation* of traditional university education under new conditions. The study revealed that the transition from traditional on-campus learning activities to videoconference-based activities was not straightforward. Using the terminology proposed by Engeström (1990), the transition required both *downward contextualization*, that is, an adaptation of activities to the limitations and affordances of the environment, and *upward contextualization*, that is, locating activities in a larger-scale organizational context. Various types and sources of breakdowns were observed, including discoordinations in synchronous communications, technological limitations, and interinstitutional barriers.

In a follow-up study (Hedestig and Kaptelinin 2005), the focus shifted to factors underlying successful integration of technology into teaching and learning and preventing breakdowns from taking place. More specifically, the study dealt with the work practice of a technician whose responsibilities formally consisted of making sure videoconferencing equipment was in working order and properly configured during videoconference sessions. It was found that successful learning in the videoconference setting was possible only because the technician also assumed a number of extra responsibilities and roles, not formally required of him, in addition to his normal duties. Owing to his extra work many potential breakdowns were avoided. The concept of *suprasituational activities* (Petrovsky 1975) was used to provide an account of the data obtained in the study and to understand conditions of successful functioning of emerging technology-based learning environments.

Suprasituational activities transcend the immediate requirements of the situation at hand. People taking part in collective activities may carry out actions which are not required of them and can even be in conflict with their individual interests. This type of behavior, which is often difficult to explain rationally, is nevertheless quite common. Rebels, dissidents, enthusiasts, and Good Samaritans come to mind, or, in the case of computer users, "gurus and gardeners" who provide technology expertise to coworkers even though it is not part of their job description (Gantt and Nardi 1992). Suprasituational activities can be considered a necessary but temporary stage in the development of an activity system. When the activity system underlying a certain practice is not completely supported by tools, rules, and the division of labor (Engeström 1990), suprasituational activities are what hold the activity system together. However, the functions served by these activities can be expected to be transformed gradually into functions served by artifacts, environments, and norms of the setting. Therefore, suprasituational activities are critically important during the initial phase when an emerging activity system has not yet crystallized into the material and organizational structure of a setting. Occasionally, when unexpected changes occur and a readjustment of the activity system is required, suprasituational activities may provide the additional degree of resilience needed to complete the change. At the same time, by keeping an activity system afloat, suprasituational activities provide a basis for improvements and developments that can ultimately make them unnecessary.

An activity-theoretical perspective on computer support for collaborative learning is distinctly different from other common approaches to designing technology-enhanced learning environments. Gifford and Enyedy (1999) explored the theoretical underpinnings of computer-mediated learning environments and identified two important approaches— domain-centered design, based on the transmission model of instruction, and learner-centered design which by and large ignores collaboration and interaction with peers. Gifford and Enyedy concluded that neither domain-centered design, which has been widely criticized (fig. 4.1), nor learner-centered design (fig. 4.2) can be considered appropriate models for CSCL:

> Developing learning environments based on the LCD [learner-centered design] model is shortsighted on several accounts. First, this model often goes too far in reducing the role that the teacher plays, denying the student access to the accumulated wisdom, experience, and empathy of expert teachers. Second, like Domain Centered Design, the LCD model ignores the social context of learning and the important role of conversation and collaboration as part of the active learning process. Third, the environments are focused on individual student misconceptions which need to be changed to the normative conceptual understanding. (Gifford and Enyedy 1999)

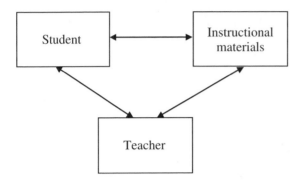

Figure 4.1
The domain-centered model of computer-mediated learning. From Gifford and Enyedy 1999. Reproduced with permission of the authors.

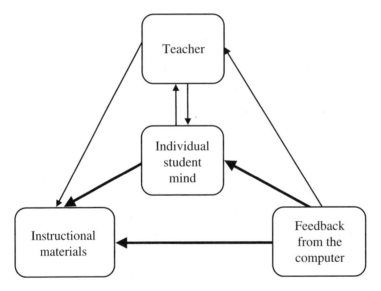

Figure 4.2
Learner-centered design. From Gifford and Enyedy 1999. Reproduced with permission of the authors.

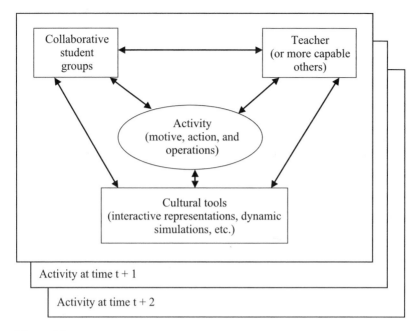

Figure 4.3
Activity-centered design. From Gifford and Enyedy 1999. Reproduced with permission of the authors.

Gifford and Enyedy further maintained that

> while the recent work of the CSCL community avoids a narrow focus on the individual, much of the research is still attempting to build on the ideas and assumptions of learner-centered design. Instead of the individual, however, at the center of the model are collaborative groups of students. (Gifford and Enyedy 1999)

To address this problem, Gifford and Enyedy introduced a new model influenced explicitly by activity theory (see fig. 4.3). This model, placing developing activity at the center, makes use of the following activity-theoretical insights:

- culturally defined tools mediate all activity, and mediation fundamentally changes the nature of the task;
- activity can be analyzed at three levels (activities, actions, and operations); and
- cognition and mediating cultural tools have their origins in social interaction.

The activity-centered design model was used to evaluate a concrete educational system, Probability Enquiry Environment. The evaluation, which showed that actual student activities corresponded only partly to intended activities, indicated problems related to the context of using tools and how they related to other artifacts in the setting.

Recently, Gay and Hembrooke (2004) studied the use of wireless laptop computers among undergraduates at Cornell University. Rather than focusing on individual learners, they examined evolving social practices surrounding laptop use, investigating a contradiction in the social system brought about by the technology. Although the wireless technology was supposed to foster learning communities, in many cases it had the opposite effect as learners began to surf the Internet, instant message with friends, and so on, during class time. Rather than bring learners together for shared projects, the technology tempted them to virtually "depart" the learning community, offering such individual excitements as day trading, reading email, and searching for personal information. Finally, the students discussed the problem as a community and came to the conclusion that some social rules were necessary to manage the technology. Thus Gay and Hembrooke used activity theory to focus on a community of learners, to examine a contradiction induced by the introduction of a particular technology, and to understand the collective response to the contradiction that allowed students to use the technology as it had originally been intended. (This study will be discussed in more detail in chap. 9.)

Activity theory has been used in a variety of empirical studies as a framework for analysis and evaluation of concrete cases of technologically mediated collaborative learning such as constructivist learning environments (Jonassen and Rohrer-Murphy 1999), workplace learning in coronary clinical work (Sutter 2002a,b), and distance education (Mwanza 2000, 2002a,b).

4.5   ANALYTICAL TOOLS FOR DESIGN AND EVALUATION

4.5.1   The Activity Checklist

The uses of activity theory described so far capitalize primarily on its potential as a broad theoretical framework. The broadness of the theory makes it possible to extend the scope of analysis and bring new dimensions into the focus of interaction design. However, could this same feature of the theory be an obstacle to practical application in design and evaluation of information technologies? Is it possible to translate the underlying concepts and principles of activity theory into concrete and practical tools that can help create better products?

We believe that the contribution of activity theory to the field of interaction design cannot be limited to theoretical developments. It is true that the approach does not provide readymade answers and solutions to concrete questions and problems. However, by changing the perspective of researchers and practitioners, activity theory can make an impact on solving practical problems by helping to find a way to address a problem and to ask the "right" questions. To make this easier, a number of analytical tools based on activity theory have been developed and used in concrete design and evaluation projects.

One of the first recognized potential uses of activity theory was to create analytical tools for structuring empirical evidence. When dealing with the diversity and richness of empirical data related to using information technologies in real-life contexts, a common problem one faces is how to break down the body of the data into manageable pieces while preserving the whole's structure and consistency. A possible approach, suggested by ethnomethodology, is to keep as much detail as possible and avoid generalizations. However, this approach is not always valued by designers and evaluators (see, e.g., Lancaster University and Manchester University 1994). Accounts based on activity theory, on the other hand, however general and theoretical, provide clues on which aspects of the phenomena under investigation are more important and how these aspects are related to each other. In other words, the conceptual framework of activity theory can be used as a descriptive and orientational framework that facilitates the handling and interpretation of empirical evidence about complex phenomena of the technological mediation of everyday practices.

We used activity theory as such a framework when developing an analytical tool, the Activity Checklist (Kaptelinin, Nardi, and Macaulay 1999). The rationale behind this tool was to make activity theory more practically applicable in specific tasks of design and evaluation. The Activity Checklist is intended to elucidate the most important contextual factors of human–computer interaction by pointing to specific areas that a researcher or practitioner should be paying attention to. In other words, the Checklist lays out a "contextual design space" by representing the key areas of context specified by activity theory.

The structure of the Checklist reflects the basic principles of activity theory as described in chapter 3:

- object-orientedness,
- tool mediation,
- internalization–externalization,
- hierarchical structure of activity, and
- development.

In Kaptelinin, Nardi, and Macaulay 1999, the principle of tool mediation was applied throughout the Checklist and systematically combined with other principles. This resulted in four sections of the Checklist, which correspond to four main perspectives on the use of the "target technology" (that is, the concrete technology to be evaluated or designed): (a) *means and ends*, the extent to which the technology facilitates and constrains attaining users' goals; (b) *environment*, the integration of target technology with other tools and resources; (c) *learning, cognition, and articulation*, that is, internal versus external components of activity and support of their mutual transformations; and (d) *development*, the transformation of components (a) through (c) over time. A detailed description of the Checklist can be found in appendix A of this volume.

The Checklist has been used for the analysis, evaluation, and design of a variety of technologies, including Apple Data Detectors (Nardi, Miller, and Wright 1998), an information system for a newspaper (Macauley 1999; Macauley, Benyon, and Crerar 2000), a Web site (Uden and Willis 2001), a videoconference-based learning environment (Hedestig and Kaptelinin 2002), and a collaborative tangible user interface (Fjeld, Morf, and Krueger 2004).

4.5.2 Using the Activity System Model in Analysis and Evaluation

Several analytical tools for interaction design were developed on the basis of the activity system model proposed by Engeström (1987, 1990,

1999a,b). The activity system model builds on Leontiev's approach but describes collective rather than individual activities. Even though Leontiev (1978) hinted at the possibility of extending the underlying ideas of his approach to supraindividual levels of analysis, he focused almost exclusively on individual activities. The model proposed by Engeström embeds the subject–object relationship that was the main focus of Leontiev's analysis into an extended model describing activity as a collective phenomenon.

Engeström defined the underlying concept of his framework as that of an

> object-oriented, collective, and culturally mediated human activity, or activity system. Minimum elements of this system include the object, subject, mediating artifacts (signs and tools), rules, community, and division of labor. (Engeström 1999a)

Therefore, activities are understood by Engeström as collective phenomena, both with respect to their object (as directed toward an object shared by a community) and with respect to their form (as carried out collectively rather than individually). Individuals, according to Engeström, can carry out actions only within a larger-scale collective activity system. Using as a point of departure Leontiev's view of activity as mediated subject–object interaction, and drawing on a variety of other sources, including biology, anthropology, and philosophy, Engeström introduced the third component of the interaction, that is, community (Engeström 1987). Adding this component resulted in a model describing a three-way interaction between subjects, objects, and community. Engeström (1987) then elaborated this model by suggesting that each of these three interactions can be mediated, and proposing three different types of mediators: tools, rules, and division of labor. The resulting model is typically represented as a triangular diagram describing the relationship between the components mentioned above (see fig. 4.4). As will be shown in the following chapters, the activity system model has become an analytical tool used in a wide range of concrete research, including studies in the field of interaction design.

The "triangular" activity system model developed by Engeström (1987, 1990) has been considered by several researchers as a promising descriptional framework for the analysis and evaluation of technologies and their use. Created as a tool for describing units of complex mediated

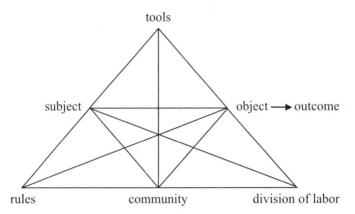

Figure 4.4
The activity system model. Adapted from Engeström 1990. Reproduced with permission of the author.

social practices, it clearly identifies key aspects of the described reality, points to potential contradictions, and provides a visual representation indicating how these aspects are related to each other (see also Kuutti 1996; Bai and Lindberg 1998). It is hardly surprising that the model had been widely used in interaction design to analyze various systems and technologically mediated activities.

Another analytical tool intended to support the design of CSCW systems was proposed by Kuutti and Arvonen (1992). This tool was a matrix (shown in table 4.1) produced by combining two sets of concepts. The first set was composed of the six nodes of Engeström's (1987) activity system model: subject, object, community, instruments, rules, and division of labor. The second set was comprised three potential uses of a CSCW system: (1) for supporting predetermined, routine procedures; (2) for supporting decision making and problem solving; and (3) for adjusting and developing technology in the process of use.

Turner, Turner, and Horton (1999) provided both theoretical arguments and a concrete example of how the main ideas of activity theory and cultural-historical psychology, and especially the activity system model, can be used in conjunction with ethnography to formulate requirements for a technology suitable for a particular work situation. Collins, Shukla, and Redmiles (2002) employed the activity system model to understand requirements for the use of SMS (short message ser-

Table 4.1
The range of relationships between an actor and a support system in an activity. Adapted from Kuutti and Arvonen 1992. Reproduced with permission of the authors.

Area of support	Role of a person toward the support system in an activity		
	Predetermined	Active	Expansive
Instrument	Routine automation	Tool	Automation or tool construction
Rules	Control	Shared meanings	Rule construction, negotiation
Division of labor	Fixed, "forced coordination"	Mutual coordination	Organizing work
Subject, "thinking"	Triggering a predetermined action	Searching information	Learning, understanding
Object	Data	Shared material	Object construction
Community	Fixed hierarchy/ network (invisible)	Malleable, visible network	Community construction

vice) as a part of the configuration of tools and technologies for customer support at a large corporation. They found Engeström's (1987) activity system model helpful for interpreting ethnographic data and formulating requirements for a new technology.

An analytical toolkit directly based on the activity system model, the "activity-oriented design method" (AODM), was developed by Mwanza (2002a,b). The method includes four tools. The first is the "eight-step model." Its steps include identifying the activity of interest and then proceeding to analyze the individual components of the model, namely, object, subject, tools, rules and regulations, division of labor, community, and outcome. The second tool is the "activity notation," employing a somewhat modified set of components making up the activity system model. The third tool is a technique for generating research questions, again by following the list of the component parts of the model. Finally, the fourth tool is the technique of "mapping AODM operational processes," which prescribes the following steps: *interpret, model,* and *decompose* the situation being examined; *generate* research questions; *conduct* a detailed investigation; and *interpret and communicate* findings.

Another example of an analytical tool that builds on the activity system model is a framework for designing *Constructivist Learning Environments* (used as a collective name for open-ended learning environments, microworlds, anchored instruction, problem-based learning, and goal-based scenarios) developed by Jonassen and Rohrer-Murphy (1999). This tool is intended to model the activity structure, tools and sign system, and sociocultural expectations that actors in a learning setting must accommodate while acting on the object of learning. The modeling is organized into six steps:

1. clarification of the purpose of activity system;
2. analysis of the activity system by identifying and describing its components (subject, object, community, tools, rules, and division of labor);
3. analysis of the activity structure (the hierarchy of activities, actions, and operations);
4. analysis of tools and mediators;
5. analysis of context; and
6. analysis of the activity system's dynamics.

To facilitate the use of the modeling tool, Jonassen and Rohrer-Murphy (1999) provided a checklist for carrying out each of the six steps, progressively clarifying the structure and functioning of activity systems.

Another analytical tool based on the activity system model is *Activity Space*, developed by Halloran, Rogers, and Scaife (2002). Activity Space is a modification of the activity system model that expands each node of the model to be able to represent potential contradictions within each of the nodes. Activity Space was used in Halloran et al.'s study to find out why a *Lotus Notes* application failed to support collaborative learning within a software design course as intended by the teacher. The analytical tool was found useful for revealing the multiple reasons behind the failure and understanding how the system could be improved.

4.5.3   The Diversity of Activity Theory–based Analytical Tools

The above analytical tools originating from activity theory are relatively new. Even though each apparently has its strengths and weaknesses, more research is needed to establish what exactly these strengths and weaknesses are. A recent study by Quek and Shah (2004) compared activity-based methods for information systems development along a number of dimensions, including the development phases supported and the use of visual models. The authors suggested that:

> existing methods need to be thoroughly tested and documented through empirical studies in practice. Further work is also needed, both to improve existing methods, as well as to produce new methods for making [activity theory] concepts applicable in practical development scenarios. (Quek and Shah 2004)

4.5.4 Organizational Prototyping

Prototyping is widely considered one of the most useful and effective techniques in the design of information technologies (see, e.g., Bødker, Grønbaek, and Kyng 1993; Hackos and Redish 1998; Preece, Rogers, and Sharp 2002). However, according to Bardram (1998), traditional prototyping has important limitations. First, prototyping typically focuses on the artifact itself, not on the practices in which the artifact is incorporated. Second, prototyping has been especially successful in the design of artifacts for individual use as opposed to groupware. Working with prototypes of groupware can be problematic because participants tend to be distributed in time and space. To address these challenges, Bardram (1998) proposed a new approach to prototyping, "organization prototyping," which draws on organizational games (e.g., Ehn and Sjögren 1991) and cooperative prototyping (e.g., Bødker, Grønbaek, and Kyng 1993).

Bardram's organizational prototyping technique integrates the following components:

1. one or more *scenarios* introducing the prototype to a concrete work practice;

2. the *prototype* itself;

3. *situation cards* describing examples of breakdown situations;

4. *action plans* for each situation card, specifying who does what, where, when, why, and by which means;

5. a *role script* for each participants; and

6. the *playground*, that is, a space where processed situation cards and action plans can be stored and categorized.

Bardram (1998) used organization prototyping to evaluate a CSCW system, the SAIK system mentioned in section 4.4.1.

4.6   DESIGN OF APPLICATIONS AND SYSTEMS

4.6.1   Toward Technological Support for Higher-Level Activities

In his book *The Invisible Computer: Why Good Products Can Fail* (1998), Don Norman told the story of a project which, if implemented, would have been one of the most revolutionary developments in the history of computing. Even though the project was not realized, it is worth mentioning here because it was strongly and explicitly inspired by activity theory.

In the mid-1990s Norman was not only a leading researcher in the area of HCI, one of the founders of the field, but also a key figure in the computer industry. In 1993, after leaving the Department of Cognitive Science at the University of California in San Diego (which he founded in the 1970s) Norman became a vice president of Apple Computer. In this capacity Norman, together with a group of prominent HCI researchers then working at Apple,[3] tried no less than to change the fundamental approach to creating software for personal computers. Instead of focusing on *applications*, which was (and probably still is) the dominant perspective in the computer industry, Norman proposed a new approach, activity-based computing (ABC), which he described as follows:

> The basic idea is simple. Make it possible to have all material needed for an activity ready at hand, available with little or no mental overhead. Tools, documents, and information are gathered together into packages maximally designed for particular activities in which they participate, without interfering with other activities. Of course, it must be possible to make changes in the choices and to switch rapidly and easily among the activities. Finally, items not needed for the current activity are hidden so they do not distract and do not take up valuable work space. (Norman 1998)

According to the ABC approach, the objective of software development was to be redefined as creating *activity spaces*, where people would work, individually and together with other people, over extended periods of time, occasionally switching to other activities and resuming the work after interruptions. Norman (1998) pointed to the ROOMS system (Henderson and Card 1986) and *Lotus Notes* as examples of software that incorporated some of the ideas underlying activity spaces. But Norman emphasized that a successful implementation of activity spaces "requires a somewhat different model of software than the current application-based framework" (Norman 1998).

Norman developed the ABC approach with explicit references to activity theory. Although the notion of activity used by the Apple ABC group was slightly different from the one developed by Leontiev, modifying the three-level hierarchy to a four-level hierarchy (activities–tasks–actions–operations), the ideas, concerns, and terminology were directly borrowed from activity theory–based HCI work of that time.

There are many possible reasons why the activity-based computing approach did not succeed; probably the actual reasons will never be established with certainty. The explanation provided by Norman is that the company, as well as, perhaps, the computer industry in general, was not ready or willing to adopt the approach, considering it too radical and risky. Another possible reason can be found in how activity-based computing was implemented. ABC was closely linked to the OpenDoc approach (a particular approach to document architectures). When the OpenDoc approach was abandoned, ABC lost some ground as well.

The story of activity-based computing shows that activity theory can in principle have far-reaching practical consequences for interaction design, even though this particular project cannot be called a success story. The idea of moving from supporting low-level tasks and applications to supporting higher-level meaningful activities is one of the main implications of activity theory, which is likely to be implemented eventually, one way or another. The Apple Computer ABC initiative has been the most ambitious attempt to employ this idea, but not the only one. In various guises, the idea has been put forward in other work based on activity theory, including theoretical analyses, empirical studies, and system design (e.g., Bødker 1991; Kaptelinin 1992, 1996a, 1996c, 2003; Nardi 1992, 1993, 1996a; Christensen and Bardram 2002; Nardi, Whittaker, and Schwarz 2002). The current work employing the ideas of "activity management" (Moran 2003) and "activity-centric computing" (Geyer, Cheng, and Muller 2003; Harrison 2004; Muller et al. 2004; Millen et al. 2005) indicates that the ideas and concerns underlying the Apple Computer ABC initiative continue to influence the search for a new computing paradigm.

4.6.2   Design and Implementation of Concrete Information Technologies

Probably the first technology to be designed using activity theory that was actually implemented as a concrete industrial prototype was a fitness system called "the bodyWise Personal Trainer." The system was designed to guide the user through the process of physical training (Blumenthal 1995). According to a design produced by a group of students in the Multimedia Design Studio at the University of Illinois at Chicago, the system comprised two components. The main component was a wristwatch-shaped device integrating a regular watch, a stopwatch, and a pulse monitor. In addition, the device contained information about the user's workout regimen. The bodyWise watch was designed to be used in combination with a device attached to a weight-training machine. The attached device could identify bodyWise watches in its proximity, read information about the trainee, and access the gym's database. The device was also equipped with a monitor displaying the suggested weights, number of sets required, and other information necessary for trainees to follow their training regimens.

The design of the system was informed by three approaches: human–computer interaction, industrial design, and activity theory. The designers concluded that the strengths of each of the approaches complemented each other. Industrial design methods and human–computer interaction techniques were combined to create an attractive, comfortable physical device with a learnable, usable interface. Activity theory had a unique impact on the device's design, an impact that cannot be attributed to either industrial design or human–computer interaction methods:

> In terms of activity theory, the motivation for working out includes the desire to appear physically and athletically competent. As a result, the primary concern expressed by the users was a fear of looking foolish in front of the other people using the weight room. This fear caused the users to avoid trying new exercises, starting an exercise regimen, or enlisting the

aid of an expert to assist them. Showing ignorance in the weight room confounds the motivation for working out. The results of this analysis was a design specification for a portable unit that could contain the user's workout regimen, as well as animated demonstrations of correct technique. (Blumenthal 1995)

The experience of using the combination of approaches led Blumenthal to conclude that the main advantage of activity theory was in determining which components and functionality the system should provide, while human–computer interaction and industrial design were found useful in deciding how a system should be implemented after its components and functionality had been specified.

Another system designed using activity theory is the computer-aided design (CAD) system BUILD-IT, developed by Morten Fjeld and his colleagues at the Swiss Federal Institute of Technology in Zurich (Fjeld et al. 2001; Fjeld et al. 2002). The system allows users to create and transform 3D computer models through manipulating physical bricks, used as input devices. BUILD-IT is an advanced system that was used in real-world projects such as planning construction of schools or factories. Providing a tangible user interface has two implications for the use of the system. First, operations with three-dimensional models are carried out via direct manipulation. Instead of setting parameters for a 3D rotation or employing a specialized control (which needs to be selected from a set of many other controls), the user rotates a brick in the desired direction and stops the rotation when it reaches the desired angle. Second, bricks as input devices provide for multiple simultaneous inputs. A co-located or distributed group of people, each person with his own brick, can cooperatively explore various designs with the system at the same time. This feature makes BUILD-IT a groupware system.

The underlying philosophy of the BUILD-IT system was explicitly influenced by activity theory, as well as by related theoretical perspectives such as action regulation theory; the notions of tool mediation, externalization, and regulation of collective actions were found particularly useful (Fjeld et al. 2002). By providing an intuitive tangible interface for working with visualizations of computer models, the BUILD-IT system supports externalization of individuals' ideas in the planning process. The system has also been found to support regulation of group actions by providing representations of objective outcomes of group work.

The UMEA (User-Monitoring Environment for Activities) system developed by Kaptelinin (2003) was designed to compensate for the lack of support for higher-level actions in existing operating systems for personal computers. This system will be described in more detail in chapter 5.

4.7   DEVELOPMENTAL WORK RESEARCH

Even though the activity system model developed by Engeström (1987) has been widely used in interaction design, most studies conducted by Engeström and his colleagues do not deal directly with the evaluation and design of information technologies. Instead, they constitute a separate area of study, namely, developmental work research. The main focus of developmental work research is on transformations of organizational work activities. These transformations may, in some cases, be induced by the implementation of technology or required by the objective needs of integrating technologies into organizations. The activity system model has been used as a tool for understanding complex effects caused by technology. The deployment of a new technology in an organization typically makes the system unstable. Through the generation and resolution of multilevel contradictions, the organization reaches a new state of temporary equilibrium. A fundamental insight of developmental work research is that this new stability is not predetermined. During transitions between relatively stable states, activity systems are especially sensitive to both positive and negative influences. Appropriate interventions during these periods can greatly contribute to the development of organizations and their activities.

One of the first examples of using the methodology of developmental work research was a study of the implementation of information technologies in a Finnish hospital (Engeström 1990). It was found that the impact of technology was not limited to the automation of time- and labor-consuming routine operations. New mediating artifacts had far-reaching consequences for coordination of work in general, the way different categories of workers defined and redefined their roles, and the way people at the hospital understood the object of their work. In other words, the whole structure of the activity system, including the nature of its individual components and their relationships, was transformed.

The methodology of developmental work research has been used by organizations to utilize the full potential of periods of change as organizations are undergoing transformation. A concrete approach developed to attain this goal was the Change Laboratory—a workshop where practitioners and developmental work research experts could meet and discuss the problems they faced and explore possible solutions. The Change Laboratory methodology has been used in a wide range of organizations, both public and industrial (Helle 2000).

In recent years, developmental work research, in addition to its traditional range of interests, has placed special focus on two issues. The first is methods for inducing developmental changes. The basic idea is that sometimes activity systems are stable not because there are no contradictions that call for changes, but because people involved in the activity systems are not aware of, or deliberately ignore, these contradictions. The method used in these cases is to collect evidence that cannot be ignored, such as video materials. Metaphorically speaking, developmental work researchers place a mirror in front of an organization, which shows there is a need for change. This "mirror" approach was employed in a variety of cases, such as reorganizing medical care. For example, one of the problems requiring a change to the whole system was the predominant orientation of medical care toward illnesses rather than patients, which was problematic for people with multiple chronic health problems. These patients were often sent from one doctor to another, round and round (Engeström 2005). Developmental work research methods were found to be helpful in revealing the problem and making major stakeholders aware of the need to search for a permanent solution rather than a quick fix.

Another key topic for developmental work research is the analysis of innovations. Innovations also destabilize activity systems. In a series of studies conducted by Miettinen and his colleagues, it was shown how innovations emerging in research organizations make their way into practice because of (or despite) political decisions and conflicts, how they become objects of activities of individuals and organizations, and how they develop over time (Saari and Miettinen 2001; Miettinen 2002; Hyysalo 2005; Saari 2003).

4.8   HYBRID THEORETICAL FRAMEWORKS

4.8.1   Instrumental Genesis

The instrumental genesis approach, proposed by Pierre Rabardel (Béguin and Rabardel 2000; Rabardel and Bourmaud 2003) has its roots in both activity theory and French ergonomics. This approach focuses on the integration of artifacts into the structure of human activities and provides perhaps the most elaborated conceptual account of such integration. The instrumental genesis approach maintains that the genuine appropriation of artifacts by human beings does not happen all at once. Typically it is an outcome of developmental transformations of artifacts, individuals, and social interactions. These transformations may take considerable time. Individuals make changes to artifacts and adjust them for their specific needs and conditions, a process referred to as *instrumentalization*. Individuals also develop skills and abilities regarding how to operate a tool, how to decide which tasks can be performed with the tool, and which methods should be applied to perform tasks effectively. This reciprocal process is referred to as *instrumentation*. Through instrumentalization and instrumentation—that is, transformations of both artifacts and persons—an artifact becomes appropriated and develops into an instrument.

In recent years, the instrumental genesis approach has gained international recognition. A number of studies have been conducted in France, Italy, and Sweden[4] (e.g., Béguin 2003; Cerrato Pargman 2003; DeCortis, Rizzo, and Saudelli 2003; Folcher 2003). Design is perhaps the most common issue addressed within the approach. The focus on design is both practical and theoretical. From a practical standpoint, the instrumental genesis approach maintains that artifacts should be designed so that they can be transformed efficiently into instruments in user practice. Several authors (e.g., Rabardel and Bourmaud 2003) emphasized the importance of designing flexible, open artifacts that can be modified by users and adjusted for various tasks, including unanticipated tasks. Another conclusion that follows from the approach is the need for designers to take into account the actual transformation of practices and the real needs of users over the course of appropriating an artifact. For instance, an empirical study of collaborative writing conducted by Cerrato Pargman (2003) allowed her to formulate high-level design requirements for collaborative writing systems such as the need to design tools for collaboration so that they support a seamless transition between individual work and collaborative efforts.

A more theoretical aspect of the treatment of design issues within the approach is related to the notion of instrumentalization. Users are assumed to be designers in a very real sense of the word. This assumption raises the question: How is design by users related to conventional design, that is, design by designers?

Béguin (2003) addressed this question through both conceptual analysis and empirical studies. He introduced the notion of "activity exchange," which underlies mutual learning by users and designers. Activity exchange is understood as a dialogical process mediated not only by words but also by intermediate outcomes of design. A design contribution of an actor, when appropriated by other actors, changes the way the designed object is experienced by them, and therefore, the appropriation may bring about changes in the activities of the other actors. Since users and designers have different experiences, including their experiences of designing artifacts, activity exchanges are a way to ensure that the designed artifact meets the requirement of instrumental genesis. Another way to differentiate between design by users and design by designers was proposed by Folcher (2003). She introduced a distinction between "design-for-use" (reflecting the designers' perspective on user practice) and "design-in-use" (reflecting the users' perspective on their own practice). These different perspectives foreground different sets of requirements for the artifact in question.

The theoretical explorations into the types and phenomena of design informed by instrumental genesis are relevant to research conducted within the participatory design tradition (e.g., Ehn 1988; Kensing 2003). Béguin's (2003) notion of activity exchange seems to be a promising conceptual tool for understanding the learning processes of users and designers that take place at the initial phases of participatory design projects.

Though the instrumental genesis approach is a relatively new framework, it has already stimulated a number of studies into how people make technology a part of their everyday lives. A priority for future development of the approach, in our view, is establishing operational criteria that can be applied to identify a concrete tool as an "artifact" or an "instrument" in a concrete use situation. Many, if not most, activities appear to be located between these extremes, and therefore can be defined as mediated by objects that are partly artifacts, partly instruments. Addressing this issue may require the introduction of a scale that would allow the placement of a concrete tool between these two extremes.

4.8.2   Genre Tracing

One of the key trends in HCI is, of course, user-centered design (see, e.g., Norman and Draper 1986). System design whose point of departure is users' needs is typically considered an ideal worth striving for. Though it is sometimes recognized that this ideal may not be realistic and is difficult to attain, the ideal itself has hardly ever been questioned. However, Spinuzzi (2003) criticized user-centered design itself as not doing justice to the creative efforts of the users it aims to support. Spinuzzi observed that an underlying assumption of user-centered design is that users are victims of poorly designed systems and need to be rescued by designers. This "victimhood trope," as he called it, ignores the everyday design decisions made by users to integrate computer artifacts into their practice.

To understand users' innovations at the workplace and take them into account when designing, evaluating, and using information technologies, Spinuzzi proposed the genre-tracing methodology. The origins of this methodology are threefold. First, it implements an ethnographic analysis of everyday practices, with its attention to the details of how people work. Second, it is based on activity theory and aims to provide an integrated understanding of processes at each level of activity, their mutual influences, and their development over time. Third, the methodology makes use of genre theory:

Genre tracing is *dialogic* (Bakhtin 1981)—it draws on the metaphor of dialogue to examine how people interact with complex institutions, disciplines, and communities; how they solve problems and disseminate solutions; and how their conversations and problem solving are instantiated in artifacts. (Spinuzzi 2003, italics in original)

A fundamental insight of genre tracing (shared with some other approaches, such as the instrumental genesis approach) is that designers can create only the preconditions for emerging user practices. Understanding these practices and the constant stream of innovations generated by end users can be an important resource for interaction design (see also Mackay 1990; Nardi 1993; Orlikowski and Tyre 1994).

4.9 INFORMATION SYSTEMS RESEARCH

Information systems (IS) as a research field has traditionally been somewhat separated from human–computer interaction and interaction design. While the main concern of human–computer interaction has been the understanding and support of individuals and groups using technology when carrying out their work or other activities, IS research deals with the processes of introducing a system into an organization, the large-scale effects of such an introduction, the activities of managers and other people who may not directly use the system, and the general functionality of systems (Baecker et al. 1995). In recent years, however, the distinction between these two areas has become somewhat blurred.

A number of factors contributed to this blurring of boundaries between information systems and interaction design. Even though there are still two separate communities, speaking in a sense different languages, some IS researchers turn to problems traditionally associated with human–computer interaction, and vice versa. Some researchers find themselves pulled across the border by a surge of interest from audiences from the other side. For instance, Orlikowski's work (e.g., Orlikowski 1992), which originated in the IS field, is widely cited in the CSCW literature. There is also organizational pressure to integrate, or at least coordinate, the two fields. Several university departments all over the world (including the departments of both authors of this book) are making an attempt to unite IS and interaction design (as well as related research fields) under the name of *informatics.*

Activity theory was introduced to information systems practically simultaneously with its introduction to HCI. In 1991, Kuutti proposed the use of activity theory and Engeström's activity system model to address the issue of context in IS research and development. Kuutti (1991) maintained that activity systems as an analytical concept provides a middle ground, a reasonable compromise between two opposite but equally counterproductive extremes: (a) taking information systems and their use out of context and (b) extending the notion of context to the point where it becomes overly complex and unmanageable. According to Kuutti:

> The solution offered by Activity Theory is that there is a need for an intermediate concept—a minimal meaningful context for individual actions—which must form the basic unit of analysis. (Kuutti 1991)

Kuutti's work stimulated further exploration of activity theory as a theoretical foundation of information systems in Finland (e.g., Korpela et al. 2002) and Sweden (e.g., Bai and Lindberg 1998). Kuutti himself can be considered a true border dweller as he continues to be an active researcher in both interaction design (Kuutti 1992, 1996; Iacucci, Kuutti, and Ranta 2000) and information systems research (Kuutti 1991, 1998, 1999).

A coordinated research program aimed at exploiting the potential of activity theory in both IS and HCI is being carried out at the Activity Theory Usability Lab at the University of Wollongong in Australia (Bourke, Verenikina, and Sharrock 1993; Hyland 1998; Hasan, Gould, and Hyland 1998). An underlying assumption of this research program is that activity theory provides an integrative perspective that allows a holistic understanding of technology, people and their tasks, and organizational contexts. The Wollongong group has conducted a series of theoretical and empirical studies of information systems and usability, informed by activity theory, including the development of an activity model of executive information systems (Hasan 1998) and the comparison of activity theory with other theoretical approaches, such as cognitive science (Gould 1998), grounded theory, general systems theory, and distributed cognition (Hasan 1998).

A recent example of an information systems research that employed activity theory is a study conducted by Wiredu (2005). The study dealt with an implementation of mobile technologies within the framework of a health-care development project and the reasons why the implementation was not successful. Wiredu analyzed contradictions in the activities of mobile professionals, such as power struggles between remote and local authorities, and proposed a model of remotely distributed activities that provided a theoretical account for the main contradictions that resulted in the implementation failure.

4.10   CONCLUSION

At the time of this writing, activity theory has been used in interaction design and related fields for over a decade. The variety of studies described in this chapter spans the theoretical revision of basic concepts of HCI, a retrospective analysis of empirical studies and system development projects, the development of conceptual tools for design and evaluation, and the design of applications and systems. In the next chapter we will describe in more detail a concrete example of using activity theory to design UMEA (User-Monitoring Environment for Activities).

5

A Design Application of Activity Theory: The UMEA System

In this chapter[1] we take a detailed look at a system whose design was informed by activity theory. The theory provided guidance in both (a) identifying a problem that the new design intended to address and (b) finding concrete design solutions. The problem that motivated the design was supporting higher-level user activities rather than low-level, application-specific tasks. The proposed solution was monitoring the user and providing digital resources for user-defined actions that can be located at any level of activity. Activity theory principles of *the hierarchical-structure of activity* and *development* were found especially useful when designing the system.

5.1 APPLICATIONS AS ENVIRONMENTS

Considering information technology a mediating artifact, rather than merely a pole of human–computer interaction, has a straightforward implication for design. If taken seriously, this notion requires that the most important design objective should be to help people attain their meaningful goals. However obvious, this objective is seldom an explicit concern for designers of digital work environments.

One of the key ideas behind the desktop metaphor underlying current operating systems, such as Mac OS and Windows, is the distinction between the file system—hierarchically organized long-term storage of information—and the desktop—a workspace where documents and applications necessary to accomplish a task are located to make them easily accessible (Smith et al. 1982). However, studies of the actual use of desktop systems (Nardi, Anderson, and Erickson 1995; Barreau and

Nardi 1995; Kaptelinin 1996d; Ravasio, Guttormsen-Schär, and Krueger 2004) have shown that the desktop, for a variety of reasons, is not being used as a space for integrating project-related tools and materials. Instead, many tools have evolved into environments that duplicate some of the features originally associated with operating systems. For instance, most Web browsers and email programs include a version of the hierarchical file system, such as the "Trash" and the "Find File" function.

There seem to be good reasons for adding operating-system functionality to applications. The lack of such functionality may cause problems to the user. For instance, it is not possible to delete a file from within Microsoft Word X for Mac. If the user searches for files using the "Find File" function of Word and discovers a file that should be deleted, he has to switch to the operating system. Once in the context of the operating system the user has to locate the file again, which can be a nontrivial task. This is a paradoxical and potentially frustrating situation: the user must again find a document which he had already located, opened, and was working on. Extending the functionality of the application by adding a "Delete" function (for instance, as it has been implemented in Microsoft Office 2000 for Windows) appears to be a way to solve problems of that kind.

However, there is a downside to applications becoming full-blown environments. Users often work in integrated, coherent workspaces while performing individual tasks completely supported by the functionality of a single application. But if they have to switch back and forth between tasks, or if several applications have to be used to accomplish a task, numerous problems may arise. For instance, to prepare and send a conference paper submission, a person might do the following:

1. go to an email program, find a message with the conference announcement, and look up the conference URL;

2. switch to a web browser, go to the conference website, add a bookmark, and download the submission template;

3. switch to a word processor, open the submission template, and format the paper;

4. switch to the web browser again, find the conference website bookmark, open the website, and look up and copy the email address to be used for sending submissions;

5. switch to the email program again, compose a message, attach the formatted paper to the message by locating the file on the hard disk, and send the message.

It is possible that the paper is located as a text file in a folder named "Conferences," the email message with the conference URL is in a mailbox also named "Conferences," and the bookmark is placed in a section titled, once again, "Conferences." In other words, the user might have three hierarchical systems within his virtual work environment—a file system, a mailbox system, and a bookmark system—each of which contains thematically related items. To complete a project that spans several applications the user would need to organize and locate appropriate resources in each system separately.

The conference submission example indicates that support provided to the user depends on the level of action in the structure of activity. There is an evident difference between *higher-level actions and lower-level actions (or tasks)*. Higher-level actions, such as submitting a paper, are those that are meaningful for the user regardless of the specific technology employed to carry out the actions. Lower-level actions, or tasks, are described in terms of an application's functionality, such as creating a list of email addresses. In the above example, the user is supported by a diverse and elaborate set of user interface features and widgets that help carry out lower-level tasks: search for a message in an email program, format a document in a word processor, and so forth. Support for higher-level actions, however, is limited. The user can click on automatically recognized email addresses or URLs (see Nardi, Miller, and Wright 1998), or issue the "Send to" command of the Word "File" menu to send the opened document as an attachment, but hardly more than that. Thus, existing systems tend to provide support for lower-level tasks rather than higher-level actions, although the latter would be helpful to the user.

5.2 SUPPORTING HIGHER-LEVEL USER ACTIONS: EXISTING APPROACHES

There have been several attempts to develop systems that support higher-level user actions by integrating diverse resources that are not limited to a single application. These systems can be divided into three main categories: personal information management systems, dedicated project spaces, and nonhierarchical information space architectures.

5.2.1   Personal Information Management Systems

Personal information management (PIM) systems, for instance, Microsoft Outlook or ACT!, are basically email programs enhanced with electronic versions of traditional organizer tools, such as address books, to-do lists, calendars, expense sheets, and memo pads. These tools are more powerful than their paper equivalents and can be used to manage various types of higher-level activities. When implemented on handheld devices such as PDAs (personal digital assistants), PIM tools can be carried around conveniently and used practically anywhere. However, the management of activities with these systems is only loosely related to the management of the files and applications necessary to carry out the activities. For instance, defining a task in Microsoft Outlook does not include finding and arranging resources for the completion of *this particular task*. A reminder about a deadline for sending a report, however helpful it may be, does not facilitate access to relevant resources. Entries in the Journal make it easier to open recent files, but relating these files to particular tasks requires an additional effort. Even the most advanced PIM systems do not create project-specific contexts containing necessary resources. And personal information management systems further increase the diversity of information hierarchies in the workspace by adding new types of hierarchies, for instance tasks and contacts (see Dourish et al. 1999).

5.2.2   Dedicated Project Spaces

Dedicated project spaces are spatially defined subsets of a virtual work environment that provide contexts for individual projects or types of tasks. Perhaps the best-known example of dedicated project spatial environments is the ROOMS system, developed by Henderson and Card (1986). This system was based on the idea of several specialized workspaces—"rooms"—associated with different classes of activities.

ROOMS was implemented as separate desktops that provided resources necessary to perform certain kinds of work (e.g., an "email communication room," a "programming room"). It was assumed that multiple workspaces would help to use screen space and memory more efficiently, since only subsets of relevant screen space consuming resources would be open at any one time. It was also assumed that reentering a room would help to restore task context so the user could more easily continue working on the task after a break.

The basic approach underlying the ROOMS system—allocating virtual spaces to individual projects where users could "place" tools and materials and thus build a special-purpose work environment—has been implemented in a number of more recent systems. For instance, the Task Gallery (Robertson et al. 2000) provided users with task windows presented as artwork hung on the walls of a virtual 3D gallery. Another example is Manufaktur, a collaborative 3D workspace intended to support design professionals in creating and maintaining the context of a task or project (Büscher et al. 1999; Shapiro 2000).

A key problem with dedicated spatial environments for tasks and projects is the overhead for the user. The user must set up an environment, place the necessary resources in it, and constantly update them. When the project is finished, the user must clean up the space. This maintenance requires time and effort (though in the case of collaborative spaces it might be "invisible" to certain users because other people take responsibility for it) (Shapiro 2000). A critically important aspect of the overhead problem is that the user is typically required to invest extra effort in creating a project context before enjoying any benefits of doing so.

5.2.3 Nonhierarchical Information Space Architectures

Both personal information management systems and dedicated virtual spaces for tasks and projects have been developed as extensions of the traditional architecture of desktop environments based on hierarchical file systems. A radically different approach to creating project contexts was used in novel architectures of information spaces, such as Lifestreams (Fertig, Freeman, and Gelernter 1996a,b) and Presto (Dourish et al. 1999).

The Lifestreams system organized documents chronologically. The user could create "substreams" of documents by entering selection criteria, such as "all mail I haven't responded to." This approach provided a simple way to organize and find documents in personal electronic spaces. People often associate events with certain time periods, and knowing the approximate time of an event helped identify the fragment of the Lifestreams sequence containing the target document. Inspecting the temporal neighbors of the document could help in directing further search if the user remembered whether these neighbors appeared before or after the target document.

The novel approach behind the Lifestreams system appears to have certain advantages over more traditional architectures. One is the possibility of combining document space management with the management of individual and group activities. For instance, a draft paper to be discussed within a group could be placed at a certain time in the future, to facilitate both access to necessary resources and coordination of individual and group activities.

The Presto system provided an infrastructure allowing for the flexible and dynamic generation of collections of documents. Documents were tagged with specific attributes defining the collections. The attributes were meaningful features of documents, such as "published paper" or "PowerPoint file." They were either extracted by the system or added by the user (Dourish et al. 1999).

Both Lifestreams and Presto were intended to help users create complex information structures that match certain criteria and can include various types of documents available to the user. However, the use of formal criteria for selecting information to be included in a project environment is problematic. Such criteria are typically difficult or even impossible to formulate, even if the user has an explicit idea of what such criteria are. For instance, when working on a paper, the user might need the email address of a person who could suggest useful references. It is much easier to just add the address to information related to the project than to determine the appropriate selection criteria that will enable the system to add the address to a "substream" or a document collection. Indeed, the systems in question allow such manual addition of objects to automatically generated collections. Allowing these additions, however, undermines the conceptual consistency of the systems. One more potential problem with nonhierarchical architectures is that users usually have not worked out explicit criteria of the information relevant to a project prior to creating a project environment; rather, such criteria may develop *as a result* of working on a project.

5.3   CREATING PROJECT CONTEXTS THROUGH INTERACTION HISTORIES: THE UMEA SYSTEM

5.3.1   The Motivation behind the UMEA System

The previous discussion indicates that the key issues for the development of systems that provide support beyond the scope of individual applications include:

- minimizing overhead and making the benefits of project environments apparent to the user;
- integrating personal information management, communication, and the management of tools and materials; and
- capitalizing upon the actual practices of users.

In the next section, we describe the UMEA system—User-Monitoring Environments for Activities—which was designed to address these issues. The system uses interaction histories to create project contexts.

In the 1990s, interaction histories were recognized as an important research issue in HCI (Hill and Terveen 1994). Interaction histories are considered a promising resource for providing users with more possibilities to control and transform objects they are working with, access information, learn, or interact with software agents (Shneiderman 1999; Rich and Sidner 1997; Wexelblat and Maes 1999). Examples of user interface components implementing the notion of interaction history include "undo" commands, active and passive histories in Web browsers, and lists of recent documents in the "File" menu of some applications.

If the user continues working with the same set of files and applications, lists of recent resources may provide convenient access to what is needed to get the work done, with no overhead. However, if the user switches between several projects and their respective sets of applications and documents, lists of recent resources may be of little help. When returning to work on a project after spending some time on a different one, the user might find, for instance, that the list of recent documents in the Word "File" menu has changed completely and that she has to locate all the necessary files on the hard disk all over again. The reason that lists of recent files are not context-sensitive is that these lists are based on a single interaction history which is the same for all types of user activities.

The key idea of the UMEA system is to map events in interaction histories to specific tasks and projects the user is working on. The mapping is accomplished by the user via indicating the beginning and the end of working on a project, in real time or retrospectively. It is assumed that on the basis of project-specific interaction histories the system will be able to provide the user with easy access to project-related resources. Users are expected to be motivated to enter project environments because this is the way for them to get easier access to resources. By entering a project users indicate that the project is active, which makes it possible for the system to continue collecting project-specific interaction histories and develop even more elaborate project contexts.

The use of interaction histories appears to be a way to address the problems with existing systems discussed above. Interaction histories can help minimize overhead by making the development of project environments a by-product of working on specific projects, at least to some degree. Since the management of both personal information and tools and materials can be monitored when the user is working on a project, both types of resources can be integrated within one project environment. And, since the system is monitoring how users actually work, the structure of the project contexts is based on the authentic work practices of users.

5.3.2   The UMEA System and Activity Theory

The design of the UMEA system was informed by activity theory in a variety of ways. First, the basic idea behind the system is that of creating environments that support higher-level user activities rather than low-level tasks. Second, the design of the system was motivated by an empirical study in which an early prototype of the Activity Checklist (Kaptelinin, Nardi, and Macaulay 1999; appendix A, this vol.) was used to determine the extent to which commonly used information technologies help information workers integrate digital resources when carrying out projects that span different applications (Kaptelinin 1996d). The study revealed a lack of such help, which led to a search for a design approach that would support the integration of resources, eventually resulting in the UMEA system. In other words, the design of the system was based on the assumption that the meaning of various objects that constitute work environments, both physical and virtual, is determined by the context of activity, that is, by the relation of the objects to a subject's motives and goals. The aim of the system was to organize resources in a natural and meaningful way, namely, around the goals of the user, no matter what those goals are.

Activity theory ideas that influenced the design of the UMEA system can be summarized as follows:

- To support the coordination of various levels of activity, a system should integrate higher-level representations of goals (such as representations provided by PIM systems) with resources needed to accomplish these goals (such as applications or documents).
- In everyday life, an individual's focus of attention is constantly switching between different conscious goals and corresponding contexts (see, e.g., Cypher 1986). Switching contexts is seldom quick and effortless; a system might make it faster and easier.
- Since human activities are situated, determined by their physical and social contexts, a system should provide support for a wide variety of actual work practices.
- The system, as a mediational artifact, should be as transparent as possible in order to allow users to focus on their meaningful goals rather than their interaction with technology.

UMEA was designed to meet these requirements by: (a) making it possible for the user to directly indicate a higher-level task, that is, a project; (b) monitoring user activities and tracking resources used when carrying out the project; and (c) automatically organizing and updating these resources to make them easily available to the user when resuming work on a project.

5.3.3   The UMEA System: An Overview

UMEA is an application that runs on Microsoft Windows. The system can be either in the foreground mode or the background mode. In the foreground mode, the system presents users with an overview of their projects. The user can select an active project and open project-related resources: documents, folders, URLs, or contacts. When the system runs in the background, it receives events, such as opening a web page, printing a file, or sending an email. When the system receives an event, the event is tagged to the currently active project. If the event is associated with a resource that has not yet been used within the currently active project, the new resource is added to an appropriate list of project-specific resources. What is added is a link to the resource; the resource itself does not change. Therefore, the same resource can be used in several different projects.

The user can switch between three views of the system: the minimized overview, the maximized overview, and project windows. The minimized overview (fig. 5.1) consists of two vertical panels: (a) the project panel, displaying project icons, and (b) the resource panel, displaying buttons corresponding to four types of project-specific resources: documents, folders, URLs, and contacts.

By selecting a project on the project panel, the user can access resources related to that project. When a project is selected, clicking on one of the resource menu buttons opens a corresponding list of resources related to that project (fig. 5.2). Choosing an item on the list opens a resource—that is, a document, a folder, a Web page, or a new email message addressed to the selected contact.

The user can edit lists of resources by manually adding or deleting items. The user can also assign ranks to various resource items displayed as a list. Items are organized into groups according to their ranks, and groups with higher ranks are displayed higher on the list.

The maximized overview (fig. 5.3) is an extended version of the minimized overview. In addition to the project panel and the resource panel, this view displays: (a) a complete list of projects, (b) a PIM/history area displaying PIM tools and the history of the active project, and (c) a control panel. PIM entries are linked to projects. Information associated

Figure 5.1
UMEA: The minimized overview window. The project panel (left) displays project icons and the "maximize" button (the triangle at the bottom). The resource panel (right) displays pull-down menu buttons that open lists of documents, folders, URLs, or contacts.

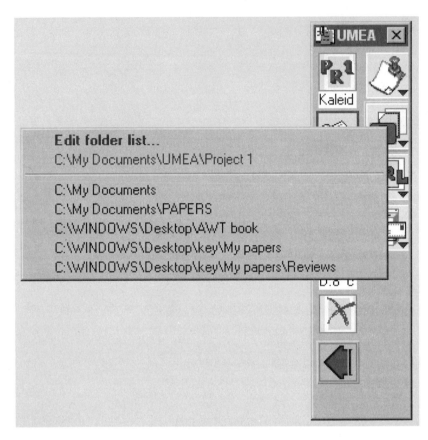

Figure 5.2
UMEA: The minimized overview window with an open pop-up menu containing
a list of folders.

with a certain date, such as a project deadline, is automatically displayed
in the calendar as a verbal description (the day view) or a bar of the
color of its respective project (the month view and the week view).

The history (fig. 5.4) is a project-specific interaction log that contains
time-stamped events describing objects (such as documents or folders)
and actions (such as printing or accessing). The history can be edited
manually by the user. For instance, the user can select a sequence of
events in a project's interaction history and delete the sequence or reas-
sign it to another project.

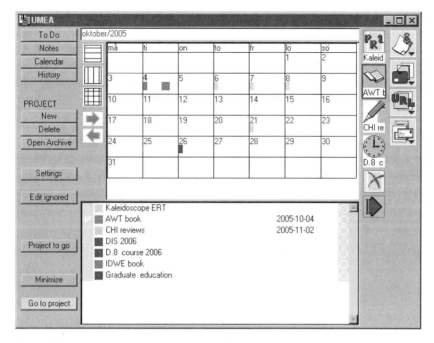

Figure 5.3
UMEA: The maximized overview window: control panel (left), PIM/history area
(top), list of projects (bottom), and resource lists (upper right).

From the maximized overview, the user can open project windows of
selected projects (fig. 5.4). Project windows look similar to the maximized overview but display information related to only one project.
When a project window is open the user can edit project attributes (the
name, associated color, icon, and deadline) or decompose the project
into subtasks. A project window opens automatically when the user creates a new project. Project-specific histories and resource lists are continuously updated in the same way regardless of whether an overview
window or a project view window is displayed.

5.3.5   A Use Scenario

Here is a possible scenario of using the system: the user launches UMEA
and opens the maximized overview window, which displays a list of all

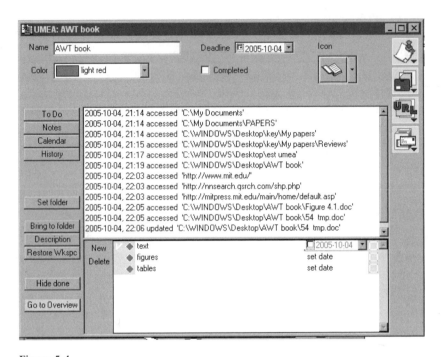

Figure 5.4
UMEA: A project window: control panel (left), project details (top), PIM/history area displaying history (center), and resource lists (upper right).

ongoing projects and a calendar. To decide which project he is going to work on, the user browses the list of projects and checks approaching deadlines in the calendar, as well as notes and to-do lists. To view notes and to-do entries associated with a project, the user clicks on the name of the project and selects an appropriate PIM tool. The user may open lists of documents related to a particular project to check its status. Once the user decides on a selected project to focus on, he can immediately continue to work on the project. All files, folders, URLs, and contacts previously used within the project are easily accessible, and the user can open these resources by selecting them on appropriate resource lists. The user may edit and save documents, send email, and browse the Web; new file names, email addresses, and URLs are automatically added to respective lists of resources related to the project. The user can also create and edit notes, to-do lists, and calendar entries, which are again automatically linked to the project. When the user wants to switch to another project, he clicks on the name of that project on the project list and gets immediate access to a new set of resources.

The user selects existing projects and reenters project environments to get access to project resources. By reentering a project context, the user makes it possible for the system to continue to create a project-specific interaction history and develop an even more elaborate project context.

If the user discovers that an incorrect project name has been selected and a part of the interaction history of project A is in fact related to project B, the user simply selects that part of the history and reassigns it to project B. The resources used in the specified sequence of events are thereby deleted from the resource lists of project A and added to the resource lists of project B.

5.3.6   Expected Benefits

Expected benefits of the UMEA system can be summarized as follows.

The system provides integrated access to documents, PIM tools, and communication facilities. The user can check a project-specific to-do list, open relevant files and Web pages, and send email messages to people on the project-specific contact list, all from the same project context.

The system does not prescribe to the user how to do her job; users can carry out tasks however they wish, without being constrained by the system. The system monitors whatever the user is doing and updates project contexts on the basis of this monitoring. Thus, the system appears to be compatible with a wide range of work practices.

The user can start enjoying benefits of the system as soon as a new project is created and given a meaningful name. Adding more information about the project, such as selecting an icon or a color, setting a deadline, or describing subtasks, opens up new possibilities for managing projects. Thus the user can gradually learn about more features of the system and correspondingly obtain more benefits.

5.4   PROSPECTS FOR FUTURE WORK

First experiences with the UMEA system indicate that it addresses a real need of users for a low-overhead integration of various types of information around higher-level, meaningful goals. The current version of the system appears to be practically useful, at least to some users. At the same time, there is a considerable potential for development of both the system and the underlying approach.

The most evident problem that needs to be solved to make the system more usable is the relatively high effort necessary to clean up lists of resources, that is, to get rid of constantly accumulating irrelevant items. A set of heuristics has been developed to avoid excessive cluttering of lists.

"Background" resources   If the user regularly performs background tasks not related to any project, such as checking the news on the web, he or she can inadvertently add irrelevant resources, such as a news website URL, to several foreground projects. A possible solution to this problem is to set up a list of background resources that can be recognized by the system as resources not to be linked to any of the user's projects.

Automatic ranking of resources   Interaction histories contain numerous clues on the relative importance of the resources used within a project. If the user saves successive versions of a document within a project, the document is probably essential to the project. On the other hand, if the user opens a document only once and closes it immediately after opening, the document is perhaps not very important and could even have been opened by mistake. If the system automatically sorts out resources by assigning them ranks, the most important resources can be displayed higher on the list to make them more accessible. Less important resources can be automatically moved down the list or hidden.

Automatic switching between project contexts   Many resources are used exclusively in one project or can be modified only within a specific project. Such resources can be automatically or manually linked to their respective projects. These linked resources can be used by the system as an indicator that the user is working on a certain project, even if the user does not explicitly indicate switching to that project. For instance, if the user is working on a document in one project context and then saves the latest version of the document in another context, the system can infer that the active project has been indicated by mistake. The system can automatically switch to the correct project or, alternatively, display a warning message and let the user select the active project.

These heuristics are expected to be implemented in the next versions of the system. Because of substantial individual differences between users, the heuristics need to be implemented so the user can select various options, such as criteria for filtering out irrelevant information or conditions for switching between projects.

Initial experiences with the system also suggest that there are two problems that present a challenge to the very idea of automatically translating interaction histories into project contexts. The first is the case of multipurpose activities, such as checking email, surfing the Web, or attending a meeting with a long list of items on the agenda. Constant switching from one topic (or project) to another is a characteristic feature of such activities. If the user must indicate each time she changes contexts, the whole activity may become disorganized. To prevent this, users should be able to postpone or avoid mapping their actions to specific projects until after a multipurpose activity session. The most promising way to support users in doing this appears to be an automatic analysis of content such as email messages and Web pages, presenting the user with suggestions on how specific fragments of multipurpose activities can be mapped to different projects.

The second problem is the limited range of activities that can be monitored. Physical activities, such as talking to a colleague, taking a book from a shelf, or drawing a sketch on a whiteboard, are critically important for many real-life tasks and projects. Most computer systems cannot monitor user behaviors in the physical world, which somewhat undermines the value of interaction histories. However, there is an increasing number of systems that allow for monitoring various types of activities beyond human–computer interaction in the traditional sense. For instance, the early Active Badge system (Want and Hopper 1992) and a number of more recent systems, such as Kimura (MacIntyre et al. 2001; Voida et al. 2002), monitor the physical locations of users. The Magic Touch system (Pederson 2001) keeps track of physical documents in the physical workspace by reading tags attached to the documents. The RoamWare system (Wiberg 2000) creates an interaction history of physical meetings by detecting mobile devices (such as PDAs, mobile phones, or laptop computers) in the user's proximity. This history is then used to facilitate and support communication with colleagues outside of meetings. The general trends toward personal technologies (Sharples 2000) and disappearing computers (Russel, Streitz, and Winograd 2005) indicate that in the future there will be more technological possibilities for creating and using rich interaction histories.

The version of the UMEA system described in this chapter represents a first step in exploring the potential of using interaction histories to support higher-level user activities. The version utilizes the interaction histories of individual users of a single computer. Extending the approach to collective and group activities is a natural next step in its development. Another direction for future work includes creating integrated and coherent work environments when the work is supported by a configuration of technologies (e.g., PCs, PDAs, and other mobile devices), probably connected to the web, through maintaining project contexts that would span different technologies.

A number of challenges need to be dealt with when taking these next steps. Creating unified project contexts on the basis of interaction histories generated by groups of users and sets of devices raises not only technological issues, such as device compatibility, but also more general issues, such as privacy, negotiation of goals and division of labor between individual users, coordination of individual and collective goals, and sharing histories and resources within a team. Dealing with these challenges will probably require a variety of conceptual tools. The experience thus far indicates that activity theory can be one of these tools. By maintaining designers' focus on developing human activities in their social context, the theory provides useful guidance in selecting strategies and setting priorities in design.

II

Advanced Issues in Activity Theory

6
Objectively Speaking

6.1 INTRODUCTION

In chapter 3 we discussed the fundamental concept of object in activity theory. In this chapter[1] we examine the concept further, exploring some of its problems and proposing extensions and revisions (see also Foot 2002a,b).

Problems with the concept of the object of activity begin with its definition. According to Leontiev:

> A basic or, as is sometimes said, a constituting characteristic of activity is its objectivity [or rather "object-orientedness"]. Properly, the concept of its object [*Gegenstand*] is already implicitly contained in the very concept of activity. The expression "objectless activity" is devoid of any meaning. Activity may seem objectless, but scientific investigation of activity necessarily requires discovering its object. Thus, the object of activity is twofold: first, in its independent existence as subordinating to itself and transforming the activity of the subject; second, as an image of the object, as a product of its property of psychological reflection that is realized as an activity of the subject and cannot exist otherwise. (Leontiev 1978)

The prominence of the "object of activity" in the conceptual framework of activity theory is hardly surprising. It appears that much of the theory's appeal lies in its view of subjective and objective phenomena as fundamentally inseparable, and of the object of activity as a crucial link relating them to each other. The object of activity thus has a dual status; it is both a projection of the human mind onto the objective world and a projection of the world onto the mind. Taking into account the object of activity means anchoring and contextualizing subjective phenomena in the objective world. It changes the theoretical perspective on both the mind and the world. Instead of being a collection of "mental processes," the mind emerges as biased, striving for meaning and value, suffering and rejoicing, failing and hoping, alive, real. On the other hand, employing the concept of the object of activity means viewing the world not just as a collection of physical bodies or organizational structures but as a place full of meanings and values, a place that can be comfortable or dangerous, restricting or supportive, beautiful or ugly, or, as is often the case, all of the above at the same time.

From a research perspective, the concept of the object of activity is an analytical tool providing a means of understanding not only *what* people are doing, but also *why* they are doing it. The object of activity can be considered the "ultimate reason" behind various behaviors of individuals, groups, or organizations. In other words, the object of activity is a *sense-maker*, which gives meaning to and determines the values of various entities and phenomena. Identifying the object of activity and its development over time can serve as a basis for reaching a deeper and more structured understanding of otherwise fragmented pieces of evidence.

At the same time, it is becoming increasingly evident that the concept of the object of activity is not without problems. It is important to understand more clearly the specific meaning or meanings of the concept in order to avoid potential misunderstandings and cases where the same term is used in different ways. In this chapter, we give an account of how Leontiev introduced the concept of the object of activity and discuss different perspectives on the concept within two influential approaches in activity theory. We argue that the concept of the object of activity can be separated from the concept of motive to provide a better theoretical account of the phenomena of poly-motivation and developmental transformations of the object of activity. In the next chapter we present an empirical example of how the separation between the notions of "object" and "motive" can help explain the complex phenomena of sense-making in collective activities at a biotechnology company.

6.2   FLAGGING A LINGUISTIC GAP: "*OBJEKT*" VERSUS "*PREDMET*"

Activity theory originates from Russian psychology of the last century, which, in its turn, has its roots in German philosophy. Because of this heritage, the main concepts of activity theory were first formulated in Russian with direct references to their German counterparts. These concepts include the concept of activity itself, which was described as corresponding to the German *Tätigkeit* rather than *Aktivität* (Leontiev 1978). The difference between these closely related words carries an important distinction between a narrow meaning of activity as a social goal-directed process and a broad meaning of activity as any process that produces effects, a concept associated with dynamics, energy, and force. That semantic difference can be adequately expressed in Russian, which, along with some other languages, has the lexical means to separate these meanings by using different words. *Tätigkeit* and *Aktivität* are translated into Russian as, respectively, *dejatelnost'* and *aktivnost'*. In English this difference is often lost because there is only one word, "activity," to express these two different meanings.

English translations of the Russian expression used by Leontiev to denote "the object of activity" run into a similar problem. In Russian there are two words, *objekt* and *predmet*, both of which are typically translated to English as "object." It is the latter, that is, *predmet*, which was used by Leontiev when he referred to "the object of activity." In Russian, *objekt* and *predmet* have very similar meanings and in many contexts they are fully interchangeable; however, there are subtle differences which are difficult to grasp even for many native Russian speakers. While *objekt* deals primarily with material things that exist independently of the mind, *predmet* often means the target or content of a thought or an action (Ozhegov 1982). For Leontiev it was important to emphasize these differences (see Stetsenko 1995). The reasons behind this distinction become apparent when tracing the introduction and the use of the concept of the object of activity in Leontiev's work.

As described in chapter 3, Leontiev developed the conceptual framework of activity theory in two books: *The Problems of the Development of Mind* (Leontiev 1981), originally published in 1959, and *Activity, Consciousness, and Personality* (Leontiev 1978), originally published in 1975. The first book aimed at providing a historical account of the mind, from the emergence of the most basic forms of psyche early in biological evolution to advanced forms of consciousness manifested in human beings. To carry out this project, Leontiev employed the concept of activity. Immediately after introducing the concept, Leontiev defined the object of activity. At that point he used the Russian *objekt* but carefully specified the meaning in which he used this word:

> Accordingly, I will limit the meaning of "object." Usually this concept has two meanings: in a broad sense, it is a thing related to other things, that is, a "thing having an existence"; in a more narrow sense, it is something that opposes (German *Gegenstandt*), something that resists (Latin *objectum*), something at which an action is directed (Russian *predmet*), that is, something to which a *living* creature is somehow related, *as an object of his or her activity*, no matter if this activity is an external one or an internal one (for example, an object of eating, an object of labor, an object of contemplation, etc.). From now on the term "object" will be used in this more narrow, special meaning. (Leontiev 1981, our translation, emphasis in original)

These concepts and ideas were then more systematically presented in *Activity, Consciousness, and Personality* (1978). There Leontiev used both *objekt* and *predmet* and carefully selected them to emphasize the appropriate dimension of meaning as described above. Both *objekt* and *predmet* played an important role in formulating the basic concepts and principles of his approach. *Objekt*, denoting the objective, material reality in general (as "things having an existence"), constituted a pole of the "subject–object" opposition through which the notion of activity as a process of mutual transformations between these poles was defined (Leontiev 1978). The term *predmet* was used to denote objective orientation of activity. The crucial role of the object (*predmet*) of activity was emphasized by Leontiev by repeatedly referring to activity as *object-oriented* activity (*predmetnaja dejatelnost*).

Therefore, the distinction between *objekt* and *predmet* was intentionally used by Leontiev to define key concepts of his approach, including the concept of the object of activity. When translating *predmet* into English there is little choice but to use the same word as the one used to translate *objekt*, that is, "object." As a result, an important conceptual distinction can be lost in English translations.

This discussion may create the impression that the task of distinguishing the Russian words *object* and *predmet* in English without extensive commentary is nearly impossible. In general, this is probably true. However, in specific cases, overcoming the linguistic barrier and reconstructing the original meanings of *objekt* and *predmet* in English is not as hopeless as it may seem. A few simple guidelines can be used by readers of English translations of Leontiev's work to identify the intended meaning of "object":

- In general, the reader should rely on the context, taking into account that "object" is likely to have the meaning of *predmet* if there is a special emphasis on concrete, social, meaningful, and integrated qualities. Running the risk of oversimplification, one can say that *predmet* is more "subjective" while *objekt* is more "objective."
- In the expression "the object of activity" and similar contexts, "object" has the meaning of *predmet*.
- In the "subject–object" distinction and related uses, "object" has the meaning of *objekt*.

Thus, even though the difficulties with translating the original meaning of the word *predmet* used by Leontiev do cause certain problems for interpretation, these problems are relatively easy to take care of if a few simple rules are kept in mind.

6.3   UNCOVERING A CONCEPTUAL GAP: HIERARCHIES VERSUS TRIANGLES

In previous chapters we discussed two influential activity-theoretical approaches, those of Leontiev (1978, 1981) and Engeström (1987, 1990, 1999a,b). As will be shown below, these two approaches provide two different views on the object of activity. These differences are often ignored. In our view, understanding these differences is important in order to avoid potential conceptual confusion and increase awareness that the same concept can have different meanings in different contexts. Articulating these differences can make existing contradictions explicit and thus stimulate further conceptual developments in activity theory.

For Leontiev, the object of activity was predominantly the object of individual activity, its "true motive" (1978). The focus on the individual was determined by the fact that Leontiev developed activity theory as a psychological framework; the category of activity was introduced and explored by Leontiev in the context of psychology. He wrote:

Human psychology is concerned with the activity of concrete individuals that takes place either in conditions of open association, in the midst of people, or eye to eye with the surrounding object world—before the potter's wheel or behind the writing desk. Under whatever kind of conditions and forms human activity takes place, whatever kind of structure it assumes, it must not be considered as isolated from social relations, from the life of society. (Leontiev 1978)

Thus, Leontiev considered activities to be social even if they are not carried out collectively. People, for instance, can work alone and yet their work is determined by social and cultural practices, tools, and values. In other words, activities can be individual or collective with respect to their form, but they are always social. With respect to the subject of activity, Leontiev focused almost exclusively on individual activities. Though he provided clear indications of the possibility of extending the concept of his approach to supraindividual levels of analysis, the concepts themselves, such as the notion of the levels of activity, were developed to provide an account of the activity of an individual human being.

Within the approach developed by Engeström (1987, 1990), the unit of analysis is defined as a collective activity system rather than individual activity (the approach is discussed in more detail in chapter 4). The object of activity is defined by the community, and it is the community that carries out the collective activity as a whole. Therefore, even though the model includes "subject" as one of its components, the effective subject within the activity system model appears to be the community. Undeniably, Leontiev's and Engeström's approaches have much in common. Both consider activity to be a relationship between subjects and their objects, and both consider all activity to be social. Both emphasize the importance of culture, development, and mediation. At the same time, there are substantial differences between the approaches, differences that are especially evident in interpretations of the object of activity (see table 6.1).

For Leontiev, the object (*predmet*) of activity is an object of activities carried out by individuals, either collectively or individually, and is related to motivation. For Engeström, the object, introduced through the "subject–object" distinction—that is, as *objekt*—is the object of *collective* activities. The object is defined as "the 'raw material' or 'problem space' at which the activity is directed and which is molded and trans-

Table 6.1
Two perspectives on the object of activity.

	Leontiev	Engeström
Form of Activities	Individual and collective	Collective
Object "Owners"	Individuals (collective object owners are not excluded)	Communities
Related Phenomena	Motivation, need ("the true motive" of activity)	Production (what is being transformed into the outcome)
Discipline	Psychology	Organizational change

formed into outcomes ..." (Center for Activity Theory and Developmental Work Research, n.d.). The concept of the object is primarily related to production though its relation to human needs and motives is also mentioned.

Arguably, the differences in the meaning of "the object of activity" within these approaches are determined by their aims. While Leontiev introduced the object of activity as a psychological concept, for Engeström this concept is an analytical tool for studying organizational change. Leontiev's and Engeström's frameworks are complementary versions of activity theory, each of which is "custom designed" to deal successfully with practical and research issues in their respective domains. Each has a different scope and can be applied fruitfully to solve different types of research and practical tasks.

6.4   REVISING THE FRAMEWORK: OBJECTS VERSUS MOTIVES

In the rest of this chapter we argue that certain problems related to Leontiev's notion of the object of activity result from inconsistencies and contradictions within his conceptual framework. In an attempt to resolve these problems we propose a revision of the concept of the object of activity. This revision does not mean a deviation from the basic principles of activity theory. Activity theory is a developing framework, and it is inevitable that certain concepts are being reformulated or abandoned, while new concepts are being introduced.

Leontiev defined the object of activity as follows:

> According to the terminology I have proposed, the object of an activity is its true motive. It is understood that the motive may be either material or ideal, either present in perception or existing only in the imagination or in thought. (Leontiev 1978)

This definition already raises questions. If the object of activity is its true motive, then two concepts—"the object of activity" and "the motive"— mean the same thing. The advantages of having a second concept that has the same meaning as "the motive" are unclear. Is the purpose of that concept perhaps to differentiate between "true" motives and "untrue" ones? However, no definition of "untrue" motives is provided.

Another problem with defining the object of activity as activity's true motive is an inconsistency in Leontiev's writing regarding a motive's ability to direct activities. In *Activity, Consciousness, and Personality*, Leontiev presents two different opinions. On the one hand, he appears to claim that motives do direct activities: "The main thing that distinguishes one activity from another ... is the difference of their objects. It is exactly the object of an activity, that gives it a determined direction" (Leontiev 1978). On the other hand, on the very next page, the directing function of the motive is questioned: "The function of excitation [general stimulation] is, of course, fully present in the motive. The function of direction is another matter: The actions that realize activity are aroused by its motive but appear to be directed toward a goal" (Leontiev 1978).

Therefore, the question of whether the motive directs activities remains open. We will return to this question later in this section.

The phenomena of poly-motivated activities present a special problem. Leontiev explicitly expressed the idea that an activity can have several motives at the same time: "activity necessarily becomes multimotivational, that is, it responds simultaneously to two or more motives" (Leontiev 1978). However, this idea had practically no impact on the fundamental analysis of needs, motives, and the object of activity carried out by Leontiev. The analysis appears to be based on an implicit assumption that there is a 1:1:1:1 correspondence between activities, needs, motives, and objects. When pointing out that the emergence of the motive is a result of a need meeting its object, or emphasizing that "an activity does not exist without a motive," Leontiev consistently avoided mentioning cases of activities with several motives.

Obviously, extending the scope of analysis to poly-motivated activities cannot be accomplished merely by acknowledging the existence of several motives of one and the same activity. A number of questions arise. How do multiple motives of an activity emerge? Do the constituting needs meet their respective objects, which results in adding new separate motives to the set associated with a certain activity? If the motives are separate, why does a set of motives define one activity instead of a multiplicity of activities? The main problem that needs to be solved to answer these questions is that of understanding the mechanisms underlying conflict resolution between different motives.

According to Leontiev, there can be two types of motives of an activity: sense-forming motives, which give the activity its meaning, and motives–stimuli, which provide additional motivation but do not change the meaning of an activity. For instance, a person may buy a car not only as a means of transportation but also because of its prestigious brand name. Motives–stimuli can elicit various behavioral and emotional reactions (sometimes coming into conflict with the general meaning of an activity), but they are of secondary importance compared to the sense-forming motives. Therefore, in case of a conflict, sense-forming motives usually prevail over motives–stimuli. A more general conflict resolution mechanism proposed by Leontiev is the "hierarchy of motives," which determines the relative importance of an individual's various motives. In case of a conflict, the hierarchy of motives is used to decide which motive should take over.

In the rest of this section we argue that the concepts proposed by Leontiev to provide an account of the phenomena of poly-motivated activities are not sufficient. The main shortcoming of the concepts is a lack of explanatory and predictive power when it comes to both moment-to-moment and long-term developmental dynamics of activity. For instance, the concepts described above predict that more important motives, that is, sense-forming motives or motives that rank higher in the hierarchy of motives, will always determine the course of activities and that objects of activity do not change over time. However, there is ample evidence that the general importance of the underlying motive is not the only factor determining the choices people make in everyday life. A relatively unimportant thing can be quite urgent, so that dealing with more important issues can be postponed. Some people are willing

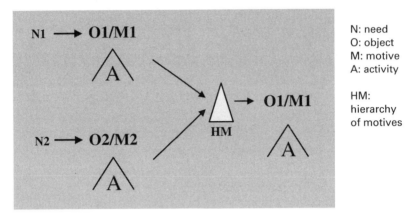

1 motive — 1 object — 1 activity

Figure 6.1
Model A. 1:1:1.

to take risks and pursue less important and even potentially dangerous motives if they think the risk level is acceptable. And the object of activity can undergo developmental changes that take place over a relatively long period of time, even though the basic motives of the activity do not change (see, e.g., Miettinen 2002; Hyysalo 2005).

The main conclusions of this analysis can be summarized as follows. First, the concept of the object of activity appears to duplicate the meaning of the concept of motive. Second, Leontiev's statements regarding whether or not the motive (and, consequently, the object of activity) can direct activities or just generally stimulate them are inconsistent. Third, Leontiev's concepts of "need," "activity," "motive," and "object" are not easily applicable to poly-motivated activities.

A possible solution to these problems is to revise the definition of the object of activity as its "true motive" and separate the notion of motive from the notion of the object of activity. The idea can be illustrated with the following diagrams. Figure 6.1 shows a 1:1:1:1 relationship between activities, needs, motives, and objects, that is: one need, one motive, one object, and one activity (Model A). This relationship appears to be implicitly assumed in most of Leontiev's analyses. If there are several needs that can come into conflict, there are also several potential activ-

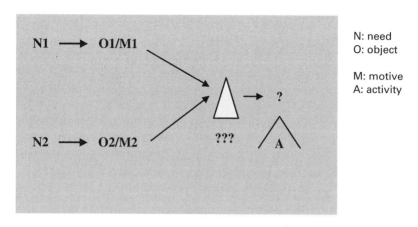

n motives — n objects — 1 activity

Figure 6.2
Model B. N:N:1.

ities, only one of which can be carried out. The selection of that activity is based on a comparison of the competing motives through the hierarchy of motives. The motive with the highest rank in the hierarchy takes over, and the activity oriented toward that motive/ object takes place.

A limitation of Model A is that it does not account for activities that have several motives at the same time. The possibility for an activity to have several motives was mentioned by Leontiev (1978) and other activity theorists (e.g., Bratus 1999), but not explicated.

Model B, shown in figure 6.2, is an attempt to represent Leontiev's ideas, scattered in his works, about the relationship between needs, motives, objects, and activities in the case of poly-motivated activities. This model is similar to Model A in that it also maintains one-to-one correspondence between needs, objects, and motives. However, Model B posits that several sets, each consisting of "one need, one motive, and one object," may converge into one activity.

Because only sketchy evidence for conflict resolution in poly-motivated activities can be found in Leontiev's works, the model is not comprehensive: the procedure for resolving contradictions between several competing motives and respective objects is not clear. One possibility is to employ the hierarchy of motives as a conflict resolution mechanism.

However, as mentioned above, the hierarchy cannot explain the moment-to-moment dynamics of priorities within the same activity. Another problem with the hierarchy of motives is that it can only make it possible for one of the competing motives to survive the selection process unmodified, while all the others are completely rejected. However, activities with several motives are likely to be shaped by the whole configuration of effective motives, not just one of them. Therefore, the main problem with Model B is that it does not elaborate enough on the integration of needs, motives, and objects into one activity.

The need to revise Leontiev's original concepts to provide for a more feasible account of poly-motivation was also emphasized by the Russian psychologist Dmitry Leontiev (1993).[2] He suggested that Leontiev's original notion of an activity having several motives at the same time be abandoned. Instead, Dimitry Leontiev proposed a model that included: (a) a one-to-one correspondence between an activity and its motive, and (b) a many-to-one correspondence between needs and a motive. In other words, it was claimed that each activity has only one motive, but this motive can be jointly defined by a set of diverse needs.

The "several needs, one motive" notion proposed by Dmitry Leontiev (1993) suggests a consistent view on how activities can be determined by a multiplicity of needs. The notion foregrounds the relationship between needs and motives and calls for further analysis of the ways motives can be contextualized in the whole system of interactions between a human being and the world. However, the proposed model also has certain limitations. First, it does not provide an account of the object of activity; it does not include "the object of activity" as a separate component. Second, the notion of "one activity, one motive" ignores Leontiev's distinction between sense-forming motives and motives–stimuli. Third, the notion is not compatible with evidence suggesting that the object of activity of a person or organization may change over time even if needs do not change (see, e.g., Hyysalo 2005).

Therefore, we believe that Leontiev's original notion of a possibility for an activity to have several motives should not be discarded in this way. Instead, we propose to separate the notion of the motive from the notion of the object of activity. This separation implies that if there are several conflicting needs, these needs can correspond to either two differ-

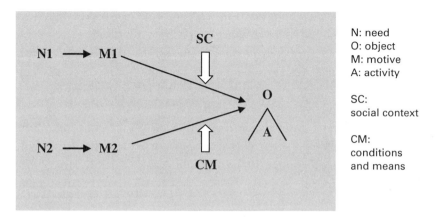

n motives — 1 object — 1 activity

Figure 6.3
Model C. N:1:1.

ent activities (which can be described by Model A) or different aspects of the same activity. The latter case can be illustrated with Model C shown in figure 6.3. The model depicts a case where the individual attempts to meet two needs (N1 and N2) in a given social context (SC), under certain conditions and having certain means (CM). In this case the individual attempts to achieve two motives, M1 and M2, at the same time. If the individual cannot simply pursue these two motives at the same time, the activity does not have a direction until the object of activity is defined. The object is different from any of the effective motives and is jointly defined by the whole set of motives the individual strives to attain in her activity.

Let us once again invoke the example of hunters to illustrate Model C. Consider the activity of a hunter, shaped by the needs of food and self-preservation. The motives are to obtain meat of a slaughtered animal as food and to survive in the upcoming encounter with the animal. If both motives are strong enough (e.g., getting food is a matter of life and death, but the prey is very dangerous), the hunter is in a state of confusion and hesitation. One of the motives can dominate, and the hunter will either flee and face the risk of starvation, or assault the animal and face the risk of being killed. It is more likely, however, that the hunter's activity will be directed toward a desired outcome that makes it possible to attain both motives. For instance, the hunter can decide to chase the animal until it is tired and no longer presents a danger. In that case both food and self-preservation influence the hunter. The object of hunting activity, however—chasing the animal and killing it after wearing it out—is what gives the activity structure and direction.

There are several distinctive features of Model C differentiating it from Models A and B: (a) there is only one object of activity, no matter how many motives are involved; (b) the object of activity is jointly determined by all effective motives; and (c) the object of activity both motivates and directs the activity.

These features of the model make it possible to address problems with Leontiev's original definition of the object of activity as its motive. First, the distinction between motives and the object of activity eliminates duplication of concepts. Second, if the functions of exciting and directing an activity are distributed between motives (exciting), the object (both exciting and directing), and goals (directing), then the contradictory claims about the directing function of the motive can be reformulated to make them logically consistent. Third, the model provides a means of dealing with poly-motivated activities.

6.5   CONCLUSION: DESIGNING THE OBJECT OF ACTIVITY

The last conclusion implies, in particular, that objects of activities are dynamically constructed on the basis of various types of constraints. These constraints include the needs that the given activity is striving to satisfy; available means; other potentially related activities; and other actors involved, with their own motives and objects. When some of these components change—for instance, the importance of a certain need increases—or new means become available, the whole configuration of constraints may require a redefinition of the object of activity to meet the new constraints (see Hyysalo 2005).

With this in mind, we can see that the process of constructing and reconstructing the object of activity can be considered a special type of design. As in any design, the outcome should meet certain criteria to qualify as a successful design product. Some preliminary criteria for "high-quality" objects of activities include (a) *balance*: the effective motives should be properly represented—if a motive is systematically ignored, the activity may face a breakdown; (b) *inspiration*: the object of activity should not only be rationally feasible but also attractive and energizing; (c) *stability*: if the object changes too often, the activity can be disorganized; and (d) *flexibility*: when factors such as motives and available means change, the object of activity should be redefined to avoid becoming obsolete and ineffective.

7

Objects of Desire

7.1 INTRODUCTION

In this chapter[1] we continue exploring extensions to the concept of object, using as an example research work in a pharmaceutical company. We focus on object formation in a collaborative setting, examining the interplay of multiple motives of multiple actors. The chapter has three aims. The first is to continue the discussion from chapter 6 on the need to distinguish between motive and object. The second is to discuss the difference between *constructing* and *instantiating* objects. The third is to begin to explore the power and passion that permeate objects. We use Weber's definition of power: "the probability that one actor within a social relationship will be in a position to carry out his own will despite resistance, regardless of the basis on which this probability rests" (Weber 1947). By passion we mean emotional attachment to an object ranging from ardent affection to intense conviction, in line with standard dictionary definitions. We argue that objects are *constructed*, *instantiated*, and *linked to one another* through relations of power and passion among actors.

The chapter presents a study examining the interplay of passionately held objects—objects of desire—in the biotechnology research department of a large pharmaceutical company. We argue that attention to such objects is important for understanding the *why* of activity and not just the *how*.

Our concern with the *why* of activity stems from two sources. First, in our empirical investigations, we have found over the course of many studies that people often speak of their activity in emotional terms, and that issues of power frequently enter the discussion. The discussion goes well beyond the practicalities of getting things done; it may involve joy, sadness, anger, fear, satisfaction, disgruntlement—a wide range of human emotions. Second, we believe a concern with power and passion is a natural extension to the fundamental question of activity theory: What is the relation between consciousness and object-oriented activity? If we are directed, impelled, motivated by objects, as activity theory says, then we are clearly in a realm that involves more than just rational calculation and logic. We are in the thick of the values, meanings, and emotions with which objects are inevitably linked. It is perhaps not surprising that Vygotsky devoted his thesis to a study of *Hamlet*, Shakespeare's tragedy about a search for meaning, about sorrow and madness. Modern activity theory is just beginning to conduct empirical studies that consider emotion, to anchor it firmly in activity rather than analyzing it as an exogenous variable as in many traditions (see Roth in press).

In the cognitive and situated approaches that are the heritage of interaction design, not only is emotion missing, but the very concept of motive has been eclipsed by a focus on lower-level actions that reveal the how but not the why of activity. As Engeström observed:

> From the viewpoint of activity theory, cognitivist and situated approaches share a common weakness, as the focus of analysis is restricted to actions, whether couched in terms of "tasks" or "situations." Neither approach is able to account for what makes people act and form goals in the first place, what creates the horizon of possible actions, what makes people strive for something beyond the immediately obvious goal or situation. What is excluded is objects and thus motives of activity—the long-term "*why?*" of actions. Without this level, theories of situated cognition run the risk of becoming merely technical theories of "*how?*"—more elaborate and flexible than mentalist and rationalist models, but equally sterile when faced with societal change and institutional contradictions that pervade everyday actions.... (Engeström 1995)

Because the empirical analysis in this chapter concerns work in a biotechnology research department, we consulted the science studies literature to locate analyses that focus on the *why* of science. As in the situated and cognitivist traditions, we found that the science studies literature also seems to emphasize the *how* of work, presenting science largely through the lens of its mechanics. Collaborative aspects of scientific research are described with notions such as articulation work, task alignment, and managing networks of people and resources (Law and Callon 1992; Latour 1996b; Fujimura 1987). Fujimura, for example, spoke of the selection of "doable problems" as a fundamental driver of scientific research. Articulation work guides science as it pulls together "everything that is needed to carry out production tasks: planning, organizing, monitoring, evaluating, adjusting, coordinating and integrating ..." (Fujimura 1987). In this framing, science proceeds as a series of tactical decisions shaped by situational constraints.[2] Considerations of motive, passion, and desire lie outside the scope of such analyses.[3]

As noted in chapter 6, the concept of object helps us understand not only what people are doing, but why they are doing it. Saari and Miettinen (2001) suggested that the why-questions of scientific work can be addressed by activity theory through its focus on motives in object-oriented activity. Hyysalo (2005) observed, "The ability to address the wider context and continuities beyond the transient actions is one of the strong points of activity theory." Developing *why* understandings will help us make sense of the *actions* of collaborative activity so carefully reported in a number of traditions including distributed cognition, situated action, computer-supported collaborative work, and science studies. To offer deeper understanding, analyses must provide adequate scope for actions to be linked to the highest level of activity, the "need or desire" to which the activity always answers, as Leontiev, and before him Vygotsky, proposed.

This chapter discusses the results of an ethnographic investigation of collaborative scientific work at a large pharmaceutical company, "Ajaxe."[4] Ethnographic research was conducted for four months, including audiotaped interviews with seventeen scientists in their offices and conference rooms, as well as informal chat at lunch and in the hallways. Most of the scientists were molecular biologists, biochemists, or immunologists. Some scientists were managers, others principal investigators or postdocs. Scientists were observed in weekly formal meetings at which important scientific and strategic decisions were made. Tours of the facility provided information on equipment and office layout.

7.2   REFINING THE CONCEPT OF OBJECT IN ACTIVITY THEORY

7.2.1   Constructing and Instantiating Objects

In the activity theory literature, there is often discussion of "constructing" an object. But what does that mean? Is constructing an object deciding what the object should be, or is it the work of attaining the object? We propose that constructing an object mean *formulating* it, that is, figuring out what it should be, and that *instantiating* an object mean realizing a particular object, achieving an outcome. These two meanings map to the emphases in the two versions of activity theory presented in chapter 6: motivation in Leontiev's activity theory and production in Engeström's. In deciding what an object should be, subjects define specific motives to meet their needs. But to actually realize or instantiate the motive, a process of production is necessary. We believe this terminology brings together the complementary emphases (as seen in table 6.1) resulting in a more unified view.

The object of the biotechnology research department at Ajaxe was to select one to two genes of therapeutic value per year for the development of profitable drugs. This object was *constructed* at some past time by management, and reflected the number of genes that could be developed into new drugs given the company's resources. Here the object was gene selection, and the motive, from management's point of view, was to increase profits for the company. The work of *instantiating* the object was a lengthy, difficult task of conducting experiments, consulting databases, reading literature, talking to people, thinking hard, and making decisions. "The biological process, it's hard and slow, and not precise," one informant commented, giving a sense of the work of instantiation in this setting.

The notion of instantiating an object draws attention to what is usually the bulk of any activity—achieving some realization of the object, attaining an outcome. At the same time, it is important to remember that objects, along with their motives, are *constructed* through social processes, and that the particular object toward which people orient their activity is of critical importance.

7.2.2   Separating Motive and Object

The original activity-theoretical notion of object seemed to suggest that object and motive are indivisibly bound. In the simple case of "one object, one motive," such a binding is not problematic, as discussed in chapter 6 (see also Hyysalo 2005). However, when analyzing collaborative work, a one object, one motive mapping immediately raises problems. Sutter (2002c) pointed out that in collective activity, many voices are heard, many actors and interests are involved. How are we to think of these many actors and interests in activity theory, of how these multiple actors orient to objects? If motives are truly important as argued by Leontiev, then we must be careful in analyzing just what the motives of an activity are.

Using data from the study at Ajaxe, we argue that actors in a collaborative activity may have radically different motives related to the same object. It seems likely that this is the common case for collaborative activity. If we do not admit the possibility that different motives of different individuals articulate in a single activity, then we must define collaborative work as a collection of individual activities that somehow coordinate with one another. In the empirical discussion, we will argue that at Ajaxe a single object was shared among members of the research department, and that the researchers related to the object via differing motives. A key finding was that the motives were *linked*; they were not isolated from one another. The motives were linked through relations of conflict, power, resistance, and acquiescence. It was the struggles to align the motives—not merely the tasks—through these relational processes that gave rise to a single activity, rather than a set of individually coordinating activities. This analysis of the articulation of motives at Ajaxe fits within Model C presented in chapter 6 although here M_n and N_n attach to different individuals (see fig. 7.1).

7.3   POWER AND PASSION IN OBJECTS OF DESIRE

In the activity theory literature, the term object tends to be used in a formal, somewhat bloodless way. While some investigators (e.g., Engeström and Escalante 1996; Holland and Reeves 1996; Sutter 2002c; Roth

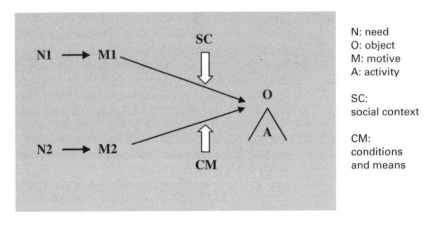

n motives — 1 object — 1 activity

Figure 7.1
Model C. N:1:1. In this application of model C, M_n and N_n can be distributed across more than one individual subject.

in press) have pointed out that power relations and conflict are central to object-oriented activity, in general, little sense of the bumptious nature of object construction and instantiation emerges from the literature.[5] In collaborative activities, objects are often said to arise from "negotiation," "discourse," "collective reflection" (Kuutti 1998; Foot 2001; Saari and Miettinen 2001). These cerebral formulations fail to capture the passions that imbue human activity. The analysis in section 7.3.1 will examine the passions that animated the activity of selecting genes at Ajaxe, emphasizing the interplay between motives and how it shaped the object itself. The analysis foregrounds institutional and emotional contradictions engendered by conflicting motives. The aim is to reveal the institutional contradictions of which Engeström spoke, contradictions that do not fit comfortably within accounts emphasizing the *how* of collaborative work (with its tasks and doable problems).

We now turn to a discussion of the process of *curating genes* at Ajaxe, and how differing motives came into play in curation.

7.3.1   "The Ability to Select What Others See": Collaborative Processes of Scientific Curation

At Ajaxe, as at many pharmaceutical companies, biotechnology research was funded in part to find genes with therapeutic value that would lend themselves to the design of drugs to combat disease. One difficulty with such an undertaking is that there are tens of thousands of genes. Ajaxe researchers commonly invoked the metaphor of a "pipeline" in discussing gene selection; many genes entered at one end of the selection process, but few emerged at the other. Early in the interviews, we began to hear the fascinating term *curation* used to describe the process of winnowing for selection. Informants spoke of a process in which genes were carefully selected from a larger set to be presented to others, just as in museum curation where objects are selected to be displayed to an audience.

Curation also extended to experimental results and scientific literature. In this analysis we focus on the curation of genes, as that was most closely tied to the research department's central object. But curation was a general process that permeated the entire scientific enterprise at Ajaxe. Beyond Ajaxe, the term curation is used in biology to describe the annotations in certain databases such as SwissProt. These databases are valued by scientists for their excellent curation in which each gene or protein is annotated with painstakingly selected, high-quality information.

Curation is a deeply social process through which materials are strategically revealed to others, or hidden from them. One high-ranking manager at Ajaxe, an accomplished scientist, explained scientific curation as "the ability to select what others see." This phrase struck us as remarkably different from the textbook explanations of how science is conducted. While science studies have long documented the many ways in which scientific practice departs from textbook formulations (going back at least to Fleck 1979, originally published in 1935), the characterization of the process of biological curation as "the ability to select what others see" was a vivid revelation, from a scientist, of the power relations central to the scientific work in the research department. Rather than replicable experiments that progressively revealed the secrets of the universe, curation pointed to carefully managed relations with other scientists as a key to scientific progress. In particular, the idea of curation underscored a scientist's power to choose the materials to be revealed to other scientists and those to be hidden. Scientists chose to hide or reveal materials based on their motives. The process of curation is the backdrop against which we describe the interplay of motives in the collective activity in the research department.

In a telling and representative example of curation, a mid-level scientist described how high-level managers sometimes developed a belief in the potential for certain kinds of genes to be profitable, heavily promoting them within the company. The scientist remarked, "[One of our VPs] likes [genes of type X]. This starts limiting what you can look at. This immediately wipes out huge pie slices. There is a filter."

This scientist's notion of "what you can look at" perfectly mirrored the manager's framing of curation as "what others see." The scientist emphasized how drastically curation could limit areas of interest for scientists at lower levels of the hierarchy.

The ability-to-select-what-others-see was differentially distributed across power levels of the organizational hierarchy at Ajaxe. We consider *top-down, bottom-up,* and *bidirectional* processes of curation as they operated to instantiate the object of delivering genes to the company. Top-down criteria for curation were established by powerful members of upper management within the research department and the larger corporate hierarchy. Bottom-up criteria came from middle managers, principal investigators, and postdocs. Bidirectional criteria derived from potentially anyone at any level. Those with the most power had more ability to select-what-others-see. However, others resisted the curated selections in some cases, generating some power from below.

Three motives animated object construction and instantiation at Ajaxe —the profit motive, scientific interest, and a humanitarian desire to help others by contributing to the development of new drugs. None of these motives is surprising. However, without considering them, and the dynamic relations between them, we cannot make sense of important collaborative processes that shaped scientific work at Ajaxe. These processes included acts of resistance by scientists against management directives, acts of "self-censoring" by lower ranking scientists, and emotional dislocations generated throughout object instantiation.

We now turn to an analysis of the specific criteria by which genes were curated, with an emphasis on how these criteria articulated the differing motives of scientists and managers engaged in the activity. The criteria are arranged to show how motives followed power relations in the hierarchy at Ajaxe.

7.3.2   Top-Down Criteria of Curation: The Profit Motive and Its Manifestations in Curation

Market direction   For a pharmaceutical company, a therapeutic gene is a potentially profitable gene. A fundamental criterion for the curation of genes at Ajaxe was the company's market direction for specific disease areas and the estimated market size for a drug. As one manager commented, "if you have a drug you're usually targeting a single [physiological] process, you're targeting a particular molecule [gene] that then has a major downstream effect on the whole physiological process.... we [need to] understand the context of the disease and therefore the target for the drug." This consideration of market direction in curating genes was clearly linked to the profit motive. In general, everyone at Ajaxe was in favor of profits, but for some managers, profit was the only motive of interest, or the main motive (in general, the higher up the hierarchy, the more salient the profit motive).

Intellectual property   Another top-down criterion for curation was Ajaxe's "IP position," that is, the intellectual property held by it and by its competitors. If Ajaxe held patents on particular genes, those patents were of great potential value. One manager noted, "these are the sets of genes that were identified, these are the things that we believe we have some sort of intellectual property position on, or we can curate our way to really nailing down the intellectual property position." "Curating our way to nailing down the intellectual property position" meant selecting genes that the company could ultimately patent.

If competitors held patents on specific genes, they might be of much less interest to Ajaxe, even if they were in the right therapeutic ballpark. Finding out which patents competitors held, or which patents might be issuing soon, was an ongoing struggle. Some managers regularly devoted time to consulting patent databases and reading news on the Internet, trying to sniff out where competitors might be headed with their intellectual property efforts.

Clinical considerations: Drug delivery mechanisms and side effects   In the initial stages of exploring a gene for potential therapeutic value, it may be difficult to know how the protein the gene codes for might be delivered as a drug or what side effects it might cause. But often something is known from previous work, so potential delivery mechanisms and side effects were considered as genes were curated. Potentially interesting genes could be shunted aside if it was likely that their proteins could not be easily delivered (e.g., in oral form) or would cause serious side effects.

Market direction, intellectual property, and clinical concerns, all relating to the business side of the work, were the basic motives management applied to the curation of genes in the research department. In the next section, we see how these motives did not stand in isolation from other motives, but interacted with them in specific ways. Even when motives were in conflict, they were bound to one another through interactions between the managers and scientists. These ongoing interactions centered on motives suggest a single activity in which one object is approached via different motives from different people in the activity, rather than a model of multiple coordinated activities.

7.3.3   Bottom-Up Criterion for Curation

Scientific interest   By far the most important bottom-up criterion for curation at Ajaxe was the scientists' interest in a particular gene (or set of related genes). One scientist remarked, "Our filter [for choosing a gene to study] is whether or not it's interesting." Genes were talked about as being interesting or boring. One scientist jokingly referred to a gene championed by upper management as "the most boring molecule at Ajaxe."

The motive of engaging in interesting scientific research energized the process of curation at Ajaxe. The scientists were passionate about their work, often spending long hours in the lab, and expressing strong emotional commitment to their research in the interviews. After some initial skepticism on the part of some scientists with respect to talking to us, as soon as they realized we were really interested, they spoke at length and with deep feeling about their work.

Intellectual and emotional energy pervaded the scientists' research. While the "pipeline" metaphor connoted rational control and linearity, other metaphors in the interviews suggested more emotional, less rational spheres of experience. One scientist described the selection of genes as "a Zen kind of thing." Another called it a "zoo" and a "bubbling cauldron." Such language expressed an energizing capacity—a quiet energy in a Zen process, chaotic energy for the zoo, heat and ferment in the bubbling cauldron. These metaphors bespeak the emotional energy animating the motives behind everyday actions that answer Engeström's question: "What makes people strive for something beyond the immediately obvious goal or situation?" They give meaning to Leontiev's original formulation of object-oriented activity: "Behind the object, there always stands a need or a desire, to which [the activity] always answers." Taking these metaphors and emotions as data, we move outside the scope of the cognitivist, situated, and science studies realm of actions to a sphere of object-oriented activity.

Management understood that despite their own interests and criteria for curation, and their considerable ability-to-select-what-others-see, no good scientific work would take place at Ajaxe unless scientists got interested in it. "No matter how much structure you have in an organization, still the only way to get people to do work is to get them excited about something," remarked one manager. A key challenge for management in instantiating the object of discovering therapeutic genes was to align their own curatorial criteria (market direction, intellectual property, clinical considerations) with the scientific interests of principal investigators and postdocs. This was of course a moving target as new scientists came into the group, interests changed, and market conditions shifted. The managers did not always succeed at alignment, as "the most boring molecule at Ajaxe" comment suggests. However, they deliberately tried to produce the best alignment they could. One manager said, "And so it [some gene or set of genes] makes sense because there's an exciting new biology, and makes sense because of the patent position around that.

Makes sense in the end economically." The manager acknowledged the scientists' motive to conduct "exciting new biology," but also the company's motives to establish intellectual property and to generate profit. To "make sense" of these disparate motives, he tried to select genes to fulfill multiple motives.

However, the situation was far from one in which the managers simply went along with what the scientists wanted. Managers were able to direct curation through their power to allocate resources. They could fund postdocs and visiting scholars, and buy reagents for the genes they considered important to the company. Often scientists chose to "self-censor," in the words of one scientist, selecting genes for which managerial resources would be forthcoming. Scientists knew that their work would be publicly examined in the formal meetings. They were not eager to be exposed as working on genes the company did not endorse. Thus, no open conflicts ensued in cases of "self-censoring"; these scientists chose work to align with company interests, acquiescing to curations from above.

Sometimes, however, the motives of scientists and managers came into more explicit conflict, and the scientists deliberately resisted the managers' direction. One scientist described a case in which a group of scientists pursued a gene of interest despite management's concerns about side effects. The scientist commented, "When a decision is made at [a high level], the upper-level people can't explicitly stop the researchers from working on anything. But they certainly have the power to steer resources one way or another." The team found itself with few resources. But they still believed in the project, so they cobbled together what resources they could, such as visiting researchers, to keep the project going. One scientist said, "We've gone from being a team to more of a club." The scientists fought back to keep the gene from being curated away—because of their scientific interest—and continued to work on it. The scientists were not choosing "doable" problems; here they chose problems explicitly defined as those that were not to be done.

While everyone recognized the importance of profits, the need to be responsive to market conditions sometimes came into conflict with doing biology as the biologists had been trained to do it. Most of the scientists' academic experience led them to choose an area and stay with it until interesting scientific contributions had been made. A scientist might remain in a single area for many years. One scientist spoke of the need, in the corporate context of Ajaxe, to learn how to dive into new areas in which he had no training but which were identified by the company as market opportunities. "Well, I knew peripherally things about [the new areas]. But that's how you have to do it here and it's certainly—this ain't your father's biology." The scientist felt conflicted about having to abandon areas of deep scientific interest to pursue potentially more profitable areas. The company's profit motive and his own scientific motives collided. The scientist aligned himself with the company's motives, accepting the curations of more powerful managers, but experienced what he referred to as "fragmentation."

Middle-level managers were in an interesting position as they attempted to balance scientific interest and curation by management. Closer than upper management to the principal investigators and postdocs (often newly minted from their ranks), yet on the management team, they had to walk a fine line. One of the most influential of these managers was known to defend the research interests of the scientists against upper management when she believed the work was important. The curation process, then, was shaped in important ways from the bottom of the hierarchy by the interests of the scientists which the managers had to take into account, and which they attempted to align with business considerations.

The "bottom-up" motive of scientific interest suggests that activities do not generate their own incentives in a simple way. Traditional activity theory provides somewhat limited guidance in considering the provenance of motives. Leontiev said: "[O]nly within the human activity system are the objects able to exist as incentive, goal or tool; outside this system they lose their existence as incentive, goal or tool.... The very conditions given by society carry the motives and goals for the activity together with its tools and methods" (quoted in Christiansen 1996). While Leontiev's statements are certainly true in one sense, in another sense they suggest a closed system of motives and goals. The Ajaxe data show that a single object can exist in relations of tension with multiple motives. These motives may enter the system from other activities; for example, the scientific "club" that insisted that their genes be part of the lab activity at Ajaxe. To say simply that society offers motives does not help in untangling conflicting motives, nor does it suggest that new motives are created and enter activities, which they certainly do. Society is perhaps the wrong level of analysis for tracing relations of motives empirically. In studying collaboration, a key challenge is to understand how activities interact with one another, and how they change over time, as different activities influence one another.

7.3.4   Bidirectional Criteria for Curation

Scientific pragmatism   The science studies literature tells us that the scientific process is shaped by the "resistance" of the materials and instruments with which science is conducted (Fleck 1979; Pickering 1995; Miettinen 1998; Saari and Miettinen 2001). Far from being purely a result of human curiosity and intellectual endeavor, science is pushed and pulled by the physical properties of the *things* it uses to investigate nature. At Ajaxe, these things were instruments, tools, reagents including lab animals, genetic material, and rare chemicals. For example, sometimes the scientists had to wait months for the proper strain of "knockout mice"[6] before they could proceed with their research.

Both managers and scientists described how practical constraints often influenced curation and how they tried to manipulate these constraints to meet their own motives. The most basic practical constraint was the availability of personnel; a gene could not be investigated if there was no one at Ajaxe—a principal investigator, a postdoc, a visiting scholar— who was interested in the gene. Managers attempted to recruit strategically to find people with expertise and interest in the genes they wanted to learn about.

Scientific progress was monitored. If sufficient progress was not being made after a certain amount of time, a gene could be dropped from the pipeline. As one principal investigator observed, "If you end up working on [a gene] longer than three to five years then you have to ask yourself, 'Is there something else I could be spending my time on?'" Managers were sensitive about resources being used for projects that did not seem promising. The availability of and knowledge about reagents also shaped the curation process. Limitations due to reagents would seem to be a purely pragmatic concern, part of the *how* of science. Indeed they were, but it was also the case that many scientists anticipated future needs for reagents and developed a "trading network" with other scientists so that when they needed a reagent, they had someone to ask. So, while the scientists were sometimes stymied by lack of access to reagents, they did not leave this process to chance. The need for reagents was known and planned for, and was managed to the best of the scientists' abilities. These actions were undertaken to fulfill the motive of conducting interesting scientific research.

Miettinen (1998) observed that "resistance should be interpreted through the structure of activity." Resistance is a relation between historically formed artifacts (such as knockout mice) and scientific objects. The management of reagents is a good example of the way a set of actions makes deeper sense as the fulfillment of a motive, rather than as the end point of analysis. In activity theory, actions such as managing reagents, and their impact on the conduct of science, are seen as sensible actions within a horizon of possible actions (Engeström 1995; Kuutti 1998) established by an object.

Humanitarian desires   Many scientists and managers at all levels of the hierarchy at Ajaxe were motivated by a humanitarian desire to see their work someday help others overcome disease. As one midcareer scientist said, "Many of us would like to go out [retire] knowing something's gone into somebody, and benefited them. It's not about writing papers, or you know, that stuff any longer. It would be really nice to be part of a drug. Even if it's just, we identified the [gene] sequence. Somebody else could have figured out what it did. I hope the whole department is thinking along those same lines."

This scientist had not only decided for himself that humanitarian motives were important for him personally; he wanted to influence his department to work for the greater social good. He had an active program of getting others to "see" genes he considered important. This scientist's desire to serve humanity, and the actions he took to do so, exemplify the passions behind a "horizon of possible actions." Such actions cannot be made sense of without incorporating a long-term orientation that gives meaning and emotional import to activity. Notions of selecting doable problems and tinkering that do not consider a long-term orientation in research work cannot account for the scientific and humanitarian commitments constructed in the scientist's declaration that "It's not about writing papers," and his avowal that he wanted to know that he had helped to develop something that's "gone into somebody, and benefited them."

The deeply felt desire to aid humanity evident in this scientist's work reveals the patently social nature of the "needs and desires" Leontiev referred to in defining activity. In activity theory, passion is not an individualistic psychological state; it is a relation of emotion to an activity with its objects. The scientist who lobbied others to join him surely experienced an emotion, which we can take to be meaningful at the individual level. But the emotion was bound to the scientist's activity in two ways. First, in attempting to recruit others to join him, he externalized the emotion into the activity as a means of transforming the activity. In expressing the emotion, the scientist was able to influence others. And second, the scientist expressed and conceptualized the object within terms derived directly from the activity. He compared helping people to writing papers. He explicated the precise nature of the humanitarian contribution that could be made in his department, that is, identifying gene sequences.

The scientist's passion for humanitarian outcomes was part of a set of motives in play within the Ajaxe culture. It was also connected to humanitarian motives attaching to the larger international social class of well-educated professionals to which the scientist belonged. Miettinen (1998) observed that the motives of research work may "connect research activity to society, integrating ecological, economic, and societal values in a vision of the future rendered by a knowledge of new technological opportunities." Humanitarian values in a successfully capitalist company such as Ajaxe show the importance of larger societal values entering local activities. Understanding the interplay of societal values and local activity is an important reason to attend to motives and not only to actions. Analyzing objects of desire enables the assessment of the forward trajectory, at a societal level, of the impact of scientific research as it emerges in the concrete everyday activity of scientists.

7.4   DISCUSSION

Curation at Ajaxe can be seen as a process in which the motives of scientists and postdocs played with and against the motives of managers. Understanding the active relations of these motives is necessary to account for the process by which a research department could curate its way from thousands of genes to one or two specific genes in a year. It is necessary to account for the phenomenon of scientific research driving for-profit innovation. Such undertakings cannot be seen merely as the outcome of adroit handling of the pragmatics of the *how* of science; they are rooted in the passionately held motives of the actors in the activity. In action-based accounts, either the long-term *why* is taken as a background given, outside the scope of detailed analysis, or it is not dealt with at all. By focusing on motives, we have tried to show how they were central to the function of the research department at Ajaxe, suffusing its activity with meaning at every step as the instantiation of gene selection was carried out.

The motives we have discussed all aligned with the organizational object of selecting one to two genes per year. That object-directed activity gave meaning to the daily actions of the scientists and managers. The conflicts we have examined derived *from the motives in relation to one another*, not the motives in relation to the object. In other words, each individual motive articulated in a relatively smooth way to the object, but, among themselves, the motives sometimes generated disruptions. Thus the object itself was not contested; it was the instantiation of the object that led to tensions, tensions deriving from incompatibilities among the multiple motives. In other cases, of course, the object itself might well have been contested. However, objects tend to be relatively long-lived entities with some stability because nothing would ever get done if people constantly contested objects. This empirical analysis suggests one locale of disruption in activity is in the instantiation of objects with multiple motives. The analysis emphasizes the importance of separating motive from object when studying collaboration.

The analysis emphasized linkages between motives, that is, the way motives played out in relation to one another. The interplay between motives knit together the activity, as against a collection of individuals pursuing individual activities. The interplay manifested itself in the emotional tenor of the scientists' work, in their fears, joys, and desires.

To speak of such emotions is not to revert to mentalist conceptions of "inner states," but to reveal the social nature of needs and desires as they are expressed in human activity. Vivid images like the bubbling cauldron or the Zen process portrayed emotional activity within a social context. And informants' discussions of the means of negotiating and transforming motives in the activity depicted the externalization of emotions in ways peculiar to and appropriate for the local setting. The scientist who remarked, "This ain't your father's biology," as he struggled with feelings of disruption, located his feelings within the intersection of the social group that had trained him and the activity, with its new demands, of which he was now a part.

The criteria for the design (or construction) of successful objects discussed in chapter 6 dovetail with Ajaxe management's view of aligning motives: "And so it [some gene or set of genes] makes sense because there's an exciting new biology, and makes sense because of the patent position around that. Makes sense in the end economically." The manager spoke of balancing scientific research with profitability, of the stability and flexibility denoted by the "patent position," which had a fairly long time horizon but which had to be responsive to the activities of competitors, and of the inspiration and energizing afforded by the "exciting biology."

Far from being merely an arena of making do with doable problems, then, or the result of sober reflection and discourse, the curation of genes at Ajaxe was indeed a "bubbling cauldron" of interwoven motives and passions: deeply felt scientific interest, naked pursuit of profit, hidden and open conflict, and emotional satisfactions and dislocations. We see, in the push and pull of top-down and bottom-up processes of curation and their attendant motives, the shaping of a particular instantiation of the research department's object. Without a consideration of the dynamic web of motives of profit, scientific interest, and humanitarian desire, we cannot understand the most fundamental processes that energized the selection of the genes, nor the emotional aspects of the work. But it is these processes that accounted for the selection of these genes—

and not those other genes—as managers and scientists worked together, though not always in harmony, to fulfill the object of selecting target genes for Ajaxe.

7.5 CONCLUSION

Just as the scientists spoke of "selecting what others see," so we all do in our own practice. We have attempted to "curate" the desires and conflicts animating the motives behind the objects in one human activity, and the power relations that move such desires and conflicts in particular ways. A corporation could not leverage the work of scientists to increase its profits through the innovation of new products if it did not learn to exploit scientists' interest in conducting scientific work. That this leveraging is not a straightforward process, but involves accommodations and adjustments on both sides, is evident. These accommodations and adjustments are not the end game of activity, as they are construed to be in many accounts. They are actions, within a horizon of possible actions, responsive to actors' motives, in varying relations of accord and discord to others' motives. As we deepen accounts of collaboration in activity, we will need to confront the objects of desire that animate activity. These objects link people in diverse relations, articulating multiple actors with multiple motives.

This chapter has attempted to reveal some aspects of object-oriented activity—power and passion—that have been obscured in the activity theory literature and ignored in other literatures. The work proceeded from a grounded theory exploration of work in a biotechnology laboratory. The exploration revealed themes of power and passion in scientific work. These themes seemed to point to areas of needed development in activity theory, i.e., deeper investigation of a concept of motive both in terms of its emotional impact and its relation to individual subjects as they negotiated collective activities. These negotiations involved complex power relations as well as individuals seeking to meet their own needs in a social setting. The analysis was, on the one hand, structured by activity theory's concept of object/motive and, on the other hand, an attempt to extend that concept to explain the data of the empirical investigation. It was felt that the data were not explained by Leontiev's original formulation of need-object-motive-activity, but that a new formulation, Model C, presented in chapter 6 (see also Kaptelinin 2005), better accounted for the data. The data also pointed to the need to find a vocabulary to distinguish object construction and object instantiation, which we have argued are two distinct but necessary and closely related processes. In sum, the analysis began with an open-ended grounded theory approach, but was shaped, as data analysis proceeded, by activity theory's core concepts. At the same time, the work made an effort to develop those concepts in response to the empirical findings.

8

Historical Currents in the Development of Activity Theory

This chapter is an excursion into some historical twists and turns in the development of activity theory. In chapter 3, the fundamentals of activity theory were presented, describing its evolution as a sequence of accumulating contributions through which it gracefully progressed from Vygotsky's early insights to Leontiev's framework. The reality has been somewhat more complicated. For readers interested in the history of activity theory, especially its Soviet origins, this chapter discusses some of the broader conceptual influences that had an impact on Leontiev's thinking, the variety of activity-theoretical frameworks in Russian/Soviet psychology, some debates between activity theory and rival approaches, and the current debate regarding the dialectics of the individual and the social. This chapter is less related to interaction design than other chapters of the book and some readers might consider skipping straight to chapter 9.

8.1 FROM VYGOTSKY TO LEONTIEV: CONTINUITY OR DISCONTINUITY?

Undeniably, Leontiev's thinking was to a large extent shaped by Vygotsky. Leontiev was Vygotsky's student and his first major study was conducted under Vygotsky's supervision (Leontiev 1931). As discussed in chapter 3, a number of Vygotsky's concepts and ideas were directly incorporated into the body of activity theory. Despite all this, Leontiev's activity theory was not a direct continuation of Vygotsky's cultural-historical psychology. Leontiev developed his own research agenda, which was in certain respects substantially different from Vygotsky's.

The bloodline of activity theory includes not only Vygotsky's ideas but other significant work as well.

The impact of the Russian psychologist Mikhail Basov on the development of activity theory was probably no less important than that of Vygotsky. In the mid- and late 1920s Basov developed a theoretical approach that was explicitly based on understanding human beings as "active agents in environments." This approach was applied to problems of psychology of volitional processes and then in child psychology. Basov's main work, *General Foundations of Pedology*,[1] featured a section entitled "Development of a human being as an active agent in an environment" (Basov 1930). This section anticipated some key ideas later developed by Leontiev.

In particular, Basov stated that an understanding of human work and development should focus on an "equation with three variables—the human being, environment, and activity" (Basov 1930). He proposed that human activity, understood as an interaction of an organism with environment, and the way the organism establishes a relationship between itself and the world, be discerned as a special object of analysis. Basov conducted concrete theoretical and empirical analyses of the structural components of activity and the way activity is stimulated by objects in the environment. Finally, Basov emphasized the importance of mediating artifacts (even though he did not use this exact terminology). For instance, concerning the development of tools and organizational forms of labor, Basov stated that not only does this development "result in changes of the forms of social organization, it also changes the individual organization of all human beings; first of all it changes their psychology (that is, human beings as actors in an environment) but also, to a certain degree, their organisms" (Basov 1930, our translation).

The approach proposed by Basov was highly valued by many of his contemporaries. Vygotsky praised the novelty of the ideas and the combination of analytical and integrative perspectives within a single approach (Merlin 1975), while Leontiev, who published a review of Basov's *General Foundations of Pedology* in a leading Soviet periodical of that time, appreciated the fact that human psychology was being approached from a natural science position (Leontiev 1929). Leontiev also positively evaluated the attempt to understand human beings in the general context of biological evolution.

According to Yaroshevsky, Sirotkina, and Danilicheva (1993), Leontiev's ideas regarding the structure of activity have their origins in the works of Basov rather than those of Vygotsky. This does not mean that Basov was a direct predecessor of Leontiev. There were substantial differences between their approaches. In particular, some concepts that were of central importance to Basov did not play an important role in Leontiev's work.

A recurrent idea in Basov's work was understanding environments as not mere collections of stimuli but as integrated wholes. This understanding applied to both physical and social environments. Objects in the physical world are interdependent and interrelated, so the ultimate physical environment of any organism, according to Basov, is the universe (see Merlin 1975). The integrative nature of environments is even more apparent in the case of social settings. For instance, knowing one thing about a person, such as her occupation, often helps in making inferences about other aspects of the social environment of that person. Since there is a two-way interaction between human beings and environments, which mutually transform each other over the course of activities, the mutual adjustments of actors and environments result in an unstable, dynamic equilibrium. Therefore, there is an essentially isomorphic relationship between human beings, environments, and activities. One implication of this idea of an isomorphic relationship was that environments are not independent of actors. Environments are dynamic entities: for the same person the environment can be different at different phases of development. According to Basov, the "radius" of an environment generally increases when a person progresses to a new developmental phase.

Another major issue for Basov was "organizational forms," or formal structures of activities. In an attempt to go beyond the elementary "stimulus–response" structure of behavior, he introduced the concept of "circular" responses, based on an idea similar to the cybernetics notion of the feedback loop. Basov differentiated three main types of dependencies between components of an action through which the action is implemented: (a) no dependency at all (the components can be executed separately from each other); (b) chain actions (execution of one component triggers the next one); and (c) flexible exploration strategies. An example of an action organized according to the last type is solving a math problem by starting with an incorrect understanding of the problem and gradually coming to a correct understanding—and a correct solution—by trying out a variety of apparently feasible solutions and discovering that they do not work.

Finally, Basov made an interesting attempt to develop a method suitable for studying people in their natural environments. He was not satisfied with the lack of interest in processes taking place in real-life settings that was typical of psychological studies of that time. He believed that psychologists should "study people not only in laboratories but also at factories, plants, and other places where people are actors in environments" (Basov 1929, cited in Yaroshevsky, Sirotkina, and Danilicheva 1993, our translation). Accordingly, Basov developed a research method based on a set of guidelines for conducting a psychological study through observations in a natural environment. The guidelines required the researcher to:

- keep separate the objective data collected during observations and the observer's inferences about corresponding subjective phenomena of observed people;
- register as much objective data about observed behavior as possible (and, if necessary, augment observations with interviews and questions);
- conduct observations continuously during the time necessary to follow how the processes in question are unfolding rather than capture a sequence of isolated low-level events; and
- keep in mind the purpose of the observation and focus on data relevant for that purpose.

These guidelines are hardly eye-openers for current interaction design researchers and practitioners. Similar guidelines have been formulated in a number of handbooks on how to conduct user studies. In particular, they are almost identical with basic principles of contextual inquiry (see, e.g., Holtzblatt and Beyer 1993; Hackos and Redish 1998; Beyer and Holtzblatt 1999). However, given that the method was developed in the 1920s, it was indeed a significant accomplishment for its time, and occurred around the same time American and European anthropologists were systematizing similar methods (see, e.g., Malinowski 1922).

Therefore, considering approaches developed by Vygotsky and Leontiev as two generations of the same framework does not take into account an important contribution made by Basov (and some other contributions, as well; see Yaroshevsky 1996). In addition, the "two generations" view underplays the differences between Vygotsky and Leontiev. Arguably, these differences are almost as deep as the similarities.

"Activity" was not a key concept for Vygotsky. He did not consider analysis of the whole structure of purposeful, goal-directed actions a necessary precondition for understanding the psychological processes that are embedded in these actions. Also, he was not especially interested in external, practical activities unless they constituted a context for phenomena of semiotic mediation by culturally developed means. His interests were predominantly in signs, meaning, art, intersubjectivity, and appropriation of culture. The very style of Vygotsky's writings, for example, his numerous allusions to poetry, suggests that he was not particularly inspired by the natural sciences. Even though Vygotsky conducted brilliant logical analyses and was a talented experimenter, he seemed to value intuition and deep insight over exactness, logical consistency, and impartiality. In these respects Leontiev appears to be almost the opposite of Vygotsky. Leontiev was committed to bringing psychology to the standards of consistency and rigor typical of natural sciences. His challenge was to build a comprehensive and coherent conceptual framework that could be used as a foundation for psychology as a true science. The objects of study preferred by Leontiev were phenomena such as perception that more easily yielded themselves to experimental investigation typical of the natural sciences.

Given the substantial differences in research perspectives and individual dispositions of the two researchers, it is hardly surprising that Leontiev did not just follow in Vygotsky's footsteps, but pursued his own agenda. While he incorporated Vygotsky's insights into the dialectics of the individual and the social, his own ambition was to understand the nature of meaningful, purposeful acting in the world.

In sum, both logical and historical evidence clearly indicate that the frameworks developed by Vygotsky and Leontiev are two distinct frameworks rather than generations of a single approach (Zinchenko 1993). Even though these frameworks are closely related and share a number of key ideas, they are also substantially different. While activity theory is based on some fundamental ideas formulated by Vygotsky and can be classified as a part of the cultural-historical tradition in a broad sense, its roots can be found in other approaches as well. While some of the most fundamental concepts of Leontiev's framework can be clearly traced to Vygotsky, Leontiev's ideas of human beings actively transforming their environments are likely to have been also inspired by other researchers, in particular Basov.

8.2   THE VARIETY OF ACTIVITY-THEORETICAL FRAMEWORKS IN RUSSIAN PSYCHOLOGY

Leontiev's approach was not the only activity-theoretical framework in Russian psychology. A prominent "alternative" activity-theoretical framework was developed by Sergey Rubinshtein, a leading Soviet psychologist and a prolific writer. He is especially well known for his *Foundations of General Psychology* (Rubinshtein 1946), the most comprehensive textbook on psychology ever written in Russia.[2] Rubinshtein was one of the first Russian psychologists who clearly articulated the need to make object-oriented activity a basic concept in psychological research. Some of the closest colleagues and students of Leontiev give Rubinshtein priority in introducing the concept of activity to psychology: "Object-oriented activity as the subject matter of psychological science was first identified by S. L. Rubinshtein. This approach was then developed by Leontiev" (Davydov, Zinchenko, and Talyzina 1982).

The differences between these two activity-theoretical perspectives in psychology, that of Leontiev and that of Rubinshtein, are seldom discussed, especially in research conducted outside Russia (Brushlinsky 1990, 1994). Some of these differences can be briefly summarized as follows.

The main conceptual disagreement between Leontiev and Rubinshtein was related to the exact meaning of activity as the subject matter of psychology. Rubinshtein maintained that activity as a whole cannot be the subject matter of psychology. Since psychology deals with *subjective experiences*, there are "psychological aspects of activity" that should be studied in psychology. Leontiev objected to that position. He emphasized that psychological research should focus on the activity as a whole in order to understand the interdependent components of the activity.

Taking some of the components, such as "nonpsychological aspects of activity," out of the context of activity would make it impossible to reconstruct the system of interdependencies between all components and would defeat the underlying logic of activity theory. Leontiev warned against a separation of activity into "psychological" and "nonpsychological" aspects. In a widely cited statement, which in fact was an implicit reply to Rubinshtein's arguments, he pointed out that "It is not a special part of activity which is of relevance to psychology, but its special function—the function of constituting the subject in the objective world" (Leontiev 1975, our translation).

Therefore, the approach developed in Russian psychology by Leontiev was not the only framework using the concept of activity to address how humans work, learn, and develop in a social context. In addition, Leontiev's colleagues within the Moscow School of Psychology developed their own approaches that were related to Leontiev's activity theory but were also different in a number of significant aspects. These approaches included, among others, Galperin's theory of stage-by-stage formation of psychological functions (Galperin 1976, 1992; Arievitch 2003), Davydov's theory of essential generalization (Davydov 1990b), and Zinchenko's microstructural analysis (Zinchenko and Gordon 1976).

Galperin's theory of stage-by-stage formation of psychological functions dealt with mechanisms and conditions of internalization. The point of departure for the theory was an understanding of the formation of new mental functions and abilities as the result of internalization. Over the course of learning, individuals develop "mental actions" by internalizing actions that can initially be carried out in an external plane and in collaboration with others. Galperin focused on the educational implications of this concept. His ambition was to reveal the underlying mechanisms of internalization and to develop an educational method, based on this understanding, which would facilitate learning by supporting internalization.

The approach proposed by Galperin can be roughly divided into two parts. The first part is based on the notion of the *orienting basis of activity*. This notion was of key importance to Galperin because his view of the human mind in general was based on the concept of orientation. Galperin started from a fundamental idea of the cultural-historical tradition, the idea of the human mind as emerging and existing in subject–object interaction. His next step was to specify the function of the mind. This function, according to Galperin, is to *orient* the subject in the world, that is, provide representations that make it possible for the subject to act in sync with reality. This view may seem to overemphasize the role of perception and mental representations and look somewhat like a version of the cognitivist approach. However, the similarity with cognitive psychology is superficial. The representation, which was of key importance to Galperin, the orienting basis of activity, is not an objective, precise model of the world. Instead, it was conceived of as highly subjective and dependent on the purposes of the subject, including only those aspects of reality relevant from the point of view of the activity at hand. Therefore, Galperin's concept of the orienting basis of activity bears more similarity to Gibson's ecological psychology (Gibson 1979) rather than to traditional cognitivist concepts of mental model and mental representation.

The orienting basis of activity is a cognitive representation of the domain, in which the action to be mastered is expected to be carried out, customized for that specific action. The representation should meet two criteria. It should be complete, that is, contain all information that is necessary to perform an action. And it should be selective, that is, irrelevant information should be filtered out. For instance, the orienting basis of driving a car in a city could include the street layout, landmarks, and road signs, but would exclude the architectural style of the buildings. According to Galperin, for an action to be successfully mastered it is crucially important that learners develop adequate orienting bases of activity by either appropriating those created by somebody else or constructing their own.

The second part of the approach is a method intended to facilitate the internalization of actions that learners need to carry out in the internal plane to reach a high level of performance. Galperin's unique approach was to organize the learning process so that the learner works with tasks presented in successively less external, material forms. Initially learners may work with physical objects, then with signs denoting the objects; then they describe the steps of solving a problem by speaking aloud; then they resort to silent speech—and eventually to no deliberate speech at all—when solving a task. For instance, the member of an emergency response team can learn how to find the shortest way to various places in an area first by actually driving a car, then by deciding on a route when using a map, then by describing a route via talking out loud, and finally by using silent speech. The underlying idea of the stage-by-stage formation of new mental actions is that proceeding through a series of increasingly "internal" tasks can break down the process of internalization into manageable steps and thus help learners undergo the transition from the external to the internal.

Even though the approach developed by Galperin has had wide-ranging implications for psychology in general (Arievitch 2003), the scope of concrete research based on the approach has been mostly limited to formal learning settings, both school learning and workplace learning. This focus is both a limitation and a strength of the approach. On the one hand, a diversity of phenomena, such as creative problem solving, do not easily lend themselves to analysis based on Galperin's framework. On the other hand, within its limited scope the approach proved to be a useful and effective tool for the development of concrete educational practices. In particular, the approach has been used successfully in skill formation, with skills ranging from motor skills, such as touch typing, to complex cognitive skills, such as error detection (Galperin and Kabylnitskaya 1974).

The framework developed by Vassily Davydov was also oriented primarily toward education. It has been—and still is—an influential approach in Soviet/Russian educational psychology, and has been widely applied to develop new types of curricula, textbooks, and other educational materials. These materials and concepts were tested in Russian schools in large-scale longitudinal evaluation studies, with very positive results. The approach developed by Davydov has its roots in Vygotsky's distinction between everyday concepts and scientific concepts (Vygotsky 1982b), Ilyenkov's dialectical logics (Ilyenkov 1977), and Leontiev's activity theory. The main idea behind Davydov's approach is that education should aim at creating optimal conditions for conceptual transformations of a special kind, called *essential generalizations*.

Essential generalization was understood as the ability to reveal the underlying principle of a concept and apply this principle to specific instances of the concept. Essential generalization, according to Davydov, is the opposite of empirical generalization, that is, generalization based on identifying an invariant property of a set of instances. Differentiating between these two types of generalization has direct implications for educational strategies for concept formation. An effective strategy to support empirical generalization is to provide learners with as many examples of a concept as possible, assuming that they will be able to extract the invariant feature or features present in all of the examples and thus reach an understanding of the concept. This strategy, however, does not always result in proper understanding and can be difficult to implement. For instance, just presenting a student with examples of light objects that float in the water and heavy objects that sink may give the student the idea that all heavy objects sink. Essential generalization, on the contrary, requires that students reach an understanding that it is the relationship between the weight and volume of an object—its density—that determines the object's floatability.

Another aspect of essential generalization is that it is based not only on immediately observable empirical data but also on understanding the relationship between the concept in question and other related concepts. For example, finding out that it is not the weight of an object but rather its density that determines the object's floatability is a significant insight. However, if one's understanding of floatability is based on empirical data only, such an understanding is rather limited. In particular, it is of little help in answering concrete questions about the difference between fresh water and salt water, about the maximum weight that can be carried by a certain boat, and so forth. The learner needs to understand Archimedes' law in order to fully comprehend the concept of floatability.

Much of Davydov's work was directed toward the development of forms, methods, and materials supporting educational activities through which learners could reach essential generalization. Just telling students the underlying principles, even though it is in some cases the only available option, was not considered the optimal learning experience. The importance of active exploration and learners' own insights was repeatedly emphasized within Davydov's approach, and the ultimate (though not completely realistic) goal of education—at least natural science education—was described as providing conditions for learners to rediscover the main ideas developed in the history of the humankind.

During the 1970s, when psychological studies based on activity theory in Russia were more intensive, diverse, and fruitful than in any other period in the history of Russian psychology, the mainstream psychological approach in the West was cognitive psychology. Despite the relative isolation of Soviet psychology, the trend toward cognitivism in the international community had an impact on activity theoretical research.

In the late 1960s and early 1970s, several research programs in the area of cognitive processes were initiated at the Department of Psychology of Moscow State University. Perception became one of the most popular objects of study in activity theory. Leontiev, then the head of the department, himself took an active part in the programs. His students conducted a wide range of both empirical and theoretical explorations into human cognition (e.g., Logvinenko and Stolin 1982; Velichkovsky 1982). From a theoretical standpoint, one of the main objectives was to analyze the potential and the limitations of the cognitivist paradigm and the possibilities for integrating cognitivist and activity-theoretical perspectives.

The interest in cognitive psychology was motivated, at least partly, by the hope of finding methods and concepts that would facilitate the study of the structure and development of concrete operations. Both logical arguments and empirical evidence indicate that automatic operations, even if executed in a very short time and without conscious control, can have complex structure and undergo developmental transformations (Leontiev 1978). However, activity theory did not have a research methodology powerful enough to analyze these transient unconscious processes. The theoretical possibility of such analysis was known to activity theorists through the work of the Russian physiologist Nikolaj Bernstein (1967). His model of the control structure of skilled behavior (such as walking), based on the idea of feedback-type control taking place at several levels at the same time, was considered an example of a successful attempt to provide an account of the structure and functioning of routine operations. But Bernstein, internationally renowned for his pioneering research in biomechanics, was not an activity theorist and not even a psychologist. His work, however relevant and insightful, could not be used directly in concrete psychological research based on activity theory. Cognitive psychology provided impressive examples of studying transient processes, closer to the home ground of psychology. Cognitive methods and concepts inspired a number of studies in Soviet psychology, especially in the 1970s.

The most elaborate attempt to combine activity theory and cognitive psychology of that time was made by Vladimir Zinchenko during the late 1960s and early '70s (Zinchenko 1971; Zinchenko and Gordon 1976). Zinchenko proposed the concept of a *microstructural analysis of human activity*. The main idea behind the microstructural analysis was to complement Leontiev's three-level model of activity with a fourth level, the level of "functional blocks," which was understood as subordinate to the level of operations. The functional blocks, as described by Zinchenko, were almost identical to the "boxes" typical of information-processing models of late 1960s, such as the model proposed by Atkinson and Shiffrin (1968). These models were introduced as a way to decompose operations, which typically have life cycles that can be measured in seconds, into smaller-scale processes, which may take up tens of milliseconds. Experimental methods developed in cognitive psychology to analyze the complex transient mental processes were proposed as a way to reveal the "hidden" structure of operations. The work by Zinchenko demonstrated that activity theory and cognitive psychology are not incompatible and that, in principle, cognitive models can be integrated with activity-theoretical accounts.

The approaches developed by Galperin, Davydov, and Zinchenko are some of the main frameworks closely associated with Leontiev's activity theory. Collectively they constituted a research community known as the Moscow School of Psychology which had its heyday in the 1960s and 1970s. Other researchers contributing to the diversity of concepts and research programs of the Moscow School of Psychology were Alexander Luria, Daniil El'konin, Alexander Zaporozhets, and Nina Talyzina, to name just a few. Most of the key figures of the community were Vygotsky's disciples. Shared Vygotskian heritage was one of the main centripetal forces that kept the community together despite numerous and varying conceptual influences from outside cultural-historical psychology. Another factor that shaped the community was the geographical proximity of the researchers. Most of the studies within the Moscow School of Psychology were conducted at two educational and research centers located just several hundred meters from each other: the Department of Psychology of Moscow University and the Psychological Institute of the Russian Academy of Education.[3] Geographical proximity, in turn, played an essential role in the development of a dense network of professional and personal relationships between the researchers. Finally, the formation of the community was partly determined by a larger-scale social context of the Soviet psychology of that time, namely, a competition between the Moscow School of Psychology and other theoretical approaches and research institutions in the USSR.

8.3 ACTIVITY AND COMMUNICATION

For several decades activity theory was undoubtedly the most prominent approach in Russian/Soviet psychology. By no means, however, was it the only one. In some of the key research centers in the Soviet Union, most notably the Psychological Institute of the Academy of Sciences of the USSR and the Department of Psychology of Leningrad (currently St. Petersburg) University, the attitude toward activity theory was not especially friendly. This was reciprocated by the prevalent attitude of the activity theory community toward its rivals.[4]

Probably the clearest and most systematic account of the main criticisms of Leontiev's approach can be found in a paper by Boris Lomov entitled "On the Problem of Activity in Psychology" (1981). The paper, published soon after Leontiev's death in 1979, was followed by a power struggle in which the proponents of activity theory lost some key administrative positions in research centers that were traditionally considered strongholds of the Moscow School of Psychology. In the paper, Lomov, the most powerful figure in Soviet psychology at the time, expressed his concern with the use of the concept of activity in psychological research. Without directly mentioning Leontiev's approach, Lomov made no secret as to the target of his criticisms.

Lomov's point was that understanding activity as a subject–object relation contradicted the Marxist view of activity as a social, historical process. According to Lomov, the analysis of individual activities should be based on an analysis of the functions of individual activities in the larger-scale social context in which those activities are embedded.

> When analyzing an activity, it is necessary to see it in a system of social relations, as connected to processes of production, exchange, consumption, ownership of the means of production, civil and political institutions, the development of culture, ideology, science, and so forth, that is, in the context of the whole entirety of the life of society. (Lomov 1981, our translation)

These philosophical arguments led Lomov to suggest a new agenda for psychological research, which he thought should be based on a more appropriate—from a Marxist view—understanding of activity as a social, historical phenomenon. Instead of focusing on the "(individual) subject–object" interaction, as Leontiev conceived it, Lomov proposed *collective* (or *joint*) *activity* as the basic object of psychological studies.

This focus of research was claimed to have two advantages. First, the analysis of the functions of an individual in a group was proposed as a research strategy that would reveal the motives, goal setting, and structure of the activity of the individual. Second, the analysis of collective activities was considered to be a way to study *communication*, which is impossible when dealing exclusively with individual activities. It was suggested that analysis of the subject–object relation (i.e., individual activity) be complemented with analysis of the subject–subject relation (i.e., communication).

Lomov's criticisms were rather general and did not result in the development of a feasible alternative to Leontiev's approach. And the criticisms effectively ignored concrete research on communication and collaboration that was being conducted from an activity-theoretical standpoint, especially studies of collective activities (Andreeva 1997). Arguably, Leontiev's framework does provide some conceptual means for the analysis of communication and social interactions in general. To begin with, a recurrent topic in Leontiev's work is an emphasis on the social nature of all types of activities, whether they are carried out individually or collectively (Leontiev 1978). In addition, following El'konin (1977), Leontiev differentiated between two types of objects—social things and social people—which made it possible to define communication as a special type of subject–object interaction. A simple argument supporting this interpretation is that even though people typically (but probably not always) interact differently with things than with other people, they still perceive other people as different from themselves. Therefore, communication can only be described as a subject–subject interaction by an external, "objective" observer, for whom both interacting subjects have the same status.

Finally, the concept of the "collective subject" was employed to make it possible to analyze human–human interactions within the activity theory framework. This concept was not elaborated by Leontiev himself, but it was widely used in concrete research conducted within the area of social psychology by his colleagues, especially by Arthur Petrovsky (Petrovsky and Petrovsky 1983) and Galina Andreeva (1997). If the subject of an activity is a group or an organization rather than an individual human being, then communication can be understood as a relationship between component parts of the compound subject. From that perspective, the suggestion that the concept of communication should have the same theoretical status as activity (Lomov 1981) can be rejected on the grounds that communication is determined by and subordinate to activity. Activity, from this perspective, is a more fundamental category that can be used to analyze communication.

To sum up, the following ideas in Leontiev's activity theory addressed the issue of subject–subject interaction, or communication: (a) a differentiation between two kinds of objects, people and things; (b) considering communication as a particular type of activity; and (c) defining communication as composed of processes that link constituent parts of the collective subject of activity. However, these conceptual means, especially in light of criticisms from outside activity theory (Lomov 1981), appeared inadequate for a concrete analysis of the social determination of individual activities. Merely pointing to the different status of people and things as objects of activity was not very helpful in understanding the underlying mechanisms and implications of the differences. The notion of the collective subject was not developed in enough detail to unambiguously guide concrete research, and it could not be applied to communication taking place outside interaction within the collective subject of a collective activity.

The outside criticisms of how Leontiev's framework dealt with the issue of communication, such as those by Lomov (1981), were widely interpreted within the Moscow School of Psychology as a part of a power struggle pursuant to political rather than theoretical objectives. For those reasons, these arguments were largely dismissed. However, even though the arguments failed to stimulate an immediate response and wide discussion in the activity theory community, the issues raised by the critics eventually and indirectly contributed to new developments in activity theory facilitated by rethinking the problems of the relationship between individual and collective activities, between activity and communication.

In the 1980s a reevaluation of Leontiev's theoretical legacy resulted in the growing realization that the approach needed to be developed further to provide an adequate account of exactly how the social nature of human activity determines its structure and functioning and why people interact with other people differently than with nonhuman things. As Radzikhovsky (1983) observed, Leontiev's three-level model "hardly explains why an activity changes because of the actual or imaginary presence of other people, or how, from a psychological point of view, 'another' human being is qualitatively different from other physical objects . . . ."

Understanding the limitations of Leontiev's framework led to a search for new concepts that could help deal with the continuous challenge of bridging the gap between the individual and the social. This search, as shown in the next section, is still in progress.

8.4   THE INDIVIDUAL AND THE SOCIAL: "LIVING IN THE MIDDLE" OF ANALYTIC PERSPECTIVES

Wertsch observed that

> analytic strategies [in human sciences] often take one of two general paths, depending on what is given analytic primacy. One path is grounded in the assumption that it is appropriate to begin with an account of societal phenomena and, on the basis of these phenomena, generate analyses of individual mental functioning. The other assumes that the way to understand societal phenomena is to start with psychological or other processes carried out by the individual. (Wertsch 1998)

According to Wertsch (1998), much contemporary research in psychology and other social sciences is based on a methodological individualism which gives analytic primacy to individuals as agents. Sociocultural analysis, including research based on Vygotsky's cultural-historical psychology, opens up a principal opportunity to overcome the individual–social antimony and "live in the middle" of several analytic perspectives. Finding a way to deal with the dialectics of the individual and the social has always been a major conceptual challenge for activity theory (and more generally for cultural-historical research). The search for a specific strategy to face this challenge accounts for much of the theoretical work conducted in the last several decades. The primary strategies can be summarized as follows:

- understanding all activities, both individual and collective, as outcomes of developmental transformations of early collective activities;
- embedding activities of individuals into collective activities; and
- studying individual and collective activities through a multilevel analysis.

Radzikhovsky (1983) suggested a revision of Leontiev's concept of activity by making collective activity the basic unit of analysis and considering all activities as originating from collective activities. This view may look similar to Lomov's (1981) idea of shifting the focus of analysis from individual activities to the activities of a group, but the two positions are actually quite different. What in fact was proposed by Radzikhovsky was reframing Leontiev's subject–object relationship by placing it in a developmental context.

The strategy of Radzikhovsky's analysis was to trace the development of individual activities to their origins in the first activities a child would carry out jointly with other people. Normally, the first activities of a child are carried out with the mother. This is a primary form of activity which is not a combination of two preexisting activities, but rather the context in which activities of a child appear for the first time. Vygotsky's law of psychological development, according to which new abilities, new psychological functions, emerge in an interaction between people (in the interpsychological plane) and are then appropriated by the individual (translated into the intrapsychological plane), apparently applies to the development of activities. The development of individual activities can be considered a result of an appropriation of ontogenetically preceding collective activities, that is, early experiences of interacting with others.

Radzikhovsky concluded that because of these roots of individual activities, any object-oriented activity of the individual should retain, in one way or another, the basic structure of the ontogenetically initial collective activities. Primary—collective—activities of the child necessarily include some forms of signs and communication. These components should be contained in any activity, if only implicitly, and can be revealed in analysis.

Radzihovsky's notion of collective activity as the basic unit of analysis capitalized on Vygotsky's ideas, but also on concepts developed by the Russian semiotician and literary critic Bakhtin (1981, 1990; see also Cheyne and Tarulli 1999), and especially on Bakhtin's notion of "hidden dialogicality." For Bakhtin, any instance of speech, including utterances directed by speakers to themselves, should be understood in the context of a dialogue, whether actual or imaginary. Any utterance is directed to "the other person" as an expression of agreement, disagreement, question, elaboration, and so forth, and its meaning can be understood only as part of an explicit or implicit dialogue. In a similar vein, Radzikhovsky maintained that any individual activity is directed not only at its object but, through the object, to another person. The activity thus intends to produce a response-action in the other person. Therefore, each activity is a semiotic activity.[5] Sign mediation and production, which are implicitly present in individual object-oriented activities, take the shape of explicit communication when activities are carried out with other people.

Another attempt to define a unit of analysis that would bridge the gap between the individual and the social in sociocultural analysis was made by Wertsch (1998). A key source of inspiration for Wertsch was the approach to human action developed by Burke (1966) which identified five perspectives on an action: Act, Scene, Agent, Agency, and Purpose. The unit of analysis proposed by Wertsch was *mediated action*, or "agent-acting-with-mediational-means." Wertsch explains that

> An appreciation of how mediational means or cultural tools are involved in action forces one to live in the middle. In particular, it forces us to go beyond the individual agent when trying to understand the forces that shape human action. (Wertsch 1998)

Wertsch used the idea of mediated action as the unit of analysis in studies of phenomena ranging from joint mother–child problem-solving to the sport of pole vaulting to narratives as cultural tools for representing the past.

The common strategy of bridging the gap between the individual and the social employed by both Radzikhovsky and Wertsch was to reveal the "hidden social and communicative" nature of activities that are traditionally considered individual. This strategy can be defined as finding genetically inherent sociality within individual activities and actions. It is, in a sense, opposed to the approach Engeström (1987, 1990) used when developing the notion of an activity system discussed in chapter 4. The solution employed by Engeström was to place the individual subject–object relationship into a larger-scale social context and extend the scope of analysis from individual activities to the whole system of social processes of production, consumption, and distribution in which the activities of the individual are embedded. This strategy of understanding the sociality of subject–object relationship by exploring phenomena surrounding this relationship—such as complex relations between mediated individual action and community understood as external to the action—has similarities to the approach proposed by Lomov (1981) as an attempt to overcome limitations of Leontiev's framework.

The different strategies used by Radzikhovsky and Wertsch, on the one hand, and Engeström, on the other hand—assigning the sociality of individual activities to certain aspects of the activities themselves (Radzikhovsky, Wertsch) or to objects and processes in a wider context (Engeström)—do not necessarily exclude each other. Instead, they can be considered complementary approaches, each having its own strengths and weaknesses. Factors critical for understanding the social nature of human activities can be found both in the activities themselves and in the social context. The most promising way to understand the relationship between the individual and the social appears to be a combined analysis of development taking place at different levels—from individual dynamics to transformations of larger-scale social context through a variety of intermediate levels (see also Cole 1996; Kaptelinin and Cole 2002; Stetsenko 2005).

8.5   CONCLUSION

Activity theory does not pretend to be a collection of ultimate truths about human nature, a source of timeless wisdom that can provide answers to any question. As shown in this chapter, the history of activity theory has been—and still is—a history of conceptual, social, and personal conflicts, discovering problems with existing concepts and exploring ways to solve them, understanding new challenges and trying to meet them by capitalizing on existing concepts or by developing new ones.

III

Theory in Interaction Design

9

Postcognitivist Theories in Interaction Design

In chapter 2 we argued that theory is important for interaction design. We observed that the development of multiple theories provides opportunities for multivoiced conversations, each theory contributing a unique set of perspectives and concepts. This chapter compares postcognitivist theories in interaction design—activity theory, distributed cognition, actor-network theory, and phenomenology. We call the theories "postcognitivist" because they have been brought into interaction design to remedy perceived shortcomings of cognitivist theory.

Distributed cognition is a well-known approach in HCI (Hollan, Hutchins, and Kirsch 2000) and CSCW (Rogers and Ellis 1994) that has highlighted the importance of tools in cognition. Actor-network theory is beginning to have significant impact (Berg 1997; Hanseth and Lundberg 2001; Holmström and Stalder 2001; Kling, McKim, and King 2003; Mahring et al. 2004; Lamb and Davidson 2005), having made vivid the power of technologies, their "push-back" in activity. Phenomenology, in insisting that everyday experience be a focus of inquiry, inspired approaches that have shaped interaction design (Winograd and Flores 1986; Suchman 1987; Dourish 2001a).[1] Distributed cognition, actor-network theory, and phenomenology share significant common ground with activity theory. They also diverge in critical ways. These commonalities and differences between the theories will be examined. We discuss actor-network theory as developed by Callon (1986) and Latour (1992), and distributed cognition as developed by Hutchins (1995), Clark (1997), and Ackerman and Halverson (1998). Dourish's (2001a) account of phenomenology is our primary resource for that tradition. Dourish's discussion is useful for our purposes because it focuses on interaction design rather than phenomenology in its entirety,[2] which is beyond the scope of this discussion.

9.1   COMMON GROUND

A major point of agreement among the postcognitivist theories is the vital role of technology in human life. Each theory incorporates technology in its own way. In activity theory, a key principle is tool mediation. Distributed cognition views cognition as distributed across people and their tools (Pea 1993; Salomon 1993; Hutchins 1995). Actor-network theory specifies the agency of technology—the way things (such as machines) are agents in their own right, interacting with humans in actor-networks (Callon 1986; Latour 1994). Phenomenology (most particularly Heidegger 1962) suggests that we understand thinking as derived from being, that is, "being-in-the-world," including the tools in the world.

Another commonality among the theories is the claim that individuals are not defined by the boundary of their skin. In activity theory, consciousness is seen as a result of practical activity with other people and with tools, so mind necessarily goes beyond the individual. And the idea of functional organs asserts a tight binding between human and tool (Ukhtomsky 1978, cited in Zinchenko 1996; Leontiev 1981). Heidegger's (1962) concept of the use of tools as "equipment" is similar to activity theory's framing of tools as mediating object-oriented activity. Equipment is a tool for some task, for a purposeful activity. Thought is bound up with the use of equipment (see Dourish 2001a). Distributed cognition defines cognition as distributed between people and tools where both are equivalent "media" in a system (Hutchins 1995). Actor-network theory places people and tools in a larger network and claims that a boundary cannot be drawn at the individual.

Postcognitivist theories are highly critical of mind–body dualism. Vygotsky's ideas of internalization and interpsychological functions explicitly sought to provide an account of the dynamic relationship between internal cognition and the external world of artifacts and people. Leontiev's criticisms of the "postulate of immediacy," in which a simple duality between stimulus and response was said to describe behavior, pointed to the need for more complex concepts: "the effects of external influences are determined not immediately by the influences themselves, but depend on their refraction by the subject" (Leontiev 1977).[3]

Phenomenology draws attention to the unity of mind and the world through humans' necessary relationship with tools. The very notion of distributed cognition (Salomon 1993; Hutchins 1995; Salomon and Perkins 1998) asserts that cognition cannot be captured with a concept of an isolated mind. Actor-network theory places all activity within the network, where nodes of any type can transact with nodes of any other type.

All of these concepts are examples of concrete analytical tools developed to move beyond dualism and to explain the fundamental unity of the mind and the world. Moving away from the cut-off Cartesian individual, postcognitivist theories came to focus on the physical and social distribution of phenomena, such as agency and cognition, that were traditionally considered to belong to the separate reality of the individual mind.

Postcognitivist theories provide an important alternative not only to cognitive science, but to authoritative theories in biology, neuroscience, and key areas of philosophy and psychology in which technology is nearly invisible. Such theories aim to describe universal human capabilities and experiences. Technology, a culturally variable phenomenon, is not foregrounded in these theories, if it is mentioned at all.

Without reviewing theory in biology and the other disciplines, we can give a few key examples regarding the invisibility of technology. In neuroscience, the brain, brain processes, and genes are seen as the locus of cognition (Edelman 1992; Crick 1993; Searle 1995). Crick (1993), for example, declared that emotions, memories, ambitions, identity, and free will are "no more than the behavior of a vast assembly of nerve cells and their associated molecules." Sociobiologists (e.g., Wilson 1975) depict genes as determinants of social activity, selected in early humankind's struggle for survival. The psychological theories of Freud, Jung, Maslow, Pavlov, and Skinner all posit panhuman processes. For example, Freud asserted universal processes such as repression, denial, and reaction formation, while Maslow suggested a universal hierarchy of needs.

Such universal formulations simply bypass the highly variable designed world and the diversity of practical activity taking place within that world. But the design and deployment of technology is a quantum leap in human evolution, involving the mobilization of vast cultural resources that do not reduce to universal biological or psychological processes. Precedents for the use of simple tools in nonhuman primates such as chimpanzees suggest how tools may have been introduced in early human communities (Köhler 1925; Goodall 1964). It appears that technology use preceded language in human evolution (Donald 1991). With increased sociality and the ability to talk about their tools as language developed, early humans made rapid advances in creating unique artifacts of immense value to human life (see Wells 2000).

The primacy of tool use in the human experience requires theorizing. Postcognitivist theories address this problem. The texture of the theories is not that of the sweeping reductionist statements about genes, neurons, dreams, neuroses, or goal hierarchies of the universalistic theories, but rather detailed depictions of the complexities of human activities. Even the most mundane activities turn out to require elaborate description (and still, it often seems there's more to say). Kirsh (1995), for example, described the surprisingly complex activity of cooks making salads. Scribner and Sachs (1990) studied training in a stockroom at a manufacturing plant. Bellamy (1996) detailed the function of technology in a middle school classroom. If postcognitivist theories have taught us anything, it is that the closer we look, the more complex ordinary activities appear, and the less amenable they are to reductionist accounts.

The project of the postcognitivist theories, then, is to provide nuanced analyses of the microgenesis of organized activity. The theories share the practice of delivering fine-grained historical accounts of activity in rich settings,[4] because, as Gherardi and Nicolini (2000) observed, "human action can only be explained in terms of the specific conditions in which it takes place...." Postcognitivist theories help us understand technology as central to human experience. They share common ground in depicting people as beings enmeshed in our own technological creations. These theories set the stage for explorations of invented worlds in which designed technical artifacts imbue human life with its distinctive character.

9.2 SORTING OUT THE THEORIES

Despite significant common ground, there are important differences among postcognitivist theories. We analyze these differences with respect to two related issues: (1) *intentionality*, and (2) *fissures in routine activity*, namely, creativity, reflexivity, and resistance. These issues engage the question of whether or not to theorize individual subjects. Activity theory is committed to developing a concept of the individual as a technologically empowered and socially contextualized subject. This commitment is questioned or jettisoned in distributed cognition and actor-network theory. Phenomenology stands with activity theory on this issue, but because phenomenology is not intended to be a psychological theory, its principles do not go as far in describing the nature of the subject as do activity theory's.

We will argue that while analysis at the level of system, network, organization, institution, culture, or other supraindividual entity is fruitful for many purposes, there are important issues of interaction design and technology use that require a notion of the individual subject. Drawing from diverse theoretical and empirical work, we argue that supraindividual entities cannot mirror, represent, stand in for, or subsume the particular ways in which individual subjects may act. We examine intentionality, a property of individual subjects that systems-level analyses do not deal with, and disruptive activities of creativity, reflexivity, and resistance that involve individual subjects as they respond to social conditions. We highlight these issues of the individual subject because some of the postcognitivist theories downplay the individual, a being whose activities we wish to keep visible in interaction design. We also discuss collaborative activity, considering a scheme developed by Raeithel (1996) that provides some ways of breaking collaboration down into a less monolithic concept.

9.2.1 Characterizing People: Intentional Beings or Nodes in a Network?

As we saw in chapter 3, activity theory begins with the idea of a purposeful subject. Only living things have needs. These needs can be met by acting in the world, by bringing together the subject's need and an object. When a need meets its object, the object becomes a motive and directs the subject's activity. For humans, needs are, in significant measure, culturally shaped. The most fundamental notion of activity theory is the motivated activity of a subject enacted in culturally meaningful ways.

Vygotsky pointed to the purposefulness of activity as the defining characteristic of the higher mental functions of mature adults. In *Thought and Language*, he observed, "A small child draws first, then decides what it is he has drawn; at a slightly older age, he names his drawing when it is half-done; and finally he decides beforehand what he will draw" (Vygotsky 1986).

Activity theory posits a "specifically human type of orientation and consciousness" that emerged as humans evolved (Miettinen 1999). Informed by the work of Luria, Leontiev, and Vygotsky, Miettinen observed that there was

> a gradual breaking of the direct, immediate, impulse-based relation to the objects of the environment. With cultural development—characterized by communication and the construction and use of tools—a specifically human type of consciousness emerged. [Such a consciousness] also implies the capability of imagining and planning what the future may hold; that is, intentionality. (Miettinen 1999)

Miettinen (1999) also noted that only humans can "tak[e] the initiative in the construction of [new assemblies of humans and materials]." We take Miettinen's concepts of intentionality as our resource for this discussion. (For more on intentionality with an interaction design slant, see Button, Coulter, and Sharrock 1995; Dourish 2001a.)

Phenomenology also posits an intentional subject. Dourish (2001a) traced the changing concept of intentionality in phenomenology, culminating in Heidegger's subject who encounters the world through purposeful practical tasks. Dourish observed that for a subject "the orientation is fundamentally a practical one; it is purposeful and active." In both activity theory and phenomenology, an active human subject engages in meaningful activity mediated by tools. Asymmetry between subject and tool gives rise to concepts such as tools that are ready-to-hand or present-at-hand (Heidegger 1962), functional organs (Zinchenko 1996), tool mediation (Vygotsky 1986; Wertsch 1998), and breakdowns and focus shifts (Bødker 1996; Koschmann, Kuutti, and Hickmann 1998).

Phenomenology and activity theory have strong links in seeing tools as mediators of human experience. Phenomenology, especially Heidegger's work, identifies tools as an important part of the way we encounter the world to accomplish our goals (Dourish 2001a). Heidegger noted that a tool is tied to a meaningful task; it is "something in-order-to" (Heidegger 1962). Heidegger distinguished tools that are ready-to-hand and those that are present-at-hand. When a tool is ready-to-hand, we have no conscious awareness of it; we simply use it to accomplish a task. This corresponds to the operational level of the activity hierarchy. When there is a problem or a breakdown, we become consciously aware of the tool and must attend to it; then the tool is present-at-hand. This sequence is the same as moving from the operational to the action level in activity theory.

Actor-network theory and distributed cognition begin from an entirely different standpoint. Where activity theory and phenomenology develop an asymmetrical notion of tools mediating human experience, actor-network theory and distributed cognition define a network or system in which symmetrical nodes can be human or nonhuman, and are treated alike.

In actor-network theory, nodes in "heterogeneous" networks are "actors"[5] that can be people, machines, or other things.[6] As Callon (1986) said, "The rule which we must respect is not to change registers when we move from the technical to the social aspects of the problem studied." Latour (1992) stated that this principle of generalized symmetry was the "most important philosophical discovery" in actor-network theory.

Actor-network theory describes networks as heterogeneous (because they contain both people and things) while at same time proposing a symmetry between nodes. Caspar (1994) suggested that there is a muddle in this formulation. Along which dimensions does the heterogeneity lie? In Caspar's words, "to argue that nonhumans should be analyzed symmetrically does not get us any closer to determining how entities are configured as human and nonhuman prior to our analyses." (See also Collins and Yearly 1992.)

Actor-network theory's principle of generalized symmetry delimits a network in which no entity has purpose or intentionality in Miettinen's sense. Technologies do not possess needs, motives, or intentions. So, in actor-network theory, we have a theory that cannot say how a system develops through cultural processes of "imagining and planning what the future may hold."

Or can it? In the midst of actor-network theory's textureless networks of generalized nodes, we unexpectedly encounter colorful princes— Machiavellian princes! It seems that actor-network theory cannot, after all, do without agents with intentions. The princes are innovators, managers, and politicians (Callon, Law, and Rip 1986). It is they who assemble the networks, enroll other actors, drive events, and push their own agendas. Specific technologies affect the course of events, but they do not instigate the networks, the projects enacted in the networks, or the technologies whose agency is felt in the networks. Miettinen (1999) observed that despite generalized symmetry as the core principle of actor-network theory: "the principle of Machiavellianism seems to dominate. These principles [generalized symmetry and Machiavellianism] contradict each other."[7]

Distributed cognition also depicts a system of like nodes where human and nonhuman are of the same type. Distributed cognition constructs a system in which tasks are performed as representational state passes from one node or "medium" to another in a system (Hutchins 1995). As in traditional cognitive science, cognition is said to be the same as computation. Computation is defined as "the propagation of representational state across representational media" (Hutchins 1995). People, tools, systems, and so on are all "media." Rather radically, Hutchins (1995) said he hoped to develop a theory that would require no change to "cross the skin." Hollan and Hutchins (2003) observed that "Distributed cognition theory is still willing to lump together cases that activity theory long ago split."

In distributed cognition, there is some slippage with respect to the strict definition of media because of a desire to provide an account of human cognition. While Hutchins (1995) clearly stated that distributed cognition constructs a system in which the analyst is to trace state across a variety of media without prejudice as to the type of media, it is also true that distributed cognition has a serious interest in *human* cognition. As Hollan and Hutchins (2003) said, "distributed cognition emphasizes cognitive aspects of human performance." Thus its theoretical underpinnings may sometimes appear to change key, especially in lengthy accounts such as that of Hutchins (1995). When the discussion turns to tool mediation and human performance, distributed cognition is more in tune with activity theory (Hollan and Hutchins 2003). When a cognitive system of like nodes is proposed, distributed cognition has more in common with actor-network theory.

Is there a difference between "distributed cognition" and activity theory's concept of tool mediation? Both suggest that cognition requires tools and that tools do important work that humans cannot do on their own. Both extend the analysis of cognition to insist on going beyond the individual mind.

One difference is that in activity theory, people mediate their relationship to reality with tools. The tool is there for purposeful, intentional activity. (Using different terms, phenomenologists have said the same.) It is reasonable in activity theory to speak of cognition as being distributed in that tools are used for human cognition. So, for example, a doctor decides whether a patient has a particular ailment partly on the basis of a reading taken from a thermometer. The cognitive work is distributed because the doctor uses the thermometer for a precise reading. However, the thermometer *mediates* the doctor's *object-oriented activity*; the taking of the temperature is part of an activity driven by a human object: it is the doctor's intention to find out what is wrong with the patient.

In distributed cognition, because of the flat system in which "media" are uniform nodes, the idea of tool mediation, which requires asymmetry, is inconsistent.[8] In a flat system, cognition is a concept that can be applied equally well to the system or to any of its nodes. If one node can exhibit cognition, then by definition, so can any other node. Tools are no longer mediators of human experience. It is here that the plausible idea of recognizing the importance of tools in cognition becomes skewed in such a way that the basic definition of cognition is changed to apply to nonhumans (such as a system). The notion of distribution, instead of acting as a helpful mnemonic to incorporate tools into the analysis, now wipes out the very concept of human cognition and replaces it with the idea that anything can potentially cognize. This is of course not inconsistent with traditional cognitive science which equates cognition with intelligence with computation (Simon and Kaplan 1989), but distributed cognition was supposed to be a challenge to traditional cognitive science (Hutchins 1995). Without a notion of asymmetry, the cognizant system of distributed cognition is equivalent to an intelligent machine.[9]

However, even within distributed cognition as proposed by Hutchins, there are suggestions that systems and people are not really the same. Hutchins (1995) spoke of the "cognitive properties" of systems. He admitted that "the larger system has cognitive properties very different from those of any individual." So at least there was an awareness of differences between what a system does and what a person does.[10] However, questions remain: why is the system said to have cognitive properties instead of functional properties or culture?[11] Human cognition, long recognized as involving attention, awareness, and judgment, is now, somehow, related to a different kind of cognition that has no capacity for attention, awareness, and judgment (see Nardi 1998). We believe it is more coherent to discuss systems as having a culture or a set of functional properties, rather than cognition. This avoids the problem of deleting attention, awareness, and judgment from theories of cognition or setting up parallel systems of cognition related to one another in unspecified ways. Rose, Jones, and Truex (2005) observed that humans have "self-awareness, social awareness, interpretation, intentionality, and the attribution of agency to others"—which are not available to nonliving things.

In activity theory, the idea of the distribution of cognition goes back to Vygotsky's universal law of psychological development: new psychological functions are first distributed between the individual and other people or tools (as discussed in chapter 3). One of Vygotsky's greatest discoveries was that subjects use mediational tools to solve problems, but over time, they stop using them and yet maintain high levels of performance. Vygotsky (1983) attributed this finding to the process of internalization. Individuals appropriate new functions which become intrapsychological.

Distribution, then, is an aspect of *development*—not a separate kind of cognition as it may sometimes appear when people speak of distributed cognition. Of course, individuals may continue to make use of other people and tools. That does not mean that developmental transformations are not occurring or that a different kind of distributed cognition takes place in parallel with individual cognition. The doctor taking a patient's temperature is doing much more than simply getting a reading from an instrument (i.e., receiving state from the thermometer medium).

She is observing the relationship of the temperature to the symptoms of various diseases she sees in different patients. She is noticing a particular temperature and the way the patient with that temperature looks and acts. She is remembering what she learned in medical school about the diseases that exhibit raised temperatures. The doctor uses the thermometer as a tool mediating her understanding of the patient's illness, an understanding that changes over time as she gains experience in her practice. After considerable practice, she may have appropriated the function of the thermometer pretty well herself and can judge a temperature without actually taking it. She may continue to use the thermometer for social reasons—the patient thinks it is proper medical practice, the insurance company requires it, her attorneys advise her to do so. The doctor transforms the role of the tool in her work, responding to social and cultural realities, rather than passively receiving state. It is important to examine developmental transformations, rather than assume that reliance on tools means we turn all functions over to them and cease to develop and transform practice. Internalization is a developmental redistribution of internal and external components. Because the internal plane is not a carbon copy of the external, its form introduces the potential for change.

The individual subject and the world   Postcognitivist theories differ in how far they go in pushing the boundaries between the individual and the world. Activity theory and phenomenology retain a commitment to the individual subject. For them, contextual analysis is a way to reach a deeper understanding of individual human beings. Distributed cognition and actor-network theory define their focus of analysis as larger-scale agentic entities that include individuals as just one type of component. Within these approaches, individuals are deprived of their unique (or even privileged) status and are seen as components of a system or network as a whole. Hollan and Hutchins (2003) observed, "From a distributed cognition perspective, goals may be properties of institutions, but need not necessarily be properties of individuals." In distributed cognition analyses, there is usually a large unchanging systemic goal such as piloting a boat safely into harbor (as in Hutchins 1995). The institutional goals that are part of a larger culture are acknowledged, but not the goals of individual subjects.

Wartofsky (1979) provided a vivid image of the nature of human intention. Observing the ubiquity of handprints in paleolithic art, he asked what these handprints could possibly mean:

> The simplest answer seems to be that such prints are the deliberate marks of presence: "I was here." ... The handprint entails a hand pressed against a wall, with the express intention of leaving its imprint there.... [T]he handprint records a gesture, an action, an intention.... The marks by means of which a species represents itself *to* itself are thus distinctive. (Wartofsky 1979)

Wartofsky compared the handprints to Robinson Crusoe's footprints. Crusoe's footprints in the sand on the beach were indeed useful for Friday as a sign of Crusoe's presence, but they were not an intentional gesture.

Without a concept of intention, of purposefulness, the handprint and footprint may be confused. Hutchins compared the development of culture to the accumulation of chemical trails left by ants. The trails enable the ant that follows its predecessors to find food more readily. "Is this a smart ant?" asked Hutchins.

> No, it is just the same dumb sort of ant, reacting to its environment in the same ways its ancestors did. But the environment is not the same.... Generations of ants have left their marks on the beach, and now a dumb ant has been made to appear smart through its simple interaction with the residua of the history of its ancestors' actions. (Hutchins 1995)

Leontiev (1974) argued that activity does not consist of reactions to an environment: "Activity is thus not a reaction or a totality of reactions, but rather a system possessing structure, inner transformations, conversions, and development." Human culture results from intentional human activity—someone raises a hand to make a mark. Crusoe's footprints on the beach were not culture any more than the ants' trails on the beach are culture. Human activity constantly changes; we do not "react" the way our ancestors did. As Luria (1972) observed, "Cognitive processes are not independent and unchanging 'abilities' ...; they are processes occurring in concrete, practical activity...." These processes grow directly from the specificity of particular kinds of practical activity, variable across cultures. Sandberg and Wielinga (1993) noted that one problem of distributed cognition theory is that a human is taken to be "a simple organism interacting with its environment and producing complex behavior through the application of simple behavioral rules." The ant analogy bears the marks of this misconception.[12]

Stetsenko and Arievitch (1997) observed of socio-constructivist theories that even though they all provide a "relational, contextualized, account of the evolving self," there are two distinct approaches. The first dissolves the self (understood as a human agent) in linguistic or social reality, while the other strives to provide a nonreductionist account. This distinction is relevant to our discussion of postcognitivist theories. Actor-network theory and distributed cognition seem to dissolve the individual by considering the individual a part of a system or network and by equating humans with nonhumans. Activity theory and phenomenology aim to construct the individual as a technologically empowered and socially contextualized subject.

Our position in this debate is unambiguously pro-individual. We believe that analysis of human embeddedness in the world, of communication and collaboration within the social context, is of fundamental importance for understanding our relationship to technology. Human beings cannot be reduced to parts of larger-scale entities determining the nature and the meaning of the parts. It is true that individuals taking part in collective activities often have to abide by the rules, roles, and routines typical of collective work. However, it is also true that individuals do not always follow the rules, roles, and routines, and sometimes they even change them. As Middleton and Brown (2002) observed, agency is "the sense that someone or something is not following some pre-established programme of action, is not simply expressing some pre-existing structure." Even though human motivation is profoundly influenced by culture and society, each individual has her own hierarchy of motives. Although both are parts of a system, individuals are different in kind from artifacts, because (a) they have their own needs and reasons to do things that go far beyond the specific activity they are involved in, and (b) they reflect on and make sense of the collective activity and their own actions.

Even within the context of a system/network/organization, the individual is acknowledged as different in kind from the organization's non-living things. Dealing with individuals and their needs and capacities becomes part of the activity in an organization. So, for example, when an organization recruits workers, a manager not only describes future work assignments but tries to make the position attractive by stressing its advantages for an individual worker, such as a creative work environment, good salary, comprehensive insurance, desirable location, and so forth (see Foot 2006). This is necessary because the individual has his own reasons for choosing to participate or not participate in the organization, his own motives and intentions. The organization's artifacts, on the other hand, have no intentions, no motivation. No one in the organization need entice the artifacts to participate by appealing to their personal motives. The humans, however, must be dealt with as motivated individuals as long as they are employed—providing raises or bonuses to good performers, offering incentives for continuing education, encouraging workers to grow and develop.[13]

Characteristic of Leontiev's view of the individual was his opposition to understanding the individual as merely a component part of social systems and processes. When discussing the idea that an individual could be completely described through a set of roles defined by the social context, Leontiev (1978) called the notion "monstrous."

In the next section, we look at the potential impact of individual subjects, with their motives and intentions, on activities central to technology and culture change.

9.3 THREE FISSURES: CREATIVITY, REFLEXIVITY, AND RESISTANCE

As designers, we are aware that technology is always changing; indeed it is the job of many of us to create such change. But how does culture change come about? Without attempting to answer such a large question, we can point to three "fissures" or disruptions that are part of the culture change of technology: creativity, reflexivity, and resistance. Creativity, reflexivity, and resistance have been identified as crucial to understanding technology by a broad range of scholars including Mumford (1934), Ellul (1964), Illich (1980), Winner (1986), and Postman (1993).[14]

By creativity we mean imaginative activity directed toward an object in which an original product emerges. By reflexivity, we mean reflection that leads to a change in practice, or potentially can lead to such change when obstacles do not prevent it. By resistance we mean opposition to a technology, or to a practice associated with a technology, that is evaluated as detrimental. In this section, we discuss creativity at length and sketch the importance of reflexivity and resistance in technologically mediated activity.

Zinchenko (1996) argued that human activities go beyond culture; indeed, they must do so, or culture would never change:

> [People] do not behave passively, and in due course they even become themselves the source and drive that is capable of developing culture and civilization, generating new ... forms and overcoming old ones.... [W]e should recognize the relations between ... human and culture to be mutually active, communicative, and dialogical. The dialog may be friendly or hostile; it may become aggressive. (Zinchenko 1996)

Such culture change manifests itself through activities of creativity, reflexivity, and resistance. To account for the very invention of technology —which undeniably involves acts of human creativity—we need a theory in which creativity follows logically from basic principles. The theory must also account for the varied responses to the deployment of a technology: a technology may be embraced, rejected, or altered by its users to better meet their needs as they reflect on its use (Mackay 1990; Orlikowski and Tyre 1994; Foot 2001; Béguin 2003; Geisler 2003; Spinuzzi 2003; Gay and Hembrooke 2004; de Souza 2005; Stahl 2006). Finally, the theory must acknowledge that people may resist technology; having reflected on its uses and consequences, the dialogue may even become hostile, as Zinchenko put it.

The Machivellian princes of actor-network theory provide ample scope for activities of culture change. Who better to scrutinize, plot, and plan than such resourceful fellows?[15] We shall leave them to their intrigues, assuming them fully capable of any necessary acts of creativity, reflexivity, or resistance.

Phenomenology posits an active subject much like that in activity theory, though as we will briefly discuss there are some differences. We use this discussion of fissures primarily to challenge some aspects of distributed cognition. (In the next chapter we do the same for certain aspects of actor-network theory.) We draw on empirical work in the activity theory tradition from Engeström (1990), Miettinen (1999),

DeCortis, Rizzo, and Saudelli (2003), Spinuzzi (2003), Gay and Hembrooke (2004), and others.

9.4 CREATIVITY

Creativity manifests itself in insights. Without a subject to have such insights, there is no creativity. The individual subject is crucial because creativity may require an instant restructuring of the whole representation of a problem (Wertheimer 1961; Csikszentmihaly 1996), a "global spontaneous reorganization of the whole body of knowledge about the problem situation" (Kaptelinin 1996b). This reorganization happens internally, not in resources distributed externally to the individual. Thus an internal process is necessary to creativity.

Even everyday activity of the most mundane sort often involves unexpected bursts of creativity in which a subject can reframe a representation to successfully solve a problem. In the well-known cottage cheese incident (Lave, Murtaugh, and de la Rocha 1984), a dieter following the Weight Watchers program was at first stumped when he had to measure three-quarters of the two-thirds cup of cottage cheese allowed by the program:

> The problem solver in this example began the task muttering that he had had calculus in college, and then, after a long pause, suddenly announced that he had "got it." From then on he appeared certain he was correct, even before carrying out the procedure. He filled a measuring cup two thirds full of cottage cheese, dumped it out on a cutting board, patted it into a circle, marked a cross on it, scooped away one quadrant, and served the rest. (Lave, Murtaugh, and de la Rocha 1984)

The dieter suddenly saw the measurement problem in a new way. He had not learned the technique he used to solve the problem at Weight Watchers, nor had he learned it in school. He used no external artifact to create the solution to the problem. While Lave et al. saw the dieter's measuring of the cottage cheese as emerging from the "situation," we note that the dieter experienced a sudden insight—he "got it"—followed by flawless enactment of the measurement. The dieter himself brought something to the situation—the subjective refraction of which Leontiev spoke. He used the resources at hand, but he was able to perform the measurement without trial and error, without interacting with the environment. He seemed to simply reassess the problem and then act, in a single smooth move. This calls to mind Köhler's chimp who "realized" it could get the bananas with a stick—no trial and error needed!

The dieter's solution was not obvious, nor was it a foregone conclusion given a "situation" of cottage cheese and a measuring cup. We can imagine other dieters confronted with exactly the same problem who would *not* come up with a solution—a less motivated dieter who might simply consume the extra cottage cheese, an elderly dieter having forgotten about fractions, a dieter with less confidence to find a solution than someone who "had had calculus in college."

The measuring cup, the cutting board, and the dieter would be considered symmetrical nodes in distributed cognition and actor-network theory, even though there is no sense in which the cooking utensils could have committed the act of creativity the dieter did. The limits of symmetry are met rapidly with an even simpler example like this one. Spinuzzi (2003) reminds us of the "inventive, wily, sly, cunning, and crafty"— descriptors of the creative human caught in the act of object-oriented activity. In considering the internal process of creativity, classical activity theory, which resolves to the individual, provides a firm footing. Other variants of activity theory that begin with a collective subject are less adapted for explaining creativity (Kaptelinin 1996b). The individual subject, with his or her unique potential to instantly restructure a representation in the context of meaningful activity, is essential for a theory of creative activity.

But perhaps the cottage cheese example is too simple? What about the fact that under many circumstances, an individual cannot accomplish as much as a group? Is there some kind of "group cognition" or "group creativity" that happens when a group works together? Is "collective creativity" qualitatively different from individual creativity? Some insight might be gained here by considering Vygotsky's concept of the zone of proximal development. While this concept was developed to explain differences in learning, it might also apply to the creative process in groups.

In the zone of proximal development, the subject learns according to the specific mediation provided by a teacher or more experienced peer. The difference between what the learner can do alone and what she can do with teacher or peer is the "zone." This zone varies according to both the individual abilities the learner brings to the learning task and the kind of mediation provided by the teacher or more experienced peer.

This zone will be different for Learner A and Learner B even when each is provided with the same mediation[16] because each learner begins with a different set of understandings and abilities. We cannot explain differences between different pairs of learners and teachers without an appeal to learners' differences. For example, although one of us spent many hours observing neurosurgeries for a study of video monitoring in a teaching hospital (Nardi et al. 1993), in no way can she claim the faintest expertise in removing brain tumors. The medical residents in the operating room, on the other hand, also observed the surgeries at the same time, but they picked up a good deal more surgical expertise than a social scientist would. What was effective mediation for medical students learning neurosurgery could not have the same impact for a nonspecialist.

The same relation between individual learner and group found in the zone of proximal development may hold for creativity. Imagine a group has convened to design new educational technology. The group consists of Lev Vygotsky, Aleksey Leontiev, Maria Montessori, and Don Norman. The designs created by the group would be different from those of a group of, let us say, first-year graduate students. And why? For two reasons: first, the designs would depend on the specific individuals present. As Leontiev observed, "the effects of external influences are determined not immediately by the influences themselves, but depend on their refraction by the subject" (Leontiev 1977). Second, the designs would be different because of the mediation provided by this group's members. Through the mediation of group conversation (and perhaps artifacts such as diagrams), members would come up with new resources for reframing problems and developing creative designs (see Fischer 2004 on the importance of conversation for "social creativity"), and these resources would vary depending on the group. We can well imagine the fruitful mediations each of these group members could provide through his or her conversation.

What we wish to point out with this thought experiment is that activity theory's concept of mediation, combined with understanding creativity as the internal restructuring of a problem representation, helps us conceptualize creativity in groups. In a group setting, the mediation of conversation from other insightful people may help individual group members to frame problems in new ways and then contribute those new insights to the group. Creative insights take place in concrete activity in which specific individual subjects converse, communicate, and respond to one another (Stahl 2006).

The designs for new technologies from our fantasy group would likely be more than merely the sum of the ideas contributed by each member if he or she were working individually.[17] But the designs cannot be explained simply by reference to the fact that they emerged in a group. The specific individual members of the group count for a good deal in terms of both their own creative abilities to restructure problems and the mediation they potentially provide to other group members. Indeed, we look to people such as those in our imaginary design group for inspiration not because of the groups they represent, but because of their fresh insights, new ways of framing problems, and surprising perspectives. We probably do not have to convince anyone in the interaction design community that an hour with Don Norman is an experience unlike any other!

We should not forget that many artists (and other creative people) work mainly independently. Their material comes from the social and physical worlds around them. They may be part of intense social worlds that shape their creativity, but they simply do not, for example, write poems or paint pictures in a group.[18] (Countless biographies clarify the circumstances under which artists produce their art. Vincent van Gogh, for example, was more attuned to the physical than social world because of his mental illness. Sylvia Plath moved in rarified intellectual circles, but wrote her best poems in solitude at 4:00 in the morning before her family awoke.)

While it is important to foster groups that enhance creativity, and this is increasingly important in science and industry, we believe that a theory that begins analysis at the group level leaves out much of importance, namely, the fissures an individual subject is capable of causing, fissures that may lead to new ways of framing problems (or to less useful disruptions, which must also be considered). From a practical standpoint, it is important to understand the kinds of mediation that can be provided by specific group members (and the need to convene groups with particular kinds of individuals), the training that may be needed for individuals to work together well in groups, and the technologies and practices (such as facilitation) that will underwrite the mediations that enable individual group members to contribute new insights. The particular expertises chosen for the group must be the right ones to produce optimal results. One person's expertise cannot be traded for another, at random. In everyday practical activity, we act accordingly, choosing this doctor and not that one, Colleague A and not Colleague B. Skilled managers observe that their job consists primarily in finding the right people and providing the resources for them to get a job done.

This insistence on positioning an individual intentional subject as a creative agent may seem to leave us open to charges of cognitivism or mentalism. But such charges would only arise from a conflation of social activity with group activity. As we hope is clear by now, activity theory constructs all activity as social, inevitably involving other people, artifacts, and culture, in various ways. Sometimes a subject acts independently (though never in social or cultural isolation) and sometimes with others. The individual subject may have agentic power, under some circumstances, to set in motion, or encourage, social processes leading to change. For example, Vygotsky was able to begin a process of framing a new theory of human consciousness that is a distinctive way of looking at the human mind. Vygotsky's work was informed by significant historical influences, but the work is unique and powerful in its own right. Precisely what Vygotsky was able to do was to take concepts from Marx, Engels, Piaget and others, and restructure them in ways that led to new theoretical understandings.

Creativity is by definition social creativity (just as all activity is social activity). There is no lone genius. In acknowledging Vygotsky's great contributions, we in no way mean to place him outside of, or above, his particular historical context. Vygotsky delivered his seminal lectures to audiences capable of appreciating them and no doubt capable of helping him work through difficult concepts. He had access to theoretical writings essential for his own theoretical development. As Seitz (2003) observed, "[A]ny creative product emerges from a unique coincidence of individual intellective abilities; the nature and relative sophistication of a scientific, artistic or entrepreneurial domain; the complexity and structure of the field of legitimization; and the distribution of power and resources within a group, community, or society." Seitz acknowledged "individual intellective abilities," situated in complex social settings involving the resources and relations of distinctive domains.

Like most members of social groups, we feel it is fitting to recognize individual contributions. We believe this penchant for recognition is social in origin. We name contributions after people—Newton's laws, Rubik's cube, Engeström's triangle. Paradoxically, the recognition of individual creativity seems a way to make the creative product a part of culture and society, to absorb it into the larger milieu by personifying it. We might just as well speak of "developmental work research triangles." Or "Rubik family cubes," as Rubik gave credit for his inventiveness to the combination of influences from his father who was an engineer and his mother who was an artist. We personify creativity for many reasons, one of which may be the uptake of new ideas in our rapidly changing culture through the drama of cultural characters.

9.4.1   Phenomenology and Creativity

Dourish (2001a) observed that "Embodied interaction is the creation, manipulation, and sharing of meaning through engaged interaction with artifacts." While this definition is broad, it points particularly to activity that is "grounded in everyday, mundane experience" (Dourish 2001a). In this emphasis on everyday, mundane experience, phenomenology and activity theory differ somewhat. Activity theory does not necessarily exclude activity that is beyond the scope of everyday, mundane experience.

It seems quite easy to come up with examples of human creations not rooted in a particular everyday, mundane experience. In the design of computer artifacts, for example, there are formal structures such as database tuples or programming languages that do not have clear antecedents in embodied experience. Walt Disney is said to have based designs for Disneyland in part on conversations with his father about his work on the Chicago Columbian World Exposition held in 1893 (Larson 2003). This dreamlike extravaganza, an enormous city-within-a-city painted snow white, with ethereal landscaping, attracting hundreds of thousands of visitors per day, did not embody mundane experience.

Discussions between father and son about the Exposition would have been of a mythic, heroic character, not a reference to prosaic activity.[19]

Fantasy is precisely the effort to get beyond the everyday. A modern example of fantasy play is computer gaming. Participating in online games calls forth acts of social and technical creativity that stretch past mundane experience. MMOGs such as World of Warcraft, Everquest, Lineage 2, and Shadowbane take users into social worlds where they cannot be said to have had embodied experience. A MMOG is a persistent computer game in which players develop a character and then advance by slaying dragons, healing the sick, performing magic, or any number of high fantasy activities. Players regularly "use" artifacts with which they have had no real-world experience. For example, in Everquest, a player could kill an enemy with a slime-coated harpoon while wearing an emerald dragonscale tunic.

Both the fantasy nature of these games and the kinds of social interaction they promote are new to users who must create not only characters for the games, but new ways of interacting. One player said:

> I don't know why I am such close friends with my EQ [Everquest] buddies. I do know that my EQ relationships are better than most of my relationships in [real life]. I think this is because when you are talking to someone online it's easier to talk about certain things since you don't have to look at a person face to face. (Yee 2002)

Such a statement about sociality defies what is learned from everyday experience about looking at others while speaking. Another player observed that in MMOGs people are "good friends due to the fact that you must throw away ... everything related to physically meeting a person" (Yee 2002). Here the player reflected that forming new kinds of social relationships was different from forming those of his embodied experience. The relationships were "better" and were constructed as *not* embodied; the player said he "threw away everything related to physically meeting a person." It is evident that new forms of social interaction were taking place. An overemphasis on "everyday mundane experience" could make it difficult to interpret virtual experiences such as those that take place in MMOGs.

MMOGs also give rise to experiences that *cannot* be embodied. One player said,

> I feel totally free in Shadowbane. I do what I want, I say what I want, and I kill who I want.... I feel at home here. Don't get me wrong, generally I'm a nice guy, but I love just letting loose in there. (Ardisson et al. 2004)

In the phenomenological tradition, "Embodiment is the common way in which we encounter physical and social reality in the everyday world. Embodied phenomena are the ones we encounter directly rather than abstractly" (Dourish 2001a). By contrast, experience in virtual games does not seem to have clear "direct" relationships to embodied experience.

9.4.2   Wartofsky's Typology of Artifacts

We have found Wartofsky's typology of artifacts useful for thinking about creativity. Wartofsky began with the observation:

> By contrast with non-human animals, human beings create the means of their own cognition. That is to say, we create cognitive artifacts which not only go beyond the biologically evolved and genetically inherited modes of perceptual and cognitive activity, but which radically alter the very nature of learning and which demarcate human knowledge from animal intelligence. The cognitive artifacts we create are models: representations to ourselves of what we do, of what we want, and of what we hope for. The model is ... a putative mode of action, a representation of prospective practice, or of acquired modes of action. (Wartofsky 1979)

A philosopher of science, Wartofsky was concerned with many issues of interest to activity theory. His work is widely cited by modern activity theorists (e.g., Cole 1996; Engeström and Escalante 1996; Hedegaard 1999; Miettinen 1999), and his ideas are consistent with much of activity theory. Wartofsky's emphasis on the *activity of representing* (as opposed to representations, emphasized in cognitive science), the concern with purposefulness, the use of Marx and Vygotsky, and the focus on artifacts will feel familiar to those conversant with activity theory.

Wartofsky proposed a scheme of primary, secondary, and tertiary artifacts. Primary artifacts are used directly in production. Secondary artifacts are "those used in the preservation and transmission of the acquired skills ... by which production is carried out." In other words, secondary artifacts tell us how to use primary artifacts; they mediate and support the development of tool-related competencies. A manual might explain how to use a software system. The software system itself might explain how to use it (in help screens or animated paper clips). So, a single artifact can have a dual character as both primary and secondary artifact. (It should be noted that neither a user manual nor a good help system automatically results in the skills necessary to use a primary artifact successfully).

Kaptelinin (1996b) proposed that metafunctional competencies enable our understanding of how to use functional organs (such as knowing tricks and work-arounds), recognizing their limitations, and knowing how to maintain and troubleshoot them. Metafunctional competencies and secondary artifacts work together to provide expertise about the actual use of functional organs. Keeping in mind that functional organs involve both internal and external resources, we can see that metafunctional competencies assess both in determining how to deploy tools in a given situation. So a physician who is a generalist knows that when confronted with a patient with an unusual allergy, he should consult his online help system which may direct him to a secondary artifact to find a particular database of interest.

Tertiary artifacts emphasize creativity. A tertiary artifact "transcends the more immediate necessities of productive praxis," giving freer rein to imagining "possible worlds" (Wartofsky 1979). Such possible worlds occur as

> models [which] are the highly specialized part of our technological equipment whose specific function it is to create the future.... [M]odels are embodiments of purpose and, at the same time, instruments for carrying out such purposes. (Wartofsky 1979)

Creativity, then, is embodied in such models, or tertiary artifacts, that specify future object-oriented activity. We can create representations of "prospective practice," as Wartofsky said, to go beyond the immediate environment. Creative activity means we are not limited to "reacting" to the environment as in distributed cognition; we have the possibility to design the environment through the creation of tertiary artifacts.

Miettinen (1999) used Wartofsky's notion of tertiary artifacts to analyze changes in ethanol production in Finland over a period of several years. Scientists attempted to produce ethanol from birch chips (such chips being plentiful in Finland). The materials proved resistant to the scientists' plans, but a simple diagram for the production of ethnanol published in 1981 guided the scientists' efforts as they worked to discover whether the birch chips could be used economically. The diagram was a tertiary artifact that "synthesize[d] and generalize[d] the modes and results of actions, carrie[d] and transmit[ed] purposes, and oriente[d] to the future" (Miettinen 1999). Thus a simple tertiary artifact, shared among the scientists, embodied a creative idea about a new form of energy production and represented a "working hypothesis and a research plan" (Miettinen 1999). The ethanol production was not successful, but the knowledge gained during experimentation turned out to be useful in other arenas as the scientists made fundamental discoveries about the chemistry of the wood chips (Miettinen 1999).

Using activity theory, Miettinen gained theoretical purchase in several ways. His analysis began with self-aware human subjects in a collective object-oriented activity, not simply generic actors (or actants) in a system or network. A human subject created the diagram. Fellow subjects (scientists) could use the diagram as a mediating artifact projecting a future model of ethanol production. Sensitive to contradictions, the analysis highlighted the material resistance of the wood chips as they defied the scientists' efforts. The wood chips were a major problem, not something that could be managed through small adjustments. In finally facing the fact that the wood chips did not have the chemistry for economical ethanol production, the scientists co-constructed the knowledge gained for other areas of application.

In a study of organizational innovation in a Finnish hospital, Engeström (1990) described the importance of tertiary artifacts in creatively changing doctors' practices. The doctors accepted a new organizational model for their work only when its larger future implications were made clear through the presentation and discussion of tertiary artifacts. The artifacts "creat[ed] a perspective for the future of the entire activity system" that motivated the doctors to move forward and clearly depicted these new directions (Engeström 1990).

Miettinen (1998) emphasized the importance of tertiary artifacts for social change. He observed that, for example, artifacts of scientific research may "connect research activity to society, integrating ecological, economic, and societal values in a vision of the future...." In a flat network, where human and thing are not distinguished, what entities could there be to have such visions?

9.4.3   Coordination, Cooperation, and Co-construction

The postcognitivist theories differ in the extent to which they emphasize creative fissures in activity. Activity theory looks for the creative possibilities of breakdowns, conflicts, and contradictions. Béguin and Clot (2004) observed that "Obstacles, disagreements [and] conflicts encountered in activity generate tension ... and invite the subject to mobilize and develop [new forms of organization]."[20] Distributed cognition tends to focus on the smooth operation of a system as it reproduces its function. For example, Hutchins (1995) emphasized such a function by describing the means by which navigation on a U.S. Navy vessel was faithfully reproduced to pilot ships safely.

To give some structure to those places where we might seek creative fissures at different levels of collaborative activity, we refer to Raeithel's (1996) three-part scheme based on earlier work by Fichtner (1984):

- coordination
- cooperation
- co-construction

Coordination is the most basic form of collaboration. It refers to cases in which people work toward a common goal, but carry out individual activities basically independently. Even though the outcome of each individual activity contributes to the outcome of a collective activity as a whole, these contributions are coordinated in a way external to activities of other individual participants (see also Engeström et al. 1987). In coordination we might find creativity in very small actions. As Béguin and Clot (2004) noted, "[E]ven the most repetitive movement of a production line worker is always unique."

Cooperation is a more advanced form of collaboration. Collaborating individuals need to relate their goals to the overall objective of a collective activity, be aware of the actions of other participating individuals, and adjust their actions to the actions of other people. Typically these are small to medium adjustments, in line with the constancy of the overall object of the collective activity. As people work together to solve problems, there is considerable scope for creativity, though changes support the established object of the activity. In cooperation, we would expect to find people changing actions to overcome disruptions that threaten the instantiation of the shared object (as in the biotechnology research described in chapter 7).

Co-construction takes place when collaborating individuals not only cooperate to accomplish a prespecified common object but can also collectively redefine the object—and the collective activity—itself. Here creative activity may lead to major alterations in the very activity, as the object is no longer agreed on and is a source of contention and reevaluation. The object may then be constructed anew, that is, co-constructed.

9.4.4   Coordination and Creativity

Distributed cognition has been the theory that places the most emphasis on coordination. The method of distributed cognition—to trace representational state as it changes in moving across nodes in a system—makes visible and salient coordination among nodes (Hutchins 1995; Clark 1997; Kirsh 2004). While Raeithel considered coordination to be part of human activity, distributed cognition expands the notion to include both people and tools. Hutchins (1995) noted, "Representational states are propagated from one medium to another by bringing the states of the media into *coordination* with one another" (emphasis in original). Consistent with Raeithel's scheme, distributed cognition highlights the external or distributed nature of the coordination.

In distributed cognition, the analysis of coordination tends to emphasize stability and the reproduction of a system (opposite in spirit to the point made by Béguin and Clot). Some of the emphasis on the smooth functioning of large systems may derive from the fact that Hutchins's (1995) theoretical work was based on a study of a U.S. military vessel, a setting where precision and predictability were sought.[21] Halverson (1993), herself a proponent of distributed cognition, said that the approach works best for "highly rationalized systems" in which elaborate coordination is likely to be a focus. Bazerman (1996) made a similar point, observing that such systems are not necessarily typical and should not be taken to be representative. Hutchins's (1995) work is a beautifully detailed ethnography of the use of modern navigational tools on a military craft, but claims regarding a general "cognition in the wild" require considerably wider ethnographic reach. A focus on coordination is but one part of the story as Raeithel's scheme indicates. And, there are differing ways of looking at coordination, as Béguin and Clot's statement suggests. Activity theory positions coordination within a larger scheme that has scope for creativity at different levels of coordination, cooperation, and co-construction. Rather than locking down activity in predictable flows of state from one medium to another in a stability-seeking system, activity theory suggests that within the enactment of actual activity there is the potential for movement and change, even in what appear to be highly regulated activities such as those of factory workers.

9.4.5   Cooperation and Creativity

The second level of Raeithel's hierarchy concerns everyday practical activity that does not require radical change, but does require some co-operative problem solving. Here we consider analyses of group activity in which subjects cooperated to advance their activity.

Spinuzzi (2003) analyzed the way automobile traffic engineers in Iowa transformed a system of accident narratives (official reports of accidents) into quantitative data. The quantitative data revealed accident patterns the engineers needed to understand to plan for better traffic management. The workers "turned thousands of narrative and diagrammatic descriptions into visual data display genres such as pie charts, bar graphs, and tables, each of which could have more impact on public policy than individual narratives could" (Spinuzzi 2003). With new ways of viewing accident data, the workers could "label dangerous stretches of road, dangerous behaviors, and dangerous classes of drivers." Spinuzzi reported that at each step in the process "workers had to decide what to include in the transformation ... and what not to include...." Such human judgments were needed to advance the task.

In Spinuzzi's analysis the workers were active subjects. Traffic safety was the collective motive in the activity. The workers "made decisions," "transformed data," and otherwise acted as aware subjects. Spinuzzi's discourse was not of small adjustments or the application of simple rules.

He described how the workers faced a mountain of narrative data—filing cabinets full of thousands of accident reports. It is a tribute to their creativity that they figured out how to transform such voluminous data. To do so, they employed specialized domain knowledge and conceptual tools including mathematical and statistical analyses to create more revealing representations of the data (Spinuzzi 2003).

Traffic safety is an apt illustration of the importance of a concept of motive and its relation to cooperative actions. Without the diligence of committed individuals who care about safety, accident rates in the United States would be higher (as they are in many other countries). Safety is not residua of prior function, or a by-product of tokens circulating in a network. In Iowa, active subjects—the workers—labored to transform accident data from one format to a very different format so that they could better fulfill the motive of improving traffic safety. The creativity that led to a cooperative transformation was motivated by a shared object.

Hutchins (1995) provided examples of sailors cooperating in response to breakdowns. Because of the social nature of cooperation, analysis at the abstract level of state propagation across representational media was inadequate at times in this analysis. For example, in describing how team members might pitch in to help one another, Hutchins (1995) began the discussion saying, "We can think of the team as a sort of flexible organic tissue that keeps the information moving across the tools of the task. When one part of the tissue is unable to move the required information, another part is recruited to do it." But then he seemed to mentally step back from this formulation as he acknowledged that the sailors' activity involved human sociability and could not be depicted simply as abstract information moving in a tissue. An anecdote entered the narrative, a shift in rhetorical tone from systems abstraction to personal reminiscence. Recalling the words of Roy D'Andrade, a well-known anthropologist, Hutchins wrote:

> As I worked with the data, something that Roy D'Andrade once said kept coming back to me. A student was making a point about what people do at work, saying that in an auto factory people mostly make cars. Roy said something like: "How do you know what they are doing? Maybe what they are making is social relationships and the cars are a side effect." (Hutchins 1995)

D'Andrade's sharply worded question suggested workers engaged in object-oriented activity—living out their own social lives as they saw fit and not just fitting into the constraints of the auto factory.[22] With D'Andrade's admonishment in mind, Hutchins (1995) observed that shipboard workers were "also constructing social relationships" as they filled in for one another. They conveyed subtle social messages by the extent to which they offered help when others needed it. A sailor would observe another's level of effort in covering for a coworker and make a judgment about what it meant: "Doing the absolute bare minimum required when others know that one has the time and resources to do more is a clear statement," Hutchins reported.

The sending and receiving of these subtle messages was not the function of a system on autopilot. Human judgment entered in, and awareness of what a worker's actions might mean—nuanced cultural meanings. Here we have human cognition, not mechanical function or abstract information flow in a system of representational media. A different level of analysis—a social level, and thus an intersubjective level—was introduced. Social processes that could not be ascribed to the ship's charts, plots, and protractors figured in the analysis (introducing asymmetry). It seems that at times distributed cognition analyses veer away from the purer forms of the theory, and bring in concepts more closely related to activity theory and phenomenology.

9.4.6   Co-construction and Creativity

Let us return to Spinuzzi's traffic engineers. The transformations in the accident data the workers created altered the larger activity. Once the workers got a taste of the quantitative data, they wanted more. They wanted to know not just how many accidents occurred at rural intersections, but at which particular intersections. What kinds of accidents? Under what conditions? The labor-intensive system of going through the narratives manually was not a practical means by which to answer such questions (Spinuzzi 2003).

In the 1970s, the Iowa State Highway Commission hired a contractor to automate the process of analyzing accident reports. A mainframe system was built. It greatly enhanced accident analysis and transformed work at the agency in many ways (Spinuzzi 2003). But it was slow and difficult to use. In 1989, a manager hired an eighteen-year-old computer science student from Iowa State University to develop a PC-based solution. The student created a system that was used for several years and yet again transformed work at the agency. In actor-network theory, the manager would have been visible as a prince (or princess, in this case), but the state college student who engineered the system might never have appeared.[23]

In distributed cognition, such a radical act of creativity would ill fit the focus on the smooth function of a coordinated system, nor would the transformative artifact created by a single individual. Distributed cognition analyses often provide especially fine descriptions of sophisticated technologies while at the same time suggesting that these technologies exist merely to reduce cognitive effort, to allow for the application of simple rules (e.g., Hutchins 1995; Halverson and Ackerman 2003). How such clever technologies themselves are invented is not discussed. Clark, a proponent of distributed cognition, approached this contradiction with a joke: "Our brains make the world smart so that we can be dumb in peace!" (1997). How "our brains" do this was left to the imagination. (And what is the difference between our brains and the rest of us that is left in peace?) Activity theory, by contrast, points to the creativity of the human subject in responding to cultural challenges, such as those described in Miettinen's study analyzing creativity in scientific activity, or Engeström's description of the doctors' response to tertiary artifacts that enabled them to improve their practice. Spinuzzi's historical analysis of an activity stretching over decades, detailing the contributions of individual subjects and groups, in a specific context, showed how the reflective and creative work of members of the activity led to the co-construction of new forms of data analysis and the larger social organization of the agency.

Spinuzzi (2003) studied the use of artifacts among technical communicators, highlighting the "idiosyncratic, divergent understandings and uses of artifacts and the practices that surround[ed] them as they develop[ed] within a given cultural-historical milieu." These divergent understandings and practices are a source of variation needed to provide material for change. Squashing individual variation forecloses the opportunity to study the microgenesis of change. As Béguin and Clot (2004) said, "[W]e need to situate action in the development of activity to retain the virtues of creativity and inventiveness ... recognize[d] in action." Such divergent understandings, creativity, and inventiveness are not fore-grounded in distributed cognition analyses. As we saw in chapter 7 in the discussion of the biotechnology researchers, what scientific research conceals may be as important as what it reveals. "Selecting what others see" is a social process that shapes scientific research. Examining what a theory leaves out may be just as important as understanding what it brings in.

9.4.7   Activity versus System

In attempting to understand creativity, we may ask: Where is the locus of control in culture? Does it lie in the system or in the enactment of activity? If it is solely "in the system," then where could creative change come from? These questions expose a central tension in social theory of the last several decades: is the real question how to explain durable, stable structure, or is it to explain development and change? In approaches such as ethnomethodology and distributed cognition, stability is the phe-nomenon to be explained. Some interesting empirical accounts in distrib-uted cognition concern the way stability is preserved in the face of technical change (Licoppe 2005). Actor-network theory's case studies have examined change, especially in studying the activities of "princes." Activity theory is also focused on development and change, attempting to position them in a cultural matrix assumed to have some stability (see, e.g., Blackler 1993).

In distributed cognition, control is seen as being primarily in the orga-nization or system, especially in its management of coordination. Hutch-ins observed:

> [M]uch of the organization of behavior is removed from the performer and is given over to the structure of ... the system. This is what it means to co-ordinate: to set oneself up in such a way that constraints on one's behavior are given by some other system. (Hutchins 1995)

Here the locus of control is outside the "performer," which has the ef-fect of downplaying—even making invisible—acts of creativity and the uniqueness of an actual activity. But, as Béguin and Clot (2004) said, "[E]ven the most repetitive movement of a production line worker is always unique." This view puts at least some control in the enactment of activity (even at the level of coordination). Béguin and Clot argued that the organization of activity is stable and predictable, *but not the activity itself* (see also Vergnaud and Récopé 2000). Even in the tiniest movement of an assembly line worker, there is scope for the new, the unpredictable. Such reasoning situates the locus of potential change in *activity* rather than in organizational structures. We saw in chapter 7 that the managers at Ajaxe dealt with the reality of organization versus creative scientific activity. As one manager said, "No matter how much structure you have in an organization, still the only way to get people to do work is to get them excited about something."

Béguin and Clot observed that in practice, activities are enacted with judgment and interpretation, so the subject is always capable of something new (see also Taylor 1985). This way of thinking opposes that of distributed cognition, which looks for constraints on activity rather than possibilities for change. Béguin and Clot's statement is interesting precisely because it directs us to look for the uniqueness of even the most apparently regular activity, and to be cognizant of the actual enactment of activity, not only to structures within which an activity is played out. In a similar vein, Emirbayer and Mische (1998) argued that it is essential to understand how "structural environments of action are both dynamically sustained by and also altered through human agency—by actors capable of formulating projects for the future and realizing them, even if only in small part...."

Ilyenkov (1982) observed:

> In reality it always happens that a phenomenon that later becomes universal originally emerges as an individual, particular, specific phenomenon, as an exception from the rule.... Thus, any new improvement of labour, every new mode of ... action in production, before becoming generally accepted and recognised, first emerges as a certain deviation from previously accepted and codified norms. Having emerged as an individual exception from the rule in the labour of one or several [workers], the new form is then taken over by others, becoming in time a new universal norm. If the new norm did not originally appear in this exact manner, it would never become a really universal form, but would exist merely in fantasy, in wishful thinking.

Hedestig and Kaptelinin's (2005) study of the video technician illustrated Ilyenkov's idea. The technician's job was technical support for an educational videoconferencing system but in actual practice, he went well beyond his formal duties. Rather than giving over his activity to the structure of the system, the technician proactively and independently took on a wide variety of cooperative roles, including cameraman, systems administrator, teaching assistant, and supervisor. Initially, the technician's extra work was not even visible in the system, and management did not understand how necessary his varied services, which exceeded the constraints set by the system, actually were to the success of the educational experience. Hedestig and Kaptelinin (2005) observed that an individual's ability to transcend the immediate situation and carry out "suprasituational" activities is key to both personal development and to the larger development of an activity. Over time, the changes made by an individual subject may become part of the way the activity is normally done, or they may be the catalyst for other changes.[24]

9.5   REFLEXIVITY

Leontiev (1974) pointed to reflexivity as "a rise of consciousness," "a reflection by the subject of reality, of his activity, of himself." The aware subject is capable of reflecting on his or her use of technology in an activity. A technology could be imagined to be better than it currently is in the context deployed; it could be used differently than intended; it could change in certain ways. As with creativity, individual reflexivity always takes place in a social context. It is never isolated from activity.

Gay and Hembrooke (2004) studied the development of learning communities and the role of technology in fostering community in an investigation of the introduction of wireless laptop computers at Cornell University. Wireless access was campus-wide, so students could use the laptops "anywhere, anytime." Gay and Hembrooke examined students' reflections on the technology through student journals and interviews with students in a communications class.

Some students reported succumbing to the "temptations" of reading email, sending instant messages, and browsing the web during class.

They said that this behavior at times became "addictive" or "obsessive." Students reflected that they were often "distracted" by the laptops, and that they had short attention spans as they switched from listening to a lecture, to reading email, to instant messaging. While interactions within the communications class were enhanced in some ways with the technology, the wireless laptops opened the door for students to participate in other activity systems having nothing to do with class, during class time. Instead of listening to a fellow student's question in a class, for example, a student could send instant messages to friends. Though the student physically sat in the classroom, with the new technology he could participate in unrelated activities. One student reported,

> I felt in some ways that [the wireless computer] acted as a gateway to many activities that brought me away from my studies.... I fell victim to searching the Web for unrelated nonacademic information that took my focus off the class. (Gay and Hembrooke 2004)

Gay and Hembrooke observed that

> Students were ... participating in ... multiple divergent ... activities that were not class related (such as day trading, communicating with family and friends, and searching for personally relevant information).... Even when carrying out group assignments in class, many groups worked individually, coming together at the last moment to compile individual contributions into a collective product.

A concept of individual subject was crucial to Gay and Hembrooke's investigation. While reflection is a social process, it is an individual subject who assesses experience, sometimes reformulating its meaning, and communicating that meaning to others. The students' reflexivity was prompted by the researchers' asking them questions and reading their journals. But it was the individual student who switched out of the classroom activity to another activity, and who could reflexively see that happening and report it. It was an individual who could, simultaneously, be "in a classroom" and, at the same time, be part of another activity, say, instant messaging with friends. It was an individual who was aware of this activity shifting, the need to coordinate the activities, and the costs such coordination imposed on each activity.

In reflecting on their own distracted behavior, some students came to the conclusion that social solutions were needed to curtail the negative aspects of the wireless technology. They suggested rules or restrictions on laptop usage. "I like the suggestion made in class the other day: the class as a whole should make a list of rules, and everyone should abide by them," said one student. Students in the disrupted activity attempted some co-construction as they recognized that the technology that was supposed to form a learning community was in fact weakening that community as other activities intruded during class time. On reflection, the students recognized that unfettered access to competing activities would divide them, rather than unite them in a cohesive learning community (Gay and Hembrooke 2004).

DeCortis, Rizzo, and Saudelli (2003) approached the design of digital tools for elementary school children with activity theory's notion of tool mediation. They designed a set of educational tools for narrative construction for children ages 6 to 8 to encourage creativity and cooperation. The tool environment, "Pogo," was found to "offer new resources to encourage thought and choice." In particular, the Pogo tools

> support[ed] both personal reflection and intersubjective comparison, help[ing] children think about and analyze their own experience. This confers a role of ... *reflexive mediation* to instruments.... (DeCortis, Rizzo, and Saudelli 2003; emphasis in original)

The children's creativity was seen to be tied to the sharing of their reflections with one another. The analysis relied on strong notions of tool mediation and asymmetry, as the tools were analyzed to show how they inspired reflection and how the children then shared their reflections to advance the creative activity of constructing the narratives (DeCortis, Rizzo, and Saudelli 2003).

Through a process of reflection, people often change the way they use technologies. They go beyond what the designers had envisioned and cast tools as mediators in new activities. Geisler (2003) provided a detailed account of the way she used her Palm Pilot to attain work–home balance, a function unforeseen by Palm designers. She noted that such usage was outside the cultural frame established for the Palm Pilot, which emphasized professionalism and efficiency at work. Reflecting on her own needs, she devised creative ways to use the device to fulfill her objects. She had used other tools in similar ways in the past. Using activity theory, Geisler's account emphasized development over time:

Activity theory calls attention to the trajectory of personal motives that lead to technological adoption. The balancing of the competing demands of work and family shaped, almost from the beginning, my choices in time management technologies from the Day-Timer through HyperCard to the Palm. (Geisler 2003)

Geisler (2003) was able to look at her own activity, assess the shifts in her activities over time, and create effective ways to use a technology designed for other purposes. Theories in which people and things are equivalent, or "lumped together," as Hollan and Hutchins (2003) put it, delete investigation of asymmetric relations such as a human reflecting on a tool and creatively changing its use, or a human developing new functions by building on the use of prior tools, as in Geisler's evolution from Day-Timer to Palm Pilot.

In distributed cognition, reflexivity is downplayed to preserve symmetry.[25] There is a "special medium" but not an active intentional agent as realized in activity theory or phenomenology. Actor-network theory has its princes, but in distributed cognition, the special medium is no aristocratic alpha male, but rather a humbler entity "that can provide coordination among many structured media—some internal, some external, some embodied in artifacts, some in ideas, and some in social relationships" (Hutchins 1995). People are seen as having more advanced abilities to coordinate than other media, but to speak of the special medium (referred to as "that," not "who") as an intentional being capable of creating, reflecting, or resisting would be to miss the essential character of the special medium which is its ability to coordinate.

And yet, distributed cognition analysts find that they encounter activities of creativity and reflexivity in the arenas they study. Ackerman and Halverson (1998) investigated a telephone hotline group. They traced the propagation of cognitive state through the hotline's organization, illuminating the use of various kinds of "organizational memory" to solve callers' problems. The research is an elegant microanalysis of a single call, providing insights into the nature of organizational memory.

But the analysis went beyond distributed cognition in drawing attention to the hotline staff's need to reflexively reconfigure work practices. The authors reported that the staff created a set of flexible informal routines to cover a wide range of hotline problems. They noted, "Indeed, the [hotline] manager repeatedly mentioned during the study that he was trying to balance flexible diagnosis and service with transaction efficiency" (Ackerman and Halverson 1998). There would be little room for such reflexivity and creativity in a truly symmetrical account. While people reflect, technologies do not. A pencil will never look at itself and say, "I could be sharper." Only people reconfigure and redesign their practices and tools. Ackerman and Halverson (1998) moved away from symmetry toward a position more akin to activity theory. They remarked that their account had "a certain social twist"—allowing distinctly human social activities of reflexivity and creativity to enter the discussion.

9.6 RESISTANCE

Resistance to technology is hardly a lively topic in the interaction design community. We are the designers and purveyors of new technology. Economically, intellectually, and spiritually, technology is at the heart of many of our favorite activities. Nonetheless, as experts, we have a responsibility to assess the impact of new technologies and to voice concerns when that is appropriate. We have a responsibility to craft theories that allow for activities of resistance, placing them within the scope of the human relationship to technology. The theories that posit flat networks of uniform nodes have the narrowest scope for describing or explaining resistance. An active subject is a necessary component of theorizing resistance, to explain how people act with technology.

Wertsch observed that an individual's

> stance toward mediational means [may be] characterized by resistance or even outright rejection.... A focus on resistance and rejection leads one to consider a host of issues that do not arise when one assumes that cultural tools are friendly helpers. (Wertsch 1998)

Like creative activity, resistance is a rupture in the smooth flow of routine collective activity. It upsets the culture; it introduces conflict and discoordination. Wertsch's making visible rejection and resistance is important because it addresses the need to "consider a host of issues" that do not arise in discussions of technology that focus only on its utility and functionality. Such issues do not arise when a theory lumps together people and things, since things themselves do not offer resistance by reflecting on something and then rejecting it. (In chapter 10 we discuss material resistance as conceptualized in actor-network theory, but that is a different kind of resistance.)

In the modern context, resistance is not so much the resistance of Luddism as the refusal to accept new technologies without broad-based analysis and discussion. Forms of such analysis have been pioneered in Europe. In Denmark, for example, the Danish Board of Technology organizes panels of citizens to study important issues regarding technology and society (Sclove 1995). The citizens study the issues and prepare an advisory report which is then consulted by government decision makers. The media report also on the panels' findings so that wider discussion can take place. Could such an approach work in larger, more diverse countries? Sclove (1995) observed that in the United States, juries routinely reach consensus on difficult legal matters. He argued that though representation on citizens' panels is not statistically meaningful, it is better to have the informed opinions of a group of citizens than to have no opinion at all, except for the opinions of those who stand to gain economically from a technology.[26]

The Danish citizens' panels have been influential throughout Europe and in the United States. Langdon Winner, an American political scientist, testified before Congress that citizens' panels should be utilized in the United States to discuss new technologies such as nanotechnology (Winner 2003). He pointed out that the possible benefits of nanotechnology are enthusiastically proclaimed by scientists studying nanotechnology and business owners who wish to promote it, while those who have concerns are derided as anti-progress. But the possibility of invisible machines tiny enough to be inhaled should certainly give anyone pause. Such activities of resistance seem to fit most comfortably within phenomenology and activity theory in which technology mediates the activities of an active, purposeful subject.

While we see the incorporation of multiple voices in discussions about the societal uses of technology as the key issue of resistance in the twenty-first century, it is also true that some outright refusals of technology take place and must be analyzed. For example, Zambia refused to accept genetically modified corn, even when it was offered as charity. No new nuclear plants have been constructed in the United States for three decades, owing to the resistance of a coalition of scientists and ordinary citizens (see Bazerman 2001). European countries do not buy genetically modified food from the United States (Winner 2003). Such social activity involving complex negotiations and discussions among diverse groups of humans requires a theory that allows for intentional activity enacted by beings capable of imagining and planning the future.

9.7   CONCLUSION

In this chapter, we discussed two topics about which postcognitivist theories have distinctive perspectives: (1) intentionality, and (2) fissures in routine activity arising from creativity, reflexivity, and resistance. Examination of these topics reveals the extent to which a technologically empowered and socially contextualized subject is theorized. Activity theory and phenomenology construct such a subject, while actor-network theory and distributed cognition focus more on the level of network or system (though they bring in empowered humans through Machiavellian princes or special media). Activity theory and phenomenology position humans as the most powerful agents, beings with purpose and intentionality. In activity theory, the aware, intentional subject, engaged in object-oriented activity, acts to fulfill specific motives, rather than reacting, applying simple rules, or just doing what the system says to do. In phenomenology, *Dasein* is a human orientation of purposeful activity in a world that includes "tools for our use" (Dourish 2001a).

By contrast, in actor-network theory's symmetrical networks, actors are equivalent agents. The agency of things, a particular emphasis in actor-network theory, is evident in that they have their own "timings, tempos and properties"; they push back in their interactions with other agents (Latour 1996a). In a contradictory move, actor-network theory introduced princes, who are subjects with intentions of the kind found in activity theory and phenomenology (Latour 1992). Distributed cognition proposed a system of state-passing media, but brought in the special medium, people. As we saw with ethnomethodology in chapter 2, formulating a theory around a radical, vivid, but circumscribed principle may result, if we were to invoke Freud, in a sort of reaction formation. That which is most ardently desired is turned on its head and its opposite put in motion. Thus actor-network theory, though it hoped to avoid "changing registers," violated its most important discovery in asserting a principle of Machiavellianism.[27] In admitting the "specialness" of people, distributed cognition gave a nod to a principle of asymmetry, but at the cost of the same theoretical contradiction Miettinen (1999) noted for actor-network theory: the humans end up being different from things after all.[28]

In examining creativity, reflexivity, and resistance, we introduced Wartofsky's hierarchy of artifacts and Raeithel's hierarchy of collaborative activity. These conceptual tools structure analyses of the different kinds of tools and the way individuals and groups orient to collective activity. We found it necessary to make arguments for the importance of a concept of the individual subject. These arguments do not mean that we wish to reinstate a Cartesian isolate, a noble cognitive savage, as it were. Activity, always social in character, is never a closed system of *cogito ergo sum*. What we propose is that changes in both the subject and the system cannot be fully explained at the system level. The individual subject develops through mediated activity in observable, measurable ways (e.g., the zone of proximal development). Systems change under the influence of observable individual actions. Deleting the individual subject deletes important sources of change, fissures that lead to transformations, and responses to fissures. An important challenge for activity theory is to better theorize transformations between individual and collective levels.

We discussed both commonalities and differences among the postcognitivist theories. There are many reasons for the differences, among them temporal and cultural. Activity theory developed in Russia, phenomenology primarily in Germany, actor-network theory primarily in France, and distributed cognition in the United States. The latter two theories are of recent vintage, the other two stretch back decades. But perhaps more important than these differences are the distinctive intellectual challenges each theory took on in its historical context, what each theory responded to as it struggled to put forth an original perspective. Activity theory sought an alternative to behaviorist notions of stimulus–response and the shortcomings Vygotsky perceived in Piaget's work. Vygotsky felt that a concept of culture was essential to psychology. Phenomenology responded to the overformalization of science and mathematics in which the everyday world of practical experience had little place. Actor-network theory was frustrated with the privileging of the social over the technical, or vice versa, depending on the account. Actor-network theory developed the notion of generalized symmetry to make visible the agency of the material world. Distributed cognition aimed to overcome the limitations of cognitive science where mental representations were the primary focus, ignoring the importance of tools. The varied intellectual predecessors of the theories are in part responsible for the distinctive "look and feel" of each.

As a group, the postcognitivist theories provide an important voice in the dialogue with universalistic theories in biology, psychology, and elsewhere. Although they do so in different ways, postcognitivist theories argue the need to analyze the microgenesis of change in particular historical contexts and to make visible the importance of technology.

It remains to be seen how each theory will influence interaction design in the future, and how the theories will influence one another. Some of the theories reproduce one another in key ways (such as activity theory and phenomenology), others contradict each other in some dimensions (such as activity theory and distributed cognition), while still others provide "probes" that can be deployed in the development of a neighboring theory. In the next chapter we take up one such probe from actor-network theory, discussing its perspectives on agency and how they might be used in the development of activity theory. We build on actor-network theory's emphasis on material agency, formulating new notions of agency from activity theory's principles of asymmetry and mediation.

10

Artifacts, Agency, and (A)symmetry

Actor-network theory's attention to the agency of things comes at a good time in this age of smart machines. Modern technology behaves independently and flexibly in ways that traditional tools do not. An email program, for example, can save the user the trouble of looking up and typing an email address if just one message has been sent to someone and the user can remember as little as the first initial of the person's first or last name. Even the humble fax machine has remarkable capabilities. Rae (1994) analyzed the way fax machines correct each other's garbled transmissions. He suggested that the machines' actions in making corrections resemble repair in human conversation (Schegloff, Jefferson, and Sacks 1977). Rae asked, "Does the capacity for repair imply that fax machines have agency?" We believe the answer is yes. The fax machines' sophisticated ability to decode incomplete or corrupted text with no human intervention is evidence of a capacity to respond intelligently to changing conditions.

This chapter draws on the work of Andrew Pickering (Pickering 1993, 1995) as well as other actor-network theorists (Callon and Latour 1981; Callon 1986; Rose, Jones, and Truex 2005; Shaffer and Clinton in press). We argue that actor-network theory is right to direct attention to the agency of things, and that traditional accounts (e.g., Emirbayer and Mische 1998; Wertsch 1998) in which it is "only people who are doing the acting" (Shaffer and Clinton in press) are not sufficient. At the same time, we explain why we reject actor-network theory's perfect symmetry.[1] Using the principles of activity theory, we propose a new way to conceptualize different forms of agency.

10.1   (A)SYMMETRY

Pickering (1993, 1995) developed a concept of symmetrical agency based on a dialectical notion of back and forth between the human and material worlds. He observed that traditional sociology sets forth "an asymmetric distribution of agency—all to human beings, none to the material world" (Pickering 1993). Pickering found such a notion absurd; humans cannot just effect whatever they want to, with no response from the material world. If ones wishes to send an email but the server is down, the email cannot be sent. Pickering concluded that a completely lopsided asymmetry is untenable.[2]

What about perfect symmetry, as in actor-network theory? As Pickering (1993) noted, actor-network theory "insists there is no difference between human and non-human agents: human and nonhuman agency can be continuously transformed into one another." As we did in chapter 9, Pickering found this problematic:

> We humans differ from nonhumans precisely in that our actions have intentions behind them, whereas the performances (behaviors) of quarks, microbes, and machine tools do not.... I find that I cannot understand scientific practice without reference to the intentions of scientists, though I do not find it necessary to have insight into the intentions of things.... We construct goals that refer to presently nonexistent future states and then seek to bring them about. I can see no reason to suppose that DNA double helices or televisions organize their existence thus.... (Pickering 1993)

Activity theory and Pickering reject perfect symmetry for the same reason: the existence and importance of human intentions.

Pickering used Galison's (1985) description of research in elementary-particle physics as empirical grounding for his discussion of agency. As Pickering recounted, in the early 1950s, physicists were interested in rare but interesting particles called strange-particles. The particles proved resistant to efforts to photograph them, so research was stalled. Donald Glaser, a scientist at the University of Michigan, became interested in the problem and invented a device called a bubble chamber that revealed the particles. He later won the Nobel prize for this research. Glaser began work on the bubble chamber by attempting to modify existing cloud chambers used to study other kinds of particles. The cloud chambers utilized vapor that failed to reveal the strange-particles. Glaser's early designs with the cloud chambers failed, but he learned from each failure, eventually discovering that if he filled a chamber with a superheated liquid under pressure it would record strange-particle tracks.

Pickering saw these events as a symmetrical "dialectic of resistance and accommodation" between two agencies: the material agency of the chambers and Glaser's intention to produce a chamber that tracked strange-particles.[3] Pickering proposed that the two forms of agency were "constitutively enmeshed in practice by means of a dialectic of resistance and accommodation." That is, the material world offers up resistance and humans find ways to accommodate it, to work around it. Pickering felt that by organizing material and human agencies as constitutively enmeshed with one another, he could rescue symmetry, allowing him to "return to the fold" of actor-network theory. With the dialectic, he said, the "picture [could] be symmetrized" (Pickering 1993).

This argument, however, presents a contradiction. It asserts the importance of human intention, on the one hand, and then attempts to symmetrize things on the other. Pickering said that human and material agencies are enmeshed in practice, so he defined material agency *in terms of human practice* (which in turn is shaped by human intentions). In Pickering's formulation, material agency is intelligible only with respect to human practice. As he said: "I argue that material agency is ... emergent in relation to practice"; "material agency is sucked into the human realm"; and "the resistances that are central ... are always situated within a space of human purposes, goals and plans" (Pickering 1993). These notions (resonant with activity theory) cannot logically be squared with a principle of generalized symmetry.

With respect to the events surrounding the invention of the bubble chamber, activity theory would suggest a history of human agency overcoming material obstacles. To say that Glaser "accommodated" the material realities is to miss the point that he kept going until he found a way to produce the strange-particle tracks. It was his passion to build a particular kind of chamber that enabled him to "circumvent the obstacles he had ... encountered" (Pickering 1993).

In activity theory terms, Glaser's object persisted, but his actions changed to meet the resistance of the materials. Pickering's account revealed as much, but the rhetoric of symmetry made him lose sight of the power of Glaser's intentions and their ability to successfully meet obdurate material resistances. Miettinen's discussion of the resistance of the wood chips in the production of ethanol is not unlike Pickering's analysis of the invention of the bubble chamber, but Miettinen was able to use activity theory to clarify the relationship between the scientists' objects and their actions. Miettinen explained how the scientists' changing understandings of the wood chips permitted them to eventually find an economic use for the chips, as they continued to explore the particularities of the resistances of the wood chips within their scientific practice.

To see the relationship between material and human agency as simply one of resistance and accommodation is to miss the role of human creativity in arenas such as science. Glaser was able to design and build a chamber that worked. Pickering seemed nonplussed by Glaser's creativity, observing, "One can speak of scientific creativity ... that along the way [Glaser] hit on the idea that led him to the bubble chamber, and so on." But Glaser did not "hit upon" the idea; he searched steadfastly for it, to fulfill the object of tracking the strange-particles.

Pickering argued that the dialectic of resistance and accommodation "amounts to ... a revision of plans and goals, a revision of the intentional structure of human agency." In activity theory terms, the actions and their associated goals change to meet the resistance of the material world. *But the object has not changed.* Glaser is still doggedly laboring to build what finally becomes the successful bubble chamber.

As we saw in chapter 7, science studies accounts concern themselves with actions, missing the longer trajectories of objects that shape the selection of particular actions. So, while the material world did indeed provide significant push-back, forcing Glaser to keep trying till he got the bubble chamber right, his intentions and creativity are evidence of asymmetrical agencies at play. We do not think it can be said that he "accommodated" the material world; rather he manipulated the material world until he got what he wanted.

Material agency as formulated in actor-network theory makes logical sense only with respect to a human activity. Vapor is not in itself "resistant." It is so only when it fails to behave as some human desires. Material things are not inherently, essentially resistant (or empowering, or any other quality). We describe them as such during the enactment of a particular human activity. Both a subject and a material object can potentially manifest an infinite number of properties under varying conditions. The particular properties of interest come to light in the whole context of an activity—which is oriented by a human-defined object.

We do not of course mean to suggest that humans can overcome any obstacle if they just persevere long enough. That is preposterous. We mean that humans have certain powerful resources at their disposal that must be accounted for theoretically. So potent are these resources that the Earth—a system billions of years in the making—has been drastically altered in only a few centuries of human activity. Vitousek and his team of biologists at Stanford University reported in the journal *Science*:

> Human alteration of Earth is substantial and growing. Between one-third and one-half of the land surface has been transformed by human action; the carbon dioxide concentration in the atmosphere has increased by nearly 30 percent since the beginning of the Industrial Revolution; more atmospheric nitrogen is fixed by humanity than by all natural terrestrial sources combined; more than half of all accessible surface fresh water is put to use by humanity; and about one-quarter of the bird species on Earth have been driven to extinction. By these and other standards, it is clear that we live on a human-dominated planet. (Vitousek et al. 1997)

Part of our concern with establishing clear concepts of human and material agency is that we see a grave danger (to all life on the planet) in underestimating the force of human agency. Actor-network theory has drawn attention to the power of things, but its suspension of the concepts of human intentionality and creativity to attain symmetry is too limiting. Our position is not a "humanist" one in which humans are seen as superior by virtue of tipping the agentic seesaw over to their side; we simply seek a characterization that draws attention to the particular potency of human agency.[4]

10.2 AGENCY

We will apply the principles of activity theory to derive typologies that we believe capture essential differences between different kinds of agents and varying forms of agency.

For Leontiev, the primary type of agency was the agency of individual human subjects. In chapter 3, we defined human agency as the *ability and the need to act.* Now we want to revisit and refine this definition. In light of the principles and ideas deliberated so far, we will explore exactly what "the ability and the need to act" means. If we want to know whether we can extend agency to nonhuman entities, we need to formulate the question in a more general way: What are the criteria of agency? Once we know that, we can examine the fit between the criteria and different kinds of entities. We begin by examining criteria of human agency. We then compare these characteristics to those of other kinds of entities.

Following standard dictionary definitions, the most basic meaning of the "ability to act" is the ability *to produce an effect.* But this meaning is too broad for our purposes. If "acting" is understood as just producing an effect, then the ability to "act" is a property of anything that exists, either physically or ideally; any object, process, or idea. A narrower definition of acting is *producing an effect according to an intention.* Acting in this sense can be applied to, for example, a Mars probe, since the probe, as opposed to, for instance, stones on Mars, produces an effect according to the intention of the people who created it. Humans can act in both these ways: producing effects, and producing effects according to the intentions of others. But humans can also do something that neither the stones nor the probe is capable of: they can develop their own intentions on the basis of their needs, and meet their needs by acting on other entities, both human and nonhuman.

The "need to act" encompasses both *biological needs* and *cultural needs.* It is important to note that we use this distinction exclusively to refer to the *origins* of needs. Of course, all human needs are social in the sense that the way they are manifested and experienced is determined by individual's development in a social context. The criteria of what an individual considers healthy, attractive, prestigious, and so forth, are determined by the immediate and general cultural environment. The meaning of objects as things (or beings) that can potentially meet the needs of an individual is established socially. For instance, religious norms can prescribe that potentially edible objects are not perceived as food.

However, humans are animals too, and, as any animals, they must meet their biological needs. Our biological needs derive from our heritage as evolved biological organisms. Throughout biological evolution, a driving force of development has been meeting the basic needs of organisms. By "biological needs" we mean the needs that ensure survival and reproduction. The invisible evolutionary background of human agency means that biological needs are deeply ingrained in the very nature of human agency. The human adaptation of culture created a unique new set of needs. Cultural needs have the potential to change rapidly and to proliferate in number far beyond basic needs.

Intentions are driven by biological needs to ensure survival and reproduction, and by cultural needs that are established socially. Humans themselves are, recursively, the realization of cultural needs expressed in the intentions of others. Our abilities to act are shaped by such cultural needs. We embody cultural needs as a result of our activity and the activity of others who act on us. The surgeon's hands, the attorney's mind, the athlete's body—such agencies are the result of culturally specific object-oriented activity. Those who act on us to make us who we are include family, friends, peers, teachers, coaches, and coworkers, as well as the wider culture. We might also act according to another's intention that challenges culture or is outside culture, even including antisocial activity outside the culture.

10.2.1   A Typology of Agents

We use dimensions of human agency as a framework within which to categorize different kinds of agents, as shown in table 10.1. These dimensions come from the basic principles of activity theory, as well as extended implications of the principles, to specify dimensions of asymmetry between different kinds of agents.

As can be seen in table 10.1, we do not propose a dichotomous scheme such as human–machine agency (Rose, Jones, and Truex 2005) or human–material agency (Pickering 1993). We consider several dimensions that distinguish agents and suggest that under varying circumstances, different kinds of agents may exhibit similar agencies. For example, humans and social entities share with some nonhuman entities the possibility to act through delegated agency. We believe a more expansive treatment of agencies is needed to capture the complexity of phenomena related to modern technologies, especially intelligent machines.

Table 10.1
Forms of agency.

Agencies	Agents	Things (natural)	Things (cultural)	Nonhuman living beings (natural)	Nonhuman livings beings (cultural)	Human beings	Social entities
	Examples	tsunamis, Northern lights, vernal pools, Martian rocks	speed bumps, sewing machines, teapots, adzes	grizzly bears, California poppies, truffles, protozoa	house cats, Dolly the sheep, GMO corn, Bourbon roses	Spinuzzi's traffic engineers, Miettinen's scientists, ANT's princes	World Trade Organization, ISO, Doctors without Borders, United Nations
Conditional agency	Produce effects	+	+	+	+	+	+
Need-based agency	Act according to own biological needs	−	−	+	+	+	−
Need-based agency	Act according to own cultural needs	−	−	−	−	+	+
Delegated agency	Realize intentions of (other) human beings	−	+	−	+	+	+

Table 10.1 first of all establishes a distinction between agents that are living and nonliving entities. In chapter 3 we established that not any entity is a subject. A subject lives in the world and has needs. Interaction between the subject and the world cannot be symmetric because nonliving things do not have needs.

Next, the table distinguishes between human and nonhuman living beings according to the kinds of needs they have. Humans have both basic and cultural needs while other living beings have basic needs only. We distinguish between different kinds of nonhuman living beings: those that are the product of cultural needs and those that are not. The category "nonhuman living beings (cultural)" includes organisms such as domestic animals, plants, and fungi; live vaccines; clones; and genetically engineered plants and animals (like the knockout mice in chapter 7). The distinction is between organisms that have evolved outside human intention and those that have been cultivated, cultured, husbanded, bred, cloned, or genetically modified. The latter are a direct result of human activity, of some cultural need.

The dimension called "realize intentions of humans" suggests things (natural) and things (cultural). Things that are the result of some human intention produced in a cultural milieu are artifacts. A speedbump slows a driver because it is designed to do so, a fence keeps in the sheep, a vaccine deters a disease, a field of corn is harvested to feed the pigs. By contrast, the ocean currents that move the scallops in the study by Callon (1986) are a form of agent with no intention. The vapor that resists the physicists' efforts is another. Crusoe's footprints produce an effect, but with no intention. We of course recognize that California poppies might be cultivated in a garden, that grizzly bears might be managed in a park, and so on. However, such living things have had, and continue to have, existence beyond human intention in certain contexts. This dimension also applies to humans, who may realize the intentions of other humans, and to social entities.

Should we also call nonhuman living things (cultural) artifacts? Do knockout mice have subjectivity or are they so engineered, has so much been knocked out, that they are simply artifacts? We do not have a ready answer to this question. In research labs where we interviewed for the study described in chapter 7, we talked with lab technicians who clearly regarded lab animals as living creatures to be treated as kindly as possible (before the inevitable end). The technicians spoke of how they clipped the animals' nails for their comfort and fed them cranberry treats. On the other hand, the animals were exposed to hazardous chemicals and lived in extremely limiting circumstances that did not permit them autonomy to meet their own basic needs. The point here is not to decide the question, but to suggest that the power of human agency may shape cultural categories in complex ways.

The final column in table 10.1 is the category of social entities. We are least sure about the status of social entities relative to the other categories. Social entities comprise entities from all the other columns. They produce effects, and they can be said to have cultural needs (if they are to survive and reproduce themselves, certain things have to happen), and they realize human intentions. But because they are a composite of the other four entities, they have perhaps evolved to a different level of abstraction for which the dimensions of the table are insufficient. However, the notion of *macro-actors* in actor-network theory suggests that social entities have "interests" and can be seen as agents in their own right. In actor-network theory, large-scale entities—for example, the European Union, Silicon Valley, the space program, high-tech organized crime—can be said to have interests. While interests are most certainly associated with these macro-actors (Callon and Latour 1981), we are unsure how they are the related to the interests of living organisms, and leave this question for future investigation.

The cells in the leftmost column of the table identify different kinds of agencies. Rows 3 through 6 identify dimensions of these agencies. Row 3 indicates that all agents can produce effects. Row 4 indicates that when producing effects, some agents realize biological needs. Row 5 indicates that when producing effects, some agents realize cultural needs. Row 6 indicates that an agent may realize the intentions of (other) humans. The Mars probe realizes the intentions of the scientists who built it. A schoolchild learning to read realizes the intentions of parents and teachers (and of course her own intentions as well, in most cases).

Living beings are a special kind of agent in that they strive to meet needs in the world, engaging other entities as they do so in a patterned way. An erupting volcano has tremendous agentic power, but it simply explodes, affecting whatever lies in its path without regard for where its cinders rain down, where its lava flows. By contrast, a plant with its biological needs reaches for the sun, it produces chlorophyll, its flowers attract bees of a particular kind, and its seeds are eaten by certain birds who scatter them in the woods.

As we saw in chapter 3, Leontiev searched for a concept to describe the context in which mind evolved, considering "life," but rejecting it as too general. He settled on activity, defining it in terms of a subject's relation to a world in which it attempts to fulfill its needs. Nonliving things are inert in not having needs. Phenomenologists have also noticed this, observing that things do not "care," as Heidegger (1962) proposed. Subjects engage in activity because they care about what will happen to them in the future (see also Emirbayer and Mische 1998). This caring is the condition of the tiniest one-celled animal struggling for a mite of algae, to that of humans attempting to solve the most difficult scientific or social problems. In her novel *Housekeeping* (1980), Marilynne Robinson put it poetically: "And there is no living creature, though the whims of eons have put its eyes on boggling stalks and clamped it in a carapace, diminished it to a pinpoint and given it a taste for mud and stuck it down a well or hid it under a stone, but that creature will live on if it can."

Thus agency should not be considered a monolithic property that is either present or absent in any given case. Producing effects, acting, and realizing intentions, while potentialities of certain kinds of agents, vary within the enactment of a specific activity. Extending the notion of agency beyond human subjects may appear to be a deviation from the asymmetry of the subject and the object postulated by activity theory. However, what we propose is a combination of (1) a strict subject–object dichotomy (and resulting asymmetry) and (2) the notion of *levels of agency*, an understanding of agency as a dimension rather than a binary attribute.

With this in mind, we can differentiate between types, or levels of agency. Our analysis, as depicted in table 10.1, suggests a preliminary typology including:

> *Need-based agency* Human beings have both biological and cultural needs. To meet their needs, they form intentions and act

from these intentions. Similar types of agency are manifested by social entities (even though they do not have biological needs) and higher animals (even though they do not have cultural needs).

Delegated agency   Various things and living beings can be said to clearly realize intentions, but these intentions are delegated to them by somebody or something else. These things and living beings are agents in the sense of acting on somebody else's behalf. For example, an animal such as a thoroughbred race horse realizes the intentions of its breeders when it wins a race. But at other times the horse realizes its own intentions, while grazing in the pasture or resting in its stall. Human society is of course set up so that humans delegate their intentions to other humans, even in the simplest societies where children help their parents, marriages are arranged to advance a clan's fortunes, and so on. The intentions of the individual subject and intentions delegated to a subject by others may be in accord, or they may create conflict and dissension.

Conditional agency   Anything and anyone can produce unintended effects. The Russian winter of 1812 did not target Napoleon's army but undoubtedly contributed to its defeat. Truck drivers do not intend to create obstacles on highways, but they repeatedly do. Even without intentions, something or somebody may constitute a force—or condition—to be reckoned with.

10.3   ARTIFACTS

Artifacts are special agents that are the product of cultural needs. Humans have gained some control over our needs through the design and deployment of artifacts that embody our intentions and desires. We are able, in the lifetime of a single individual, to create new solutions to meet needs as conditions change. As we saw in chapter 3, artifacts empower people through the use of technical and psychological tools. Activity theory conceptualizes the potency of human agency in part through the principle of mediation: tools empower in mediating between people and the world. People "appropriate" tools in order to empower themselves to fulfill their objects (Bakhtin 1981; Wertsch 1998). The principle of mediation clearly suggests that things have agency, because if they did not, they could not act as mediators. In a vivid example, Zinchenko (1996) observed, "Communist and fascist symbols acquired such fanatic energy that … they nearly devoured the great cultures of Russia and Germany."

Functional organs are a special kind of mediator. Zinchenko (1996) discussed the cellist Rostropovich and the quality of mediation provided by his cello. When asked in an interview about his relationship to his cello, Rostropovich replied:

> "There no longer exist relations between us. Some time ago I lost my sense of the border between us…. In a portrait [by the painter Glikman] … there I was—and my cello became just a red spot at my belly…." (Quoted in Zinchenko 1996)

A functional organ is a relation between human and thing that is different from that between nodes in an actor-network. A functional organ brings human and thing close together, in a relation more intimate than a system of like nodes. A red spot at the belly is an apt metaphor for how we experience our most cherished technologies. As discussed in chapter 3, functional organs are subsystems that are integral parts of a subject who still decides when to use functional organs and whether they have to be altered or even abandoned.

Actor-network theory speaks of artifacts as having "delegated competences" (e.g., Latour 1993). Interests are "translated" between elements in the network, that is, performances and competences move back and forth between nodes in a symmetrical network. For example, a user's competence at typing a URL can be translated to a computer that can guess at the string intended by the user (as long as a few clues are provided) and complete the typing for the user.

In the scheme proposed in table 10.1, delegation flows from humans to all other kinds of agents (including other humans). But in actor-network theory, a nonhuman entity might delegate to a human. So a cell phone demands fresh batteries. It enlists the human to put them in by beeping when the battery is low. Activity theory sees this scenario differently. There is no delegation from thing to human; the human has decided that in order to use the mediating technology, she will supply the batteries. The human has other possibilities. She can turn off the beeper; she can throw away the cell phone; she can cancel her contract with the phone company. At any time she can resist; she can modify; she can alter her relationship to the technology based on her desires. The cell phone, by contrast, does what it was programmed to do; it is without desire and intention. The cell phone's agency is manifest in its ability to beep but it is an agency designed and delegated by humans.

Artifacts can be designed to produce effects to replace human labor at the level of operations and actions. Leontiev (1978) observed that operations are destined to become the functions of machines, and indeed the proliferation of such machines created since the Industrial Revolution has continued unabated (as the Luddites also foresaw). Automatic gearboxes, electric mixers, dishwashers, and text completion are examples of artifacts taking on some particularly tedious operations.

At the level of actions, programmable artifacts have proved enormously efficient and even intelligent. As early as the beginning of the nineteenth century, Jacquard looms driven by punched cards created elaborate fabrics (and provided the inspiration for the design of Babbage's Analytical Engine as well as Hollerith's Census Machine used to conduct the U.S. Census in 1890). A modern washing machine can carry out an impressive sequence of actions. And of course computers are the exemplar of programmable artifacts, interpreting languages that permit flexible sequences of actions (and operations) on a new scale of complexity.

While mediators can be designed to autonomously assume human operations and actions, they cannot, in themselves, create meaningful activities. Artifacts cannot decide what they want; they cannot form an intention, or say what is meaningful and what is not. Rae's fax machines, clever though they were, were not subjects with needs; they took no pleasure in correcting one another's mistakes and would never have done so without a human having programmed them.

Though we can't think of any actual artifacts with intention or desire, such artifacts are alive and well in the human consciousness. The Golem, Frankenstein's monster, the robot Maria in Lang's *Metropolis*, HAL in *2001*, and the Terminator, to name a few, inhabit a narrative universe in which cyborgian desires exert powerful influences in human life. These humanoid characters, while compelling, appear to be rather obvious projections of human desires and fears. A more likely source of artifacts with intention may be research in artificial life, an area to which we will look for interesting future developments (Reynolds 1987).

Mediators empower in ways specified by human designers, but the agency of artifacts may also be conditional, producing unintended effects. Winner (1977, 1986) has explored the unintended consequences of technology in several empirical investigations. Shaffer and Clinton (in press) pointed to the studies of Postman (1993) and Tenner (1997) in observing that "[things] have a way of exceeding or changing the designs of their makers." Unintended consequences of artifacts may be of value to people (such as the discovery of penicillin) or they may be tragic (such as an explosion at a nuclear power plant).

10.4   CONCLUSION

Actor-network theory has fruitfully challenged traditional accounts that restrict agency to humans. Using activity theory's basic principles and definitions, we have proposed a formulation that builds on actor-network theory's accomplishment but offers a different categorization of agents and agency, one that retains the asymmetry of the subject–object dichotomy. The subject–object dichotomy does not imply that activities should be understood in terms of a lone subject acting in a passively resisting environment. An extended notion of agency provides for creating richer representations of real-life settings. It takes into account human beings, who can help and support or resist and oppose: as representative of organizations, as individuals, and as physical bodies. It includes individual human beings and social entities, composing, for example, complex networks of activity systems (Engeström 1999b). And how about animals? Any pet owner would probably agree that animals have agency (to spare). Finally, the notion of things having a kind of agency can be found in virtually all cultures, from the ancient tradition of giving things (such as ships) and natural phenomena (such as hurricanes) human names, to the modern anthropomorphizing of the computer and the use of metaphorical language to describe machine behavior.

We identified different kinds of agents according to whether they are driven by the demands of life and whether they embody cultural needs. We found that these qualities indicate that a simple symmetry between people and things leaves out far too much. In particular, it leaves out the power of human agency and the way humans regulate their own activity through the creation and use of new agents, both living and non-living. Table 10.1 also suggests an interesting tension: every agent is capable of producing effects for which there is no intention. The more cultural things (living and nonliving) we have in the world, based on human design and intention, the more possibilities we introduce for conditional agency, that is, for new kinds of unintended effects.

11
Looking Forward

In concluding this book, we return to the hope expressed in chapter 1 that activity theory will expand its distinctive role in the continued development of interaction design. We believe that activity theory provides a snug theoretical fit with the sensibilities emerging in an interaction design oriented to the "design of spaces for human communication and interaction" (Winograd 1996). As a psychological theory that constructs a technologically empowered and socially contextualized human subject, activity theory has the potential to guide exploration in research and product development in interaction design in arenas of interest such as emotion in design, connected presence, pleasurable interactive products, persuasive technologies, technology as personal jewelry, technology as experience, context-aware computing, affective design, and design as performance. Emotion, experience, social connection, pleasure, persuasion, performance, awareness, affect, personal adornment—these require a human being with a body. The technologies that beckon are not merely carriers of information in systems, but potentially transformative artifacts capable of providing people with diverse new cognitive, emotional, social, aesthetic, and physical experiences.

Bannon (2005) observed that the thrust of today's interaction design is toward "a more holistic view of human-systems interaction that begins to privilege the human, social, and cultural aspects of computing." The privileging of the human aspects of computing runs counter to theories of flat networks or systems, but is receptive to asymmetrical theories in which technology mediates human activity. The flow in interaction design toward what is human—society, culture, emotion, awareness, affect—is compatible with activity theory's view of subjects enacting culturally meaningful activity in complex social arenas.

This flow reflects an expansive view of the individual—an individual who is growing, developing, changing, expanding in response to new opportunities and experiences, including technological ones. Such a view of the individual is bedrock in activity theory, going back to Vygotsky's studies of the development of children and his optimism for the promise of education. With foundations in biology, activity theory has retained a commitment to the individual organism. Along with this commitment was Vygotsky's insistence on the importance of culture. This powerful combination sets activity theory apart from strictly sociological accounts (such as actor-network theory or ethnomethodology), purely cultural accounts (such as those in cultural anthropology), systems-level accounts (such as distributed cognition), and psychological accounts focused on internal processes (such as many theories in traditional psychology). Activity theory integrates a psychological account of individual development with a historical account of the development of culture. These two lines converge and mutually influence one another. Culture provides resources but does not entirely constrain development—which is always open to the creativity of individuals who can restructure representations in original ways. The person is seen as capable of expansion socially, cognitively, even spiritually (Zinchenko 1996).

11.1   DEVELOPMENT OF ACTIVITY THEORY

Activity theory is in an active state of development and ferment, partly because the experience of using it in interaction design has revealed a need for elaboration and revision. With this stimulus, activity theory will continue to produce theoretical insights that are likely to be found useful in interaction design.

The basis for continued development is found in the principles of activity theory themselves which work together in an integrated framework. Theorizing in which work proceeds from an integrated set of core principles is different from a "one from column-A and two from column-B approach" which is sometimes offered up in the spirit of theoretical bricolage.[1] Leontiev (1974) argued that such approaches do not succeed in the long run because they lack foundation:

> Although the term "eclectic" is accorded highest praise by [certain] authors, eclectic positions have never been successful. A scientific synthesis of various kinds of complexes, psychological facts, and generalizations cannot be achieved by simply binding them together in the same book. It demands a further elaboration of psychology's conceptual framework and a search for new scientific categories that can mend the splitting seams in the structure of psychological science. (Leontiev 1974)

Activity theory has had the benefit of over eighty years of continued development, as well as grounding in older European philosophical traditions, as a basis for formulating "new scientific categories."

While there are many areas in which activity theory can and should continue to develop, interaction design as an application domain has provided some clear indications of future directions for development. In particular, there is a need to develop activity theory by extending the meaning of mediation, providing an account of multiple actions and activities, developing analytical tools for creating procedural representations of activities, differentiating between actual and potential goals, further delineating the relationship between individual and collective activities, and integrating the study of emotions. In the next sections we discuss these suggested areas of development.

11.1.1   Beyond Tool Mediation

The concept of tools does not describe all types of technologies. A computer application or system can be considered more an environment than a tool. Ducheneaut and Bellotti (2001), for example, argued that email is a habitat where people spend much of their working time doing all kinds of things, not merely performing a single task with a single tool.

Therefore, it seems some artifacts are not tools. Can the use of artifacts that are not tools be described as mediation? Currently activity theory is not quite clear on this issue. On the one hand, the notion of mediation in activity theory is clearly not limited to tools. For instance, the activity system model proposed by Engeström (1987) includes three types of mediators. Besides tools (mediating the relationship between the subject and the object) the model also describes rules (mediating the relationship between the subject and the community) and the division of labor (mediating the relationship between the community and the object). In principle, nothing prevents us from considering environments as mediators of human interaction with the world.

On the other hand, it appears that in activity theory environments are primarily understood as the world with which the subject is interacting. This understanding would exclude considering environments as mediators. But as designers, we construct environments to help people get something done; we think of them as mediators of activity. Making the relationship between artifacts, environments, and the world an object of analysis and extending the notion of mediation beyond tools are promising and much-needed directions for the further development of activity theory. Future work in this direction is likely to make activity theory a more powerful approach for studying a variety of information technologies such as media spaces, electronic workplaces, and games.

11.1.2   Dealing with Multiple Activities

A recurring theme in studies of office work is the need to manage multiple activities—to deal with interruptions, to prioritize, and to balance competing interests (Cypher 1986; Gallie et al. 1998; Nardi et al. 2002; González and Mark 2005; Mark, González, and Harris 2005). And people are acting in many contexts beyond work—at home, school, and in multiple communities and networks both online and off. To manage all these activities, people deploy a diverse assemblage of both digital and nondigital technologies in offices, homes, public spaces, and mobile contexts. Can activity theory provide an account of multiple activities including an understanding of their structure and dependencies? In principle, yes. However, the conceptual apparatus of activity theory currently does not provide an elaborated set of concepts for the analysis of multiple activities. Even though it is emphasized that human life can be described as a flow of various activities (Leontiev 1978), and that activities constitute networks within which activities or their individual components are related to other activities and their components (Engeström 1990; Kuutti 1996), the focus of analysis is usually on particular activities rather than on the flux of multiple activities typical of everyday settings and practices. There is a need to develop analytical tools that can help understand why people at certain a moment select a particular goal and carry out a particular action, why and how they move from one action to another, how they coordinate multiple actions, why they abandon certain goals, and how they develop new objects. It is hardly possible to provide adequate technological support for the coordination, flexibility, and mobility required in modern work and nonwork activities without such an understanding.

To meet this challenge of dealing with complex real-life processes, activity theory requires some new concepts. A move is needed from a preoccupation with separate activities to a focus on the complex interplay of several dynamically coordinated activities. Research methodologies that make it possible to study multiple activities empirically are also needed. Microlevel methods, such as interaction analysis (Jordan and Henderson 1995), or shadowing with detailed recording of informant actions (González and Mark 2004), might be points of departure for the development of such a methodology.

11.1.3   Procedural Representations of Activity

In order to understand the real-life use of technologies, analysis should focus not only on the structure of activities as modeled in the activity hierarchy, but also on how the activities are carried out, how they proceed through the phases of their respective lifecycles.

In interaction design, models of task structure are combined with procedural representations such as scenarios (Carroll 1995; Preece, Rogers, and Sharp 2002). In activity theory research, a few procedural models have been developed as well. For instance, Bødker (1996) developed a technique to translate video recordings to a diagram, providing a microlevel description of how an activity progresses over time. The diagram is a timeline, a two-dimensional representation with one dimension being time and the other corresponding to the level of activity. Such representations provide an overview of an activity as a process. They can help reveal the main phases of an activity, identify critical points in the process, and identify actual and potential problems.

Hyysalo (2005) developed a timeline representation depicting organizational activity extending over a long period of time (approximately a decade). This representation was intended to capture the dynamics of several aspects of activity simultaneously. More specifically, the diagram represented the change of the object of activity at various phases of its development, as well as contextual factors that to a large extent determined the direction of development of the activity.

However, more work on procedural representations of activity is needed. Development of modeling frameworks representing the unfolding of concrete activities is essential for relating the concepts of activity theory to specific concerns of researchers and practitioners.

11.1.4   Actual Goals, Potential Goals, and Engagements

More conceptual work is needed to advance understanding of goals in activity. Goals structure the flow of ongoing activity. The subject cannot be aware of all possible goals at the same time (Leontiev 1975; appendix A, this vol.) but can be conscious of only one goal at any given moment of time. Therefore, a hierarchy of goals could be more accurately described as a hierarchy of *potential* goals that temporarily become actual goals one at a time (Wertsch 1998).

Working with a representation of potential and actual goals might help designers understand some conundrums of user behavior. For example, it is puzzling that short-term efficiency seems to continually trump long-term efficiency for users of computer systems. Users continue to eschew excellent features built into software systems that would save them considerable time over the long run, such as the use of macros and scripting languages, customizable user interfaces, and tools for managing application preferences. Systems such as ROOMS or the Coordinator required low investment of time and effort for maintaining work environments (Henderson and Card 1986) or categorizing email messages (Winograd and Flores 1986)—investments likely to have brought substantial long-term benefits—but these systems did not become success stories because of seemingly irrational user biases. Users were apparently not convinced that being sidetracked from their actual goals was worth the effort of setting up and maintaining the systems, despite the logic of long-term gains.

Of course, users only seem irrational. The ability to focus on attaining a concrete goal is a prerequisite for efficiency, creativity, and having the experience of immersion and flow (Csikszentmihaly 1996). The need to take into account general concerns and explicitly place the task at hand in a larger-scale context can break concentration and force a person into a "reflective mode" in which they are stepping back and thinking about the larger activity, even if they wish to stay in an "experiential mode" to get the actual work done (Norman 1993). So the tendency of users to focus on rather narrow tasks and ignore big-picture concerns is not necessarily negative. Nor is it surprising, given the multiple activities that people are juggling. A means of dealing with this contradiction should be to attempt to coordinate potential goals and actual goals.

However, currently it is not clear how to coordinate in this way. A straightforward solution is to have the user define the overall structure of her activities and then select a specific goal to focus on. This approach, which underlies most project management systems, is successful when project management is an explicit goal of dedicated people. In supporting individual activities, the approach appears less suitable. Creating a comprehensive description of a person's activity can be an overwhelming task perceived as a major distraction from actually getting down to work. A possible alternative is to take the opposite approach, that is, to start with concrete goals to create a structural representation of a larger-scale activity. For instance, users can be allowed to define their actions and goals without any restrictions on the content and level of abstraction. They can retrospectively relate previously defined goals into persistent structures and eventually develop a representation of the overall structure of their activities. A sequence of such views can gradually reveal—most importantly, to users themselves—the emerging underlying structure of the activities. This approach is adopted, for instance, in the UMEA system described by Kaptelinin (2003) and in chapter 5.

Another approach to understanding goal selection more fully is the modification of the activity hierarchy to include an intermediate level between activities and actions, a level called "engagements" (González and Nardi 2005). Engagements are chains of thematically connected actions, oriented toward a particular purpose, and framed within a particular object-oriented activity. In an office setting, examples of engagements might include long-term projects, the solution of crises, or special events such as speeches or parties. Engagements are typically named, often informally (e.g., the Wilson account, the server meltdown, the beach party for the sales group). They provide a level of structure and sense-making missing from discrete actions and high-level objects. Engagements relate to goals by helping people decide what goal to work on next, providing a more local context or sense of activity than objects or particular actions.

The need for such a concept is indicated in interaction design research in which designers have tried to identify means of helping users manage collections of documents and other items. Starting with ROOMS (Henderson and Card 1986), these systems enabled users to organize thematically collected digital artifacts such as email messages, text documents, and spreadsheets. These collections are associated with particular "working contexts" (MacIntyre et al. 2001), "higher-level tasks" (Kaptelinin 2003), or "thrasks" (thematically connected email threads, according to Bellotti et al. 2003). The idea of engagements is preliminary and requires empirical analysis and conceptual elaboration before it can be useful in activity theory.

11.1.5   Individual and Collective Activities

Even though it is widely accepted that one of the main advantages of activity theory is the potential to combine the individual and the collective within a coherent framework, this potential is far from being fully realized. Current activity-theoretical approaches have a relative emphasis on either the individual or the collective. For instance, the approach developed by Leontiev focuses on the individual, on psychological phenomena, while the approach developed by Engeström is oriented toward sociological issues.

The lack of research into concrete mechanisms underlying the relationship between the individual and the collective in current activity theory is, in a way, paradoxical. Among the first and the most important accomplishments of the cultural-historical approach were the notions of the zone of proximal development and the universal law of human development, as discussed in chapter 3. Stetsenko (2005) argued that activity theory has been primarily concerned with the impact of the collective on the individual, while the influence of the individual on the collective has not been elaborated enough. According to Stetsenko, individual and collective planes of activity should be understood as inseparable aspects of activity cycles, and while the basic principles of activity theory make this understanding possible, the approach needs to be further developed to adequately deal with this issue.

The general possibility to bridge the divide between the individual and the collective opened up by the cultural-historical tradition (see Cole 1985; Cole and Engeström 1993; Kaptelinin and Cole 2002) appears to be especially relevant to current developments in interaction design. Arguably, the traditional divide between HCI and CSCW and their concerns with, respectively, individual use of technology and collaboration, shows its limitations. Issues that lie at the intersection of the individual and the collective are central to interaction design. These issues include integration of private and common information spaces (Bannon and Bødker 1997), individual and group workspaces (Cerrato Pargman 2003), and linking individual expertise to organizational needs (Ackerman and Macdonald 1996).

John Seely Brown (1996) suggested the following vision for the future development of technology and society:

> I could create an envisioning of the year 2020 ... that just felt like ... sitting on my porch at home, able to be on the borderline between public and private. Being able to see what's happening around me, being able to interact with my neighbors, with my community when I want. Being able to sit back and read quietly, sense the tranquility yet connectedness, the ability to get perspective on big problems and yet be a part of the local scene....

Activity theory's general perspective on the borderline between public and private is in many respects different from the vision proposed by Brown. In particular, it questions the very existence of the border between two different worlds. To make a real contribution to current discourse on the issue, however, this general perspective needs to be elaborated and translated into concrete research.

11.1.6   Emotion

We believe activity theory can provide important insights about the role of emotion in the design and use of information technologies. Leontiev (1978) understood emotions as indicators of the relationship between a subject's motives and the "success, or the possibility of success" of an action in meeting the motives. Even if motives are not conscious, they still express themselves to the subject "in the form of the emotional coloring of the action" (Leontiev 1978). Different motives can be in conflict with one another, which may result in complex emotional experiences (e.g., "bittersweet" emotions). Leontiev (1978) suggested that a promising approach to understanding the problem of emotion is to investigate the "intermotivational" relationships that, taken together, characterize the structure of personality, and, together with it, the sphere of emotional experiences that reflect and mediate its functioning.

By pointing to the role of emotions in human activities, activity theory suggests that one way to understand emotion is to study the objects that give meaning to individuals' activities. In chapter 7, we analyzed a case that revealed that subjects do not view objects of their activities only as rational foundations of their actions. Objects of activities are generators of a wide range of feelings and emotions; they are in fact "objects of passion" and "objects of desire." And activity theory points out that understanding emotions requires an understanding of the culture, in a broad sense, and the social context in which people use technology. The same clothing, building, or car can be considered beautiful or ugly, frightening or ridiculous, depending on connotations of fashion, value, expectations, or power.

However, a view of emotions, their nature, functions, and underlying mechanisms, has not been elaborated in activity theory to the extent it can serve as a theoretical basis for understanding emotions in interaction design. Creating a more adequate conceptual apparatus for dealing with emotions is a challenge for future development in activity theory.

11.2   BUT ISN'T ACTIVITY THEORY JUST COMMON SENSE?

We would like to take a moment to address one more question that rarely, if ever, emerges in formal discussions but is quite common in less formal communication. This question, which activity theory (as well as other theories of interaction design) has to deal with every now and then is, "But isn't that just common sense?" This is a tricky question, in part because it is elusive and vague and therefore difficult to address in a systematic manner. In particular, the meaning of "common sense" is never specified. The question is also problematic because theory and common sense are contrasted, as if they are incompatible. In fact, the outcomes of applying a theory in interaction design—such as concepts, principles, or design ideas—often look obvious with twenty–twenty hindsight. Practically any outcome of using a theory, especially if it is stripped of professional jargon and described in plain language, is exactly what one would expect using common sense. For instance, hierarchical models produced by task analysis can be seen as essentially the same as common recipes (Hackos and Redish 1998). The Coordinator system (Winograd and Flores 1986) can be seen as an attempt to formalize common sense by putting explicit labels on the types of messages which any participant in a collective activity distinguishes anyway. Understanding technology as mediating artifacts can also be categorized as intuitively self-evident.

The idea of activity theory as "common sense in disguise" certainly has some face value. However, let us take a closer look at this idea. Should a theory contradict common sense in order to be useful and worthy? Probably not. Going against common sense can arguably create worse problems than being in agreement with it. After all, interaction design strives to support the use of common sense by users of information technologies. Designing systems based on counterintuitive ideas is likely to be counterproductive. Therefore, if interaction design concepts, methods, and design ideas developed on the basis of a theory obtain a clean bill of health from common sense, it can be considered evidence supporting the theory rather than an argument against it. The real criticism lies not in the claim that a theory's contributions are in agreement with common sense, but rather in an implicit or explicit assumption that the contribution could easily be made by using common sense alone, without employing any theory at all. Formulated this way, the notion of the supremacy of common sense itself yields, in turn, to criticisms.

Does common sense provide a solid enough basis for interaction design? There are reasons to believe it does not. While common sense can easily be applied retrospectively, it is not much help in making actual decisions. Common sense can be used to justify diverse, even contradictory statements. It's not really so "common" after all. People referring to common sense may (and often do) disagree, and there are no obvious ways of deciding, by using common sense only, which view is correct. A measure of healthy skepticism is appropriate when dealing with claims based on common sense. The relationship between interaction design theory and research in general, on the one hand, and common sense, on the other hand, can be defined as: "common sense follows research." Ideas developed in interaction design research tend to be considered common sense after the fact.

11.3   DESIGN AND DEVELOPMENT

In this final chapter we want to present one more example of a technology design influenced by activity theory. This work was dedicated to an expansive view of the individual, designing and implementing a system to increase the independence and development of people with cognitive disabilities. The authors cited work in both activity theory and distributed cognition as influences on the design. They used activity theory for the development of specific conceptual points, while distributed cognition suggested the importance of recognizing a system of people and tools.[2]

Carmien et al. (2004) created the MAPS-LifeLine system which combines a mobile, wireless system for people with cognitive disabilities and a web-based monitoring and intervention system for their caregivers. The handheld wireless "prompting" device reminds users with cognitive disabilities ("clients") of the steps in the tasks they are trying to accomplish. The Web-based application allows caregivers to monitor client activities remotely. The prompting is programmed in a simple scripting language by a caregiver who knows the client and understands her tasks, needs, and level of development.

For example, suppose a client wishes to travel on the city bus system independently. She would use the prompts on the handheld device to remind her of the steps of the task (have correct change, buy ticket, remember where to get off the bus, and so forth). At the same time, she is connected to a caregiver via a cell phone that is part of the handheld device. The client can make or receive a call. The client might become confused and decide she needs to talk to the caregiver. Or, as he monitors the client, the caregiver might realize that something is amiss. He would phone the client to address the next steps she should take. The system is designed with the understanding that no matter how much is known about the steps of a basic task, there are many possible breakdowns and contingencies most effectively handled by human interaction.

The MAPS-LifeLine system allows the client considerable independence while incorporating a "lifeline" to human help. Carmien et al. pointed out that other similar systems provide the equivalent of the information on the handheld device but without the web-based monitoring. With such systems, the client has too little human support and cannot afford the risks involved in undertaking independent activities. The MAPS-LifeLine system provides the opportunity for clients to expand their learning as they engage in independent activity instead of curtailing development by foreclosing new activities likely to involve breakdowns. This was an explicit design decision, and one not made in other systems. It is a design consistent with the principles of activity theory in encouraging development.

The authors observed that some clients will continue to work with the system in place and that others "will learn to perform tasks to the point where the aid is no longer needed" (Carmien et al. 2004). In activity theory terms, some clients will internalize the relevant practices, moving from interpsychological to intrapsychological function, while others will continue to need the external support of the technology and caregivers. In the latter case, at least some internalization may also take place as clients improve at their tasks, even if they still use the technology to some extent. While the system is initially distributed, over time it becomes less so as clients internalize tasks through practice guided by MAPS-LifeLine.

A seemingly simple activity such as taking the bus is a breakthrough for users with certain kinds of cognitive disabilities. Rather than reducing cognitive effort (as argued in Hutchins 1995), clients are pushed to do more, to take risks, to develop, to reach beyond themselves. Clients cannot learn to take the bus merely by following rules; more complex interactions covering unexpected cases come into play, and rules themselves do not always wear their semantics perfectly on their sleeves, but require interpretation and judgment (Taylor 1985). The MAPS-LifeLine system was designed to accommodate the complex interactions necessary for advanced cognitive function for the system's clients by mediating their encounter with reality both technologically and socially.

Consonant with activity theory's emphasis on development, the evaluation of MAPS-LifeLine will extend over lengthy periods to see how much independence users can attain as they engage in new experiences afforded by the system (Carmien et al. 2004). The system itself is a highly creative collaborative effort. The subtle, complex technology was based on a thorough investigation of the arena of cognitive disabilities, including social, legal, and political aspects (Carmien et al. 2004, 2005).

We have argued for keeping the individual subject visible in interaction design. Users with cognitive disabilities are a case in point. While there are diagnostic categories of disabilities (autism, Down syndrome, and so forth), when the aim is to design a system to afford developmentally sophisticated activities, it is critical to take into account the specific level of individual development. Each individual in effect needs a unique system, as each individual's zone of proximal development is different. MAPS-LifeLine provides that unique system through the monitoring by caregivers—family members, vocational rehabilitation counselors, group home workers—who watch over and interact with those they know well. The caregivers design and implement the prompts to meet the requirements of each user. To get the design right, it would not be enough to describe a user merely as belonging to a community of users. Each user's zone of proximal development is considered by the caregiver and taken into account to expand development as new tasks are tried.

The MAPS-LifeLine system was informed by activity theory in several ways. The design takes an optimistic view of the possibilities and potential of clients with cognitive disabilities, expanding, not reducing, their cognitive effort. The system is organized so that clients progress in their usage, moving to more independence over time as they can. In other words, it is designed to allow for development. MAPS-LifeLine incorporates the understanding that the client's individual zone of proximal development is best understood by caregivers who are given tools to implement special prompts for individual clients. And the system was designed to use technology to mediate reality for clients in the particular cultural-historical climate of the community of people with disabilities in the United States.

While people with cognitive disabilities might seem a special case for interaction design, we believe it is not a special case at all. All users have their own comfort zones, their own need for technologies to enhance their activities, to expand their particular horizons. End user programming systems, intelligent agents, context-aware computing, affective computing, and other paradigms speak to the need to find ways to more closely match human and computer. In providing an expansive concept of the individual and concrete conceptual tools for analysis, activity theory supports efforts to develop technologies to expand and extend what people can do as they act with technology.

This type of research seems to be an indication that interaction design is entering a new phase of development. In 1990, Grudin observed that the computer was "reaching out"; the scope of human–computer interaction was expanding to include larger-scale, longer-term phenomena of computer use (Grudin 1990). From an activity theory perspective, the development of interaction design can be described as moving up the hierarchy of human activity mediated by information technologies: from algorithmic operations to goal-directed actions to complete activities. In recent decades the field has progressed from being almost exclusively concerned with operations to becoming much more interested in higher-level actions. Activity theory was one of the influences that promoted this change. The study by Carmien et al. (2004) suggests that interaction design can progress to a new phase where researchers are concerned with activities. At this stage, people who use technology are not only operators struggling with the interface, not only customers consuming and (hopefully) enjoying high-tech products, but developing human beings who create meaning in their lives through acting with technology.

11.4 ACTIVITY THEORY AS A COMMUNITY RESOURCE

Activity theory will have its fullest impact when it becomes a community resource for interaction designers. In chapter 2, we spoke of the need for shared vocabulary and understandings as advocated by Carroll (2003). This book is an effort to provide a systematic exposition of activity theory to promote common vocabulary and concepts as part of the development of the interaction design community. When we do not have to begin a conference paper that uses activity-theoretical concepts with a recap of the basic principles, that will be something to look forward to! When the general principles are known, the conceptual power of activity theory will be more widely available. This does not of course mean that everyone will accept or endorse activity theory, but that we will have a sufficient level of literacy to conduct interesting discussions about activity theory and the other postcognitivist theories discussed in chapter 9. The solution to the risk of a diminished impact for activity theory appears to be a coordinated effort to eliminate lack of understanding, inconsistent terminology, and poor communication. Our desire is to sustain dialogical conversation, vigorous theoretical development, and fruitful practical application of activity theory in the interaction design community. Looking forward, we anticipate that activity theory will continue its growth as a vital resource for deepening understanding of how people act with technology.

Appendix A: The Activity Checklist

There have been several attempts to come up with tools and techniques to support taking context into account in the design and evaluation of computer technologies.[1] The existing approaches to context are for the most part "bottom-up" ones. They start with an empirical analysis of contextual factors and gradually develop concepts, which later on can be put in an appropriate theoretical framework. From our point of view, this "bottom-up" or empirically driven strategy can be complemented with a "top-down" one, that is, starting with an abstract theoretical representation of context and then situating this representation in the reality of design and evaluation.

An example of a tool which is directly shaped by activity theory is the Activity Checklist (Kaptelinin, Nardi, and Macaulay 1999). The Activity Checklist is intended to elucidate the most important contextual factors of human–computer interaction. It is a guide to the specific areas that a researcher or practitioner should be paying attention to when trying to understand the context in which a tool will be or is being used. The Checklist lays out a kind of "contextual design space" by representing the key areas of context specified by activity theory.

The Activity Checklist is intended to be used at early phases of system design or for evaluating existing systems. Accordingly, there are two slightly different versions of the Checklist, the "evaluation version" and the "design version." Both versions are implemented as organized sets of items covering the contextual factors that can potentially influence the use of a computer technology in real-life settings. It is assumed that the Checklist can help to identify the most important issues, for instance, potential trouble spots that designers can address.

The Checklist covers a large space. It is intended to be used first by examining the whole space for areas of interest, then focusing on the identified areas of interest in as much depth as possible. The general strategy, then, is a breadth-first consideration of the relevant areas of context enumerated in the Checklist, followed by a "drilling down" into specific areas that should yield rich results given the tools and problems at hand.

The structure of the Checklist reflects the basic principles of activity theory. Since the Checklist is intended to be applied in analyzing how people use (or will use) a computer technology, there is a heavy emphasis on the principle of *tool mediation*. This principle has been applied throughout the Checklist and systematically combined with four other principles. It results in four sections corresponding to four main perspectives on the use of the "target technology" to be evaluated or designed:

1. *Means and ends*—the extent to which the technology facilitates and constrains attaining users' goals and the impact of the technology on provoking or resolving conflicts between different goals.

2. *Social and physical aspects of the environment*—integration of target technology with requirements, tools, resources, and social rules of the environment.

3. *Learning, cognition, and articulation*—internal vs. external components of activity and support of their mutual transformations with target technology.

4. *Development*—developmental transformation of the above components as a whole.

Taken together, these sections cover various aspects of the way the target technology supports, or is intended to support, human actions ("target actions").

The Activity Checklist is not the only attempt to deal with context in the field of HCI, and it is not intended as a substitute for other approaches. From our point of view, the Checklist can be most successfully used together with other tools and techniques to efficiently address issues of context.

We think that the main advantage of the Activity Checklist is that it is a general framework that can be used to (1) provide a preliminary overview of potentially relevant contextual factors, (2) select appropriate tools for further exploration, and (3) evaluate the limitations of those

Table A.1
Preamble.

Means/ends (hierarchical structure of activity)	Environment (object-orientedness)	Learning/cognition/ articulation (externalization/ internalization)	Development (development)
Human beings have hierarchies of goals that emerge from attempts to meet their needs under current circumstances. Understanding the use of any technology should start with identifying the goals of target actions, which are relatively explicit, and then extending the scope of analysis both "up" (to higher-level actions and activities) and "down" (to lower-level actions and operations).	Human beings live in the social, cultural world. They achieve their motives and goals by active transformation of objects in their environments. This section of the checklist identifies the objects involved in target activities and constituting the environment of the use of target technology.	Activities include both internal (mental) and external components, which can transform into each other. Computer systems should support both internalization of new ways of action and articulation of mental processes, when necessary, to facilitate problem solving and social coordination.	Activities undergo constant developmental transformations. Analysis of the history of target activities can help to reveal the main factors influencing the development. Analysis of potential changes in the environment can help to anticipate their effect on the structure of target activities.

Table A.2
Evaluation version of the Activity Checklist.

Means/ends	Environment	Learning/cognition/articulation	Development
People who use the target technology	Role of target technology in producing the outcomes of target actions	Components of target actions which are to be internalized	Use of target technology at various stages of target action "life cycles"—from goal setting to outcomes
Goals and subgoals of the target actions (target goals)	Tools, other than target technology, available to users	Knowledge about target technology which resides in the environment and the way this knowledge is distributed and accessed	Effect of implementation of target technology on the structure of target actions
Criteria for success or failure of achieving target goals	Integration of target technology with other tools	Time and effort necessary to master new operations	New higher-level goals which became attainable after the technology had been implemented
Decomposition of target goals into subgoals	Access to tools and materials necessary to perform target actions	Self-monitoring and reflection through externalization	Users' attitudes toward target technology (e.g., resistance) and how they change over time
Setting of target goals or subgoals	Tools and materials shared between several users	Use of target technology for simulating target actions before their actual implementation	Dynamics of potential conflicts between target actions and higher-level goals
Potential conflicts between target goals	Spatial layout and temporal organization of the work environment	Support of problem articulation and help request in case of breakdowns	
Potential conflicts between target goals and goals associated with other technologies and activities			
Resolution of conflicts between various goals			

Integration of individual target actions and other actions into higher-level actions	Division of labor, including synchronous and asynchronous distribution of work between different locations	Strategies and procedures of providing help to other users of target technology	Anticipated changes in the environment and the level of activity they directly influence (operations, actions, or activities)
Constraints imposed by higher-level goals on the choice and use of target technology	Rules, norms, and procedures regulating social interactions and coordination related to the use of target technology	Coordination of individual and group activities through externalization	
Alternative ways to attain target goals through lower-level goals		Use of shared representation to support collaborative work	
Troubleshooting strategies and techniques		Individual contributions to shared resources of a group or organization	
Support of mutual transformations between actions and operations			

Table A.3
Design version of the Activity Checklist.

	Means/ends	Environment	Learning/cognition/articulation	Development
USE	People who will use the target technology	Role of existing technology in producing the outcomes of target actions	Components of target actions which are to be internalized	Use of tools at various stages of target action "life cycles"—from goal setting to outcomes
	Goals and subgoals of the target actions (target goals)	Tools available to users	Time and effort necessary to learn how to use existing technology	Transformation of existing activities into future activities supported with the system
	Criteria for success or failure of achieving target goals	Integration of the target technology with other tools	Self-monitoring and reflection through externalization	History of implementation of new technologies to support target actions
	Decomposition of target goals into subgoals	Access to tools and materials necessary to perform target actions	Possibilities for simulating target actions before their actual implementation	Anticipated changes in the environment and the level of activity they directly influence (operations, actions, or activities)
	Setting of target goals or subgoals	Tools and materials shared between several users	Support of problem articulation and help request in case of breakdowns	Anticipated changes of target actions after new technology is implemented
	Potential conflicts between target goals	Spatial layout and temporal organization of the work environment	Strategies and procedures of providing help to other users of target technology	
	Potential conflicts between target goals and goals associated with other technologies and activities	Division of labor, including synchronous and asynchronous distribution of work between different locations		
	Resolution of conflicts between various goals			
	Integration of individual target actions and other actions into higher level actions			
	Constraints imposed by higher-level goals on the choice and use of existing technology			

Alternative ways to attain target goals through lower-level goals Troubleshooting strategies and techniques Support of mutual transformations between actions and operations Goals that can be changed or modified, and goals that have to remain after new technology is implemented	Rules, norms, and procedures regulating social interactions and coordination related to target actions	Coordination of individual and group activities through externalization Use of shared representations to support collaborative work	
DESIGN　Parties involved in the process of design Goals of designing the target technology Criteria of success or failure of design Potential conflicts between goals of design and other goals (e.g., stability of the organization, minimizing expenses)	Resources available to the parties involved in design of the target technology Rules, norms, and procedures regulating interaction between the parties	Representations of design that support coordination between the parties Mutual learning of the content of the work (designers) and possibilities/limitations of technology (users)	Anticipated changes in the requirements to the target technology

Table A.4
Sample questions.

Means/ends	Environment	Learning/cognition/articulation	Development
Are all target actions actually supported?	Are concepts and vocabulary of the system consistent with the concepts and vocabulary of the domain?	Does the system require a large investment of time and effort in learning how to use it?	What was the effect of implementation of target technology on target actions? Did expected benefits actually take place?
Is there any functionality of the system that is not used? If yes, which actions were intended to be supported with this functionality? How do users actually perform these actions?	Is target technology considered an important part of work activities?	Does the system help to avoid unnecessary learning?	Did users have enough experience with the system at the time of evaluation?
Are there actions, other than target actions, that are not supported, but users obviously need such support?	Are resources necessary to carry out target actions integrated with each other? Is target technology integrated with other tools and materials?	Is externally distributed knowledge easily accessible when necessary?	Is the whole "action life-cycle," from goal setting to the final outcome, taken into account and/or supported?
Are there conflicts between different goals of the user? If yes, what are the current trade-offs and rules or procedures for resolving the conflicts?	Are characteristics of target technology consistent with the nature of the environment (e.g., central office work vs. teleworking)?	Does the system provide representations of user's activities that can help in goal setting and self-evaluation? Does the system provide problem representations in case of breakdowns which can be used to find a solution or formulate a request for help?	Did the system show increasing or decreasing benefits over the process of its use? Are users' attitudes toward the system becoming more or less positive?

What are the basic limitations of the current technology?

Is it necessary for the user to constantly switch between different actions or activities? If yes, are there "emergency exits" which support painless transition between actions and activities, and, if necessary, returning to previous states, actions or activities?

Are there external representations of the user's activities which can be used by others as clues for coordinating their activities within the framework of a group or organization?

Are there negative or positive side-effects associated with the use of the system?

tools. In other words, the Checklist can help to leverage the various strengths of empirically based approaches.

The fact that the Checklist is comprehensive and wide-ranging should not mislead its potential users. It would be impossible to investigate all the areas it covers without a multiyear study, but that is not how it is intended to be employed. For most uses of the Checklist, users should first do a "quick-and-dirty" perusal of the areas represented in the Checklist that are likely to be troublesome or interesting (or both) in a specific design or evaluation. Then, once those areas have been identified, they can be delved into more deeply. The breadth of coverage in the Checklist will help to ensure that designers do not miss areas that might be important for understanding the tool they are working on.

Appendix B: Online Resources on Activity Theory

Acting with Technology

Http://mitpress.mit.edu/
A book series published by MIT Press that explores developments in postcognitivist theory and practice concerning technology. It encompasses research from the fields of sociology, communication, education, and organizational studies, as well as from science and technology studies, human–computer interaction, and computer-supported collaborative work.

Activity Theory

Http://carbon.cudenver.edu/~mryder/itc/activity.html
A collection of links to online resources in activity theory, created and maintained by Martin Ryder at the University of Colorado, Denver.

Activity-based Computing: A New Paradigm for Ubiquitous Computing

Http://www.activity-based-computing.org/
The website of the Activity-Based Computing (ABC) project at the Centre for Pervasive Healthcare at the University of Aarhus, Denmark.

Activity Theory Usability Lab, University of Wollongong, Australia

Http://infosys.uow.edu.au/atul/main.php/
A research center employing activity theory as a theoretical foundation for research in information systems and human–computer interaction.

Activités: Revue électronique

Http://www.activites.org/
An electronic journal publishing a wide range of studies dealing with goal-oriented activities in work and everyday life settings. While the primary fields of published research are ergonomics and psychology, the scope of the journal is interdisciplinary. The papers are published in French or simultaneously in French and English.

Center for Activity Theory and Developmental Work Research, University of Helsinki, Finland

Http://www.edu.helsinki.fi/activity/
A research unit at the University of Helsinki established in 1994 by Yrjö Engeström. The Center carries out a large-scale program of research on work, technology, and organizations going through transformations. The website informs about research conducted by the Center and contains a rich collection of resources on activity theory, especially on activity systems, expansive learning, and developmental work research.

Centre for Astronomy and Science Education

Systemic-Structural Theory of Activity (SSTA): Introduction and Basic Concepts Http://case.glam.ac.uk/CASE/StaffPages/SteveHarris/Research/SSTA.html/
An introduction to a version of activity theory, systemic-structural theory of activity (SSTA), and an overview of its applications in ergonomics. Provides links to full texts of articles on SSTA.

Centre for Sociocultural and Activity Theory Research, University of Birmingham, UK

Http://www.education.bham.ac.uk/research/sat/default.htm/
The Centre was established in 2000 for conducting interdisciplinary research dealing with human practice, technologies, and education, especially with design, development, and evaluation of sociotechnical systems and learning environments.

Interaction Design Centre, University of Limerick, Ireland

Http://www.idc.ul.ie/
The Centre conducts a variety of interdisciplinary projects in the area of human-centered design of information and communication technologies. Activity theory is one of the theoretical approaches influencing the research at the Centre.

InterMedia, University of Oslo, Norway

Http://www.intermedia.uio.no/index_en.html/
An interdisciplinary research center at the University of Oslo, Norway, conducting studies of design, communication, and learning in digital environments. The studies employ activity theory as one of the conceptual tools.

InterMedia, University of Bergen, Norway

Http://www.intermedia.uib.no/
The center conducts interdisciplinary studies of knowledge dissemination and learning supported by information and communication technology, with a special focus on social and cultural aspects of the use of new media.

International Society for Cultural and Activity Research (ISCAR)

Http://www.iscar.org/
An international association established in 2002 as a result of integration of two international associations, the International Society for Cultural Research and Activity Theory (ISCRAT) and the Society for Socio-Cultural Studies (SSCS). The website provides information about the current activities of the association as well as links to conferences conducted by ISCRAT and SSCS (http://www.iscar.org/history/).

Psychology and Marxism

Http://www.marxists.org/subject/psychology/index.htm/

This resource serves as a reference point in exploring the relationship between Marxism and psychology. The resource features full texts of a number of classical works of Vygotsky, Leontiev, Luria, Ilyenkov, and others, as well as modern commentaries on the works.

Special Issue of *Journal of Computer-supported Cooperative Work: Activity Theory and Design*

Http://www.ics.uci.edu/%7Eredmiles/activity/final-issue.html
Links to papers published in a special issue of the *Journal of Computer-supported Cooperative Work* on activity theory and design.

The Fifth Dimension

Http://www.5d.org/
A web portal of the Fifth Dimension network. The Fifth Dimension is a model for creating mixed-activity intergenerational learning settings supported by technology. The portal provides links to research papers, resources for practitioners, and Fifth Dimension sites located all over the world.

The Laboratory of Comparative Human Cognition (LCHC), University of California, San Diego

Http://lchc.ucsd.edu/index.html
The website of an internationally recognized research center in cultural research and activity theory. LCHC was founded in 1978 by Michael Cole. It publishes *Mind, Culture, and Activity: An International Journal* (http://lchc.ucsd.edu/MCA/Journal/index.html/) and sponsors the XMCA mailing list (http://communication.ucsd.edu/MCA/Mail/index.html/) for online discussions on cultural research and activity theory.

Wikipedia, the Free Encyclopedia

Http://en.wikipedia.org/wiki/Activity_theory
A Wikipedia article on activity theory.

Notes

Chapter 1

1. HCI, CSCW, and CSCL comprise a set of related fields. In the past HCI was often shorthand for the whole collection, but it appears that "interaction design" and more recently "informatics" are increasingly used as general references including these fields as well as others such as digital design.

2. *The Middle Length Discourses of the Buddha*, a new translation of the Majjhima Nikaya (Boston: Wisdon Publications, 1995).

Chapter 2

1. The notion of recovering practice calls to mind Miranda's parable "On Exactitude in Science," included in Borges's *Collected Fictions* (1999). In the parable cartographers create a map that coincides with a geography "point for point."

2. Some ethnomethodologically inspired accounts are moving away from pure conversation/interaction analysis to incorporate analysis of artifacts (e.g., Middleton and Brown 2002; Goodwin 2003). This incorporation of artifacts represents a convergence with activity theory, although the emphasis in the ethnomethodological studies is still on the production of order rather than the dynamics of development as in activity theory.

3. See Béguin and Clot 2004 for an insightful discussion of problems of the situated action approach. They conclude that "action is not so much situated in the situation as in the activity."

Chapter 3

1. See http://pinkmonkey.com/dl/library1/faust.pdf/.

2. This warning, in our view, should be extended to the widespread use of the distinction between technical and psychological tools, assigned to Vygotsky, in current research. This useful conceptual distinction is difficult to apply in

concrete, real-life cases. The same object can be a technical or a psychological tool depending on the way it is used. For instance, a knife is a technical tool when it is used to slice a sausage, but it is a psychological tool when it is used by a robber to frighten his victim into submission. Therefore, the border between technical and psychological tools is not clear-cut. These concepts should rather be considered two different aspects of the same artifact, often intertwined in a complex way. For instance, a pen is a technical tool in the sense that it is used to change a thing (e.g., to write a note on a piece of paper), but at the same time it is a psychological tool, since it is used to write a message intended to affect people's beliefs.

3. Vygotsky often referred to internalization as "growing inside" (*vraschivanie*), especially in his earlier works.

4. Originally published in 1959.

5. Such transformations are not always well understood. In the case of the typist, the intelligence of how to type seems to transfer at least partly "into the muscles." A complex motor process is developed.

Chapter 4

1. SAIK is a Danish abbreviation for "Collaborative Informatics in Clinical Practice" (SamarbejdsInformatik I Klinikken).

2. See www.5d.org.

3. Thomas Erickson, Charlie Hill, Austin Henderson, Dan Russell, Harry Saddler, and Mitch Stein (see Norman 1998, p. 287).

4. Some of these studies composed a special double issue of the *Interacting with Computers* journal published in 2003.

Chapter 5

1. The chapter is a revised version of an earlier paper (Kaptelinin 2003).

Chapter 6

1. This chapter is based on an earlier paper published in *Mind, Culture, and Activity: An International Journal* (Kaptelinin 2005).

2. Aleksey Leontiev's grandson.

Chapter 7

1. This chapter is based on an earlier paper published in *Mind, Culture, and Activity: An International Journal* (Nardi 2005).

2. The notion of "doable" problems is, of course, one of perspective. In conducting fieldwork in the laboratory and taking a university course in molecular biology, one of the authors (Nardi) was awed by the daunting challenge molecular biologists have set for themselves. Working with entities rarely viewed under a microscope, researchers are constantly making inferences from minute, difficult-to-establish changes in biological quantities. These inferences require meticulously designed experiments of immense precision. The scientists aim to understand complex phenomena that nature has been evolving for billions of years. Rather than being "doable," the problems of molecular biology seem almost impossibly difficult, among the most challenging humankind has ever undertaken. Penetrating these problems requires tremendous dedication and desire as well as the full deployment of a sophisticated international scientific establishment. The newer field of proteomics is orders of magnitude more difficult than genomics (because of the influence of complex contextual factors as proteins are synthesized), and will require even more passion and power to achieve breakthroughs. Thus the use of terms such as "tinkering" (to describe working on doable problems) misses the mark when the work is viewed in the wider context of motivated object-oriented activity.

3. Psychology has a rich literature in motivation (see, e.g., Herzberg 1959; Maslow 1970; McClelland 1988). However, these approaches are not activity-based. They deal with supposedly universal hierarchies (Maslow) or sets of specific motivations (Herzberg, McClelland). These theories are insightful and have been widely applied, but do not address issues of the working out of specific objects/motives in a particular context, and dealing with the related dynamics.

4. All names used in this discussion of the research site are fictitious.

5. Knorr Cetina (1997) observed of the objects used in expert work that they elicit nonalienation and identification. While her use of the term object is not congruent with that of activity theory, she draws attention to an emotional resonance attaching to objects of work, in line with what we are getting at by developing the passionate side of objects in activity theory.

6. Knockout mice have been bred with selected genes "knocked out."

Chapter 8

1. "Pedology" was used in Russia until the late 1930s as a name for a multidisciplinary field dealing with learning and development. The field integrates psychology, pedagogy, physiology, and other disciplines to reach a comprehensive understanding of children and their upbringing. The work in pedology was effectively terminated in 1936, when its practical applications were severely criticized in an official document issued by the Communist Party's Central Committee. Many leading pedologists were prosecuted, and for several decades reference to their works was prohibited.

2. In 2000 the book was awarded a prestigious national prize as the most widely read book in Russian psychology of the twentieth century.

3. Formerly the Institute of General and Educational Psychology, Academy of Pedagogical Sciences of the USSR.

4. A characteristic feature of the theoretical discussion between activity theory and its rivals up until the 1990s was a combination of conceptual debates, power struggles, ideological references, and personal conflicts, all taking place in the unique social context of the Soviet Union before perestroika. As a result, for the most part, discussions did not really look like discussions, at least in the printed media. All sides tried to avoid direct comments and rarely addressed their opponents directly. If comments were made, they were likely to be ignored or answered with elliptical counterarguments. During late 1970s one of the authors (Kaptelinin) was an undergraduate in the Department of Psychology of Moscow University. At that time the division between "us" and "them" was always present in the background of all educational and research activities at the department. This confrontation between the Moscow School of Psychology and its opponents ran out of steam in the 1980s and 1990s, when key figures personifying the confrontation were no longer active and more pressing issues, especially problems caused by the ideological and economic collapse of the Soviet Union, overshadowed the old conflict.

5. A similar notion was recently employed by de Souza (2005) in her semiotic engineering approach to human–computer interaction. The approach is based on the idea that interaction between users and systems can be interpreted and designed in terms of communication between users and designers, taking place at the time of interaction.

Chapter 9

1. The discussion in this chapter is limited to theories that significantly engage technology as a key component and which have been influential in interaction design. Lave's work was discussed in Nardi 1996a. Work such as that of Bourdieu (1998), Foucault (1984), de Certeau (2002), and others is of interest, but is not central to our approach to interaction design.

2. Providing brief characterizations of others' theories is a risky business. We have found that the theories we examined are not always internally consistent, making generalization difficult. For example, Nicolini, Gherardi, and Yanow (2003) note that actor-network theory "has never been codified into a full-fledged theory" but is, rather, "an interpretive sensitivity and a literary genre." There are many avenues into something as open as a sensitivity or genre. We have taken a few select paths and recognize that other readings are possible. See also Rose, Jones, and Truex 2005 on this point.

3. Leontiev was implicitly referring to Rubinshtein's work, pushing for further elaboration on the question of the specific nature of the relationship between the influences and the subject.

4. This is somewhat less true of earlier work in phenomenology, but that work led to ethnomethodology whose *modus operandi*, is, of course, one of minutely detailed accounts of activity (see Dourish 2001a).

5. Nodes may be actors or even "actants," a word suggestive of nonliving things (actants as narrative structures, reactants) or distortions of living things (mutants).

6. In the prodigious tradition of French scholarship, actor-network theory itself has moved on from networks to new concepts such as rhizomes. However, it is not clear how different the new work is from the body of work known as actor-network theory.

7. Although Latour (1988) broached the subject of things as princes, the argument was conceptual and no convincing empirical examples were given. Latour recounted a late-nineteenth-century dispute between Parisian transportation planners and the national railroad in which the former attempted to squelch the power of the latter through the design of narrow subway tunnels and tracks. The railroad eventually dug up the tracks and tunnels at great expense. This seems a weak example since the railroad princes were able to defeat their counterparts at the subway simply by throwing money at the problem. The tracks and tunnels can hardly be called princes in this case. Winner's (1986) work is more suggestive of the power of technology, although Winner blames humans for the negative consequences of human-designed and human-deployed technology.

8. Hutchins (1995) began to use the notion of mediation toward the end of his discussion, but the main idea in the book, a flat system of nodes propagating state, does not support a concept of mediation. As noted earlier, distributed cognition does not always follow its most radical tenets in specific analyses. Hutchins's discussion of tool mediation is consistent with that of activity theory.

9. Without going further into a very large debate, it seems clear that machine intelligence, while impressive, is programmed by humans and does not (yet) exhibit anything close to human cognitive abilities to create, theorize, and analyze. We believe this is partly because computers lack desire. The needs that stir living things to transform themselves and their surroundings do not stir nonliving things. This is a topic for a cozy fireside chat which we cannot of course undertake in this footnote.

10. It appears that there may be a confusion between culture and cognition in distributed cognition analyses. Hutchins (1995) said, "All human societies face cognitive tasks that are beyond the capabilities of any individual member.... The performance of cognitive tasks that exceed individual abilities is always shaped by a social organization of distributed cognition." However, it seems that Hutchins is speaking here of the cultural division of labor (Smith 2003 [1776]). There is no need to assert a new term "cognitive task," when "cultural task" is perfectly adequate and does not require us to suppose that things are cognizant. The "social organization of distributed cognition" is the same as the cultural division of labor. (See chapter 3.)

11. On p. 226, Hutchins (1995) discussed the "cognitive properties of [a] navigation team" that are said to be "at least twice removed from the cognitive properties of the individual members of the team." The struggle to preserve a concept of cognition (which is computation) for the team (vs. individual team members)

through maneuvers such as suggesting "removes" (which are at different levels of analysis) does not seem to lead to clarity.

12. Even allowing for the application of simple rules, we must ask how rules are actually applied in practice. Taylor (1985) observed, "A rule doesn't [just] apply itself; it has to be applied, and this may involve difficult, finely tuned judgments.... There is a ... gap between the formula and its enactment." Emirbayer and Mische (1998) pointed out that social actors engage in reflective and interpretive work, even in highly structured environments. They noted that Aristotle put forth three reasons why rules cannot capture practice: "the mutability of the particular, its indeterminacy (complexity and contextual variety), and its inherent nonrepeatability" (Emirbayer and Mische 1998). It is precisely the intentional subject who is responsive to the dimensions of the particular enumerated by Aristotle, allowing for flexibility and nuance in actual activity.

13. Slavery is of course the attempt to turn humans into things whose motives are not acknowledged in the activities of the system. This has proved impossible, and the motivated resistances, large and small, of slaves in the United States during the antebellum era are well documented.

14. There has also been some limited discussion in interaction design (e.g., Suchman and Trigg 1992; Shneiderman 2002; DeCortis, Rizzo, and Saudelli 2003; McCarthy and Wright 2004).

15. In practice, actor-network theorists bring in concepts not only of princes, but also of communities of practice and identity that make it increasingly difficult to speak of networks in which distinctions between human and nonhuman are not being made (e.g., Gherardi and Nicolini 2000). Middleton and Brown (2002) adopted actor-network theory (with some reservations) in a fascinating study of neonatal care. They attempted to preserve symmetry yet edged back toward distinguishing the human side, e.g.: "Agency is a kind of ambiguity, a break with what we expect. The exercise of agency is ... a rendering of oneself as otherwise than what was previously understood to be the case." The act of "expecting" and the reference to "oneself" are sensible only in a human category.

16. Likewise, a single learner would have a different zone of proximal development if given a different kind of mediation by Mediator A and Mediator B.

17. Of course, we have all been in groups where no group process catches fire—no useful mediation takes place—and the group does not advance the problem.

18. Andy Warhol mocked the artistic traditions of the independent artist, setting up the "Factory" which produced art that was both commercially and artistically successful. Warhol was seeking to make visible, satirize, and subvert the most entrenched practices in the art world of his day. Perhaps Warhol's creation of the Factory is as good a statement on the habits of the independent artist in the Western tradition as we could want. Of course, we can also say that despite the group work at the Factory, it is impossible to imagine the Factory without the unique presence of Warhol himself. Could any group have invented the persona he invented for himself?

19. The first Disneyland, in Anaheim, California, opened in 1955, a vastly different time and place than Chicago in 1893. The degree of imagination needed to take ideas from the "White City" and make them work for 1950s middle America defies explanation, but it seems safe to say that mundane reality was breached. The notion of a Disneyland Paris is even harder to grasp, but it is the number one tourist destination in Europe. Walt Disney of course drew heavily from European folktales in his productions, mining rich sources of the fantastic to international acclaim and immense profit.

20. In sociology, Emirbayer and Mische (1998) made a similar observation: "[W]e have stressed the reconstructive, (self)-transformative potentialities of human agency, when faced with contradictory or otherwise problematic situations."

21. Military operations can of course involve disastrous disruptions, as revealed throughout human history, and, more recently, in the events of the war in Iraq perpetrated by the U.S. military.

22. D'Andrade's construction of the workers' activity strikes us as just the sort of startling reframing of a problem that creative people are good at, which happens in social settings but is still internal to an individual subject. D'Andrade's comment was a conversational mediation that caused Hutchins to rethink his problem.

23. In actor-network theory, princes recruit and enroll other actors; they scheme and plan. The state college student simply sat down and designed a new system.

24. Such suprasituational activity has been observed in the changing conditions of warfare in the U.S. war in Iraq (Baum 2005). A generation of soldiers, schooled in the use of the Internet, seems to have initiated some surprising changes in military conduct. While the Army had been worried before the war that its training encouraged "reactive instead of proactive thoughts, compliance instead of creativity," as a military historian quoted in Baum (2005) put it, junior officers in Iraq have unexpectedly made fruitful use of information on restricted Army websites to deal with conditions of war for which they were not trained. Discussion threads on the sites consider matters such as how to manage Humvees, interacting with locals, what to do with pregnant soldiers, and which candies do not melt in the desert heat (Tootsie Rolls). Officers have Internet access even in very remote locations and, according to Baum, they find time to check relevant sites almost every day. The use of some of the sites began as unauthorized activity, but it is apparently being absorbed into accepted military practice.

25. This manifests itself in much use of the passive voice, e.g., by Hutchins (1995), "When one part of the tissue is unable to move the required information, another part is recruited to do it." Who or what is "recruiting"?

26. Latour (1988) scorned the idea of "empty talk about the 'participation of the public in technical decisions,'" suggesting that princes sit back laughing in their palaces "weaving at leisure human and non-human actors" for their ends. Latour seemed to want what he called "the People" to assert similar powers. But he gave no clues as to how the People could gain control of new actors. Latour's analysis,

grounded in the idea that a few princes are in control and that that is how networks work, does not suggest ways forward for the People.

27. And, in bringing in princes as the focus of empirical study, less visible actors, especially users, remain outside actor-network analysis (Miettinen 1999). The idea of following networks is certainly an interesting one, and it has been used in conjunction with activity theory without any suggestion of symmetry (e.g., Miettinen 1999; Nardi et al. 2002b).

28. Miettinen (1999) observed that symmetrical vocabularies have a bad track record, for example, behaviorism. Miettinen quoted Watson, a leading behaviorist theorist: "The behaviorist, in his effort to get a unitary scheme of animal response, recognizes no dividing line between man and brute." Colorful Victorian terminology aside, this rhetoric is remarkably similar to that of actor-network theory (Miettinen's point) and distributed cognition.

Chapter 10

1. This chapter analyzes one key principle of actor-network theory, the principle of generalized symmetry. We recognize that scholars influenced by actor-network theory may not subscribe to this aspect of the theory, utilizing instead concepts such as alignments, mobilizations, and so forth. But Latour (1992) identified the principle of generalized symmetry as the "most important philosophical discovery" in actor-network theory. The impact of this principle is significant; it has led to sociological and philosophical discussions of agency useful in highlighting the interplay of human activity and the material world (see Schatzki, Knorr Cetina, and von Savigny 2001). New versions of actor-network theory are in the works, but the "old" version is most widely used and likely to be influential for some time to come (see, e.g., Rose, Jones, and Truex 2005; Shaffer and Clinton in press).

2. Berg (1998) similarly critiqued structuration theory for overprivileging human agency.

3. Barad (1998) argued that the term "material agency" is misleading because humans are material beings. While we agree, we use the term in this part of the discussion because it is clear what it means in Pickering's example. Later in the chapter we propose new terminology.

4. This is not to say that a giant asteroid striking the Earth might not have far more agency than human activity, but simply to point to the need to theorize the considerable planetary change brought about by human agency.

Chapter 11

1. Holmström (2005) remarked, "When it comes to theories, one cannot only take the good bits and leave the bad bits behind. If a researcher does not understand enough of the theoretical tradition from its original setting, s/he is likely to

open the work up to any of the same criticisms of that theory that have already been voiced in the original discipline."

2. In our view, the version of distributed cognition in this paper is the one closest in spirit to activity theory, as discussed in chapter 9.

Appendix A

1. Appendix A is a revised version of an earlier paper (Kaptelinin, Nardi, and Macaulay 1999).

References

Issues of many Russian journals are organized by year; there are no separate volume numbers. When referring to papers published in such journals we give the year of publication in place of a volume number.

Aboulafia, A., and L. Bannon. 2004. Understanding affect in design: An outline conceptual framework. *Journal of Theoretical Issues in Ergonomics Science* 5: 4–15.

Ackerman, M., and C. Halverson. 1998. Considering an organization's memory. In *Proceedings of the 1998 ACM Conference on Computer-Supported Cooperative Work*, pp. 39–48. Seattle, Washington, November 14–18.

Ackerman, M., and D. McDonald. 1996. Answer Garden 2: Merging organizational memory with collaborative help. In *Proceedings of the 1996 ACM conference on Computer-Supported Cooperative Work*, pp. 97–105. November 16–20.

Agre, P. 1997. *Computation and Human Experience.* Cambridge: Cambridge University Press.

Albrechtsen, H., H. Andersen, S. Bødker, and A. Pejtersen. 2001. *Affordances in Activity Theory and Cognitive Systems Engineering.* Risø-R-1287 (EN). Roskilde: Risø National Laboratory. (Retrieved from www.risoe.dk/rispubl/SYS/syspdf/ris-r-1287.pdf on September 3, 2005.)

Allwood, C. 1989. Computer usage by novices. In A. Kent and J. Williams (eds.), *Encyclopedia of Micro-computers*, vol. 4, pp. 37–56. New York: Marcel Dekker.

Andreeva, G. 1997. K istorii stanovlenija sotsialnoj psikhologii v Rossii [On the history of development of social psychology in Russia]. *Vestnik MGU. Serija 14. Psikhologija* 1997 (4): 6–17. (In Russian.)

Ardisson, M., M. Schieff, P. Baron, and K. Lai. 2004. Social interaction in MMORPGs. Unpublished paper. University of California, Irvine.

Argyris, C., and D. Schön. 1996. *Organizational Learning II: Theory, Method, and Practice.* Reading, Mass.: Addison-Wesley.

Arievitch, I. 2003. A potential for an integrated view of development and learning: Gal'perin's contribution to sociocultural psychology. *Mind, Culture, and Activity: An International Journal* 10: 278–288.

Arievitch, I., and R. Van der Veer. 1995. Furthering the internalization debate: Gal'perin's contribution. *Human Development* 38: 113–126.

Atkinson, R., and R. Shiffrin 1968. Human memory: A proposed system and its control processes. In K. Spence and J. Spence (eds.), *The Psychology of Learning and Motivation*, vol. 2, pp. 89–195. New York: Academic Press.

Baecker, R., J. Grudin, W. Buxton, and S. Greenberg (eds.). 1995. *Human–Computer Interaction: Towards the Year 2000. Second edition.* San Francisco: Morgan Kaufmann.

Baerentsen, K., and J. Trettvik. 2002. An activity theory approach to affordance. In *Proceedings of the Second Nordic Conference on Human–Computer Interaction*, pp. 51–60. Aarhus, Denmark, October 19–23.

Bai, G., and L.-A. Lindberg. 1998. Dialectical approach to systems development. *Systems Research and Behavioral Science* 15: 47–54.

Baker, K., G. Bowker, and H. Karasti. 2002. Designing an infrastructure for heterogeneity in ecosystem data, collaborators, and organizations. In *Proceedings of the 2002 National Conference for Digital Government Research*, pp. 5–7. Los Angeles, California, May 19–22.

Bakhtin, M. 1981. *The Dialogic Imagination: Four Essays by M. M. Bakhtin.* Ed. M. Holquist. Austin: University of Texas Press.

Bakhtin, M. 1990. *Speech Genres and Other Late Essays.* Ed. C. Emerson, and M. Holquist. Austin: University of Texas Press.

Bannon, L. 1990. A pilgrim's progress: From cognitive science to cooperative design. *AI & Society* 4: 259–275.

Bannon, L. 1991. From human factors to human actors: The role of psychology and human–computer interaction studies in system design. In J. Greenbaum and M. Kyng (eds.), *Design at Work: Cooperative Design of Computer Systems*, pp. 25–44. Hillsdale, N.J.: Lawrence Erlbaum.

Bannon, L. 2005. A human-centred perspective on interaction design. In A. Pirhonen, H. Isomaki, C. Roast, and P. Saariluoma (eds.), *Future Interaction Design*, pp. 31–51. London: Springer-Verlag.

Bannon, L., and S. Bødker. 1991. Beyond the interface: Encountering artifacts in use. In J. Carroll (ed.), *Designing Interaction: Psychology at the Human–Computer Interface*, pp. 227–253. Cambridge: Cambridge University Press.

Bannon, L., and S. Bødker. 1997. Constructing common information spaces. In *Proceedings of ECSC'97, Fifth European CSCW Conference*, pp. 81–96. Lancaster, UK, September.

Bannon, L., and V. Kaptelinin. 2002. From human–computer interaction to computer-mediated activity. In C. Stephanidis (ed.), *User Interfaces for All: Concepts, Methods, and Tools*, pp. 183–202. Mahwah, N.J.: Lawrence Erlbaum.

Barad, K. 1998. Getting real: Technoscientific practices and the materialization of reality. *Differences: A Journal of Feminist Cultural Studies* 10: 87–128.

Bardram, J. 1997. Plans as situated actions: An activity theory approach to workflow systems. In *Proceedings of the Fifth European Conference on Computer Supported Cooperative Work*, pp. 17–32. Lancaster, UK, September 7–11.

Bardram, J. 1998. Collaboration, coordination, and computer support: An activity theoretical approach to the design of computer supported cooperative work. Ph.D. thesis. Aarhus: Aarhus University, computer science department. (DAIMI PB-533).

Bardram, J., and O. Bertelsen. 1995. Supporting the development of transparent interaction. In B. BIumenthal, J. Gornostaev, and C. Unger (eds.), *Selected Papers from the 5th International Conference on Human–Computer Interaction. EWHCI'95*, pp. 79–80. Lecture Notes in Computer Science 1015. London: Springer.

Barreau, D., and B. Nardi. 1995. Finding and reminding: File organization from the Desktop. *ACM SIGCHI Bulletin* 27: 39–43.

Barthelmess, P., and K. Anderson. 2002. A view of software development environments based on activity theory. *Computer Supported Cooperative Work: The Journal of Collaborative Computing* 11: 13–37.

Basov, M. 1930. *Obschie Osnovy Pedologii*, 2-e izdanie [General Foundations of Pedology, 2nd ed.]. Moscow: Gos. Izdatelstvo. (In Russian.)

Bateson, G. 1972. *Steps to an Ecology of Mind.* New York: Ballantine.

Baum, D. 2005. What the generals don't know. *New Yorker* (January 17): 42–48.

Bazerman, C. 1996. Review of *Cognition in the Wild* by E. Hutchins. *Mind, Culture and Activity: An International Journal* 3: 51–54.

Bazerman, C. 2001. Nuclear information: One rhetorical moment in the construction of the information age. *Written Communication* 18: 259–295.

Bazov, M. 1929. Ocherednye problemy psikhologii [Impending problems of psychology]. *Estestvoznanie i Marxizm* 3: 54–82. (In Russian.)

Beaudouin-Lafon, M. 2000. Instrumental interaction: An interaction model for designing post-WIMP user interfaces. In *Proceedings of the 2000 ACM Conference on Human Factors in Computing Systems*, pp. 446–453. The Hague, Netherlands, April 1–6.

Beck, B. 1980. *Animal Tool Behavior: The Use and Manufacture of Tools by Animals.* New York: Garland STPM Press.

Bedny, G., and D. Meister. 1997. *The Russian Theory of Activity: Current Applications to Design and Learning.* Mahwah, N.J.: Lawrence Erlbaum.

Bedny, G., and W. Karwowski. 2004. Meaning and sense in activity theory and their role in the study of human performance. *Ergonomia, International Journal of Ergonomics and Human Factors* 26: 121–140.

Béguin, P. 2003. Design as a mutual learning process between users and designers. *Interacting with Computers* 15: 709–730.

Béguin, P., and Y. Clot. 2004. Situated action in the development of activity. *Activités* 1: 50–63. Available at http://www.activites.org/.

Béguin, P., and P. Rabardel. 2000. Designing for instrument-mediated activity. *Scandinavian Journal of Information Systems* 12: 173–190.

Bellamy, R. 1996. Designing educational technology: Computer-mediated change. In B. Nardi (ed.), *Context and Consciousness: Activity Theory and Human–Computer Interaction*, pp. 124–146. Cambridge, Mass.: MIT Press.

Bellotti, V., N. Ducheneaut, M. Howard, and J. Smith. 2003. Taking email to task: The design and evaluation of a task management centered email tool. In *Proceedings of the 2003 ACM Conference on Human Factors in Computing Systems*, pp. 345–352. Ft. Lauderdale, Florida, April 5–10.

Berg, M. 1997. On distribution, drift, and the electronic medical record: Some tools for a sociology of the formal. *Proceedings of the Fifth European Conference on Computer Supported Cooperative Work*, pp. 141–156. Lancaster, UK, September 7–11.

Berg, M. 1998. The politics of technology: On bringing social theory into technological design. *Science, Technology, and Human Values* 23: 456–490.

Bernstein, N. 1967. *The Co-ordination and Regulation of Movements*. Oxford: Pergamon Press.

Bertelsen, O., and S. Bødker. 2002. Interaction through clusters of artifacts. In *Proceedings of the 11th European Conference on Cognitive Ergonomics: Cognition, Culture, and Design*, pp. 103–110. September.

Bertelsen, O., and S. Bødker. 2003. Activity theory. In J. Carroll (ed.), *HCI Models, Theories, and Frameworks: Toward a Multidisciplinary Science*, pp. 291–324. Amsterdam: Morgan Kaufmann.

Beyer, H., and K. Holtzblatt. 1999. Contextual design. *interactions* 6: 32–42.

Blackler, F. 1993. Knowledge and the theory of organizations: Organizations as activity systems and the reframing of management. *Journal of Management Studies* 30: 864–884.

Blackler, F. 1995. Activity theory, CSCW, and organizations. In A. Monk and G. Gilbert (eds.), *Perspectives in HCI: Diverse Approaches*, pp. 223–248. London: Academic Press.

Blumenthal, B. 1995. Industrial design and activity theory: A new direction for designing computer-based artifacts. In B. Blumenthal, J. Gornostaev, and C. Unger (eds.), *Selected Papers from the 5th International Conference on Human–Computer Interaction. EWHCI'95*, pp. 1–16. Lecture Notes in Computer Science 1015. London: Springer.

Bødker, S. 1987. *Through the Interface—A Human Activity Approach to User Interface Design*. (DAIMI PB-224). Aarhus: University of Aarhus.

Bødker, S. 1989. A human activity approach to user interfaces. *Human Computer Interaction* 4: 171–195.

Bødker, S. 1991. *Through the Interface: A Human Activity Approach to User Interface Design.* Hillsdale, N.J.: Lawrence Erlbaum.

Bødker, S. 1993. Historical analysis and conflicting perspectives: Contextualizing HCI. In L. Bass, J. Gornostaev, and C. Unger (eds.), *Selected Papers from the 3rd International Conference on Human–Computer Interaction: EWHCI'93,* pp. 1–10. Lecture Notes in Computer Science 753. Berlin: Springer.

Bødker, S. 1996. Applying activity theory to video analysis: How to make sense of video data in HCI. In B. Nardi (ed.), *Context and Consciousness: Activity Theory and Human–Computer Interaction,* pp. 147–174. Cambridge, Mass.: MIT Press.

Bødker, S., and E. Christiansen. 1997. Scenarios as springboards in CSCW design. In G. Bowker, S. Star, W. Turner, and L. Gasser (eds.), *Social Science, Technical Systems, and Cooperative Work: Beyond the Great Divide,* pp. 217–233. London: Lawrence Erlbaum.

Bødker, S., K. Grønbaek, and M. Kyng. 1993. Cooperative design: Techniques and experiences from the Scandinavian scene. In D. Schuler and A. Namioka (eds.), *Participatory Design: Principles and Practices,* pp. 157–175. Hillsdale, N.J.: Lawrence Erlbaum.

Borges, J. 1999. *Collected Fictions.* New York: Penguin.

Bourdieu, P. 1998. *Practical Reason.* Stanford: Stanford University Press.

Bourke, I., I. Verenikina, and E. Gould. 1993. Interacting with proprietary software users: An application for activity theory? *Proceedings of the 1993 East-West International Conference on Human–Computer Interaction,* vol. 1, pp. 219–225. Moscow, Russia, August 3–7.

Bowers, J., G. Button, and W. Sharrock. 1995. Workflow from within and without: Technology and cooperative work on the print industry shopfloor. In *Proceedings of the Fourth European Conference on Computer Supported Cooperative Work,* pp. 51–66. Stockholm, Sweden, September 11–15.

Bowker, G., S. Star, W. Turner, and L. Gasser (eds.). 1997. *Social Science, Technical Systems, and Cooperative Work: Beyond the Great Divide.* London: Lawrence Erlbaum.

Bratus, B. 1982. Obschepsikhologicheskaja teorija dejatelnosti i problema edinits analiza lichnosti [General-psychological activity theory and the problem of units of analysis of personality]. In A. Zaporozhets, V. Zinchenko, O. Ovchinnikova, and O. Tikhomirov (eds.), *A. N. Leontiev i sovremennaja psikhologija* [A. N. Leontiev and Contemporary Psychology], pp. 212–220. Moscow: Izdatelstvo MGU. (In Russian.)

Bratus, B. 1999. Lichnostnye smysly po A. N. Leontievu i problema vertikali soznanija [Personal meanings according to A. N. Leontiev and the problem of the vertical of consciousness]. In A. Vojskunsky, A. Zhdan, and O. Tikhomirov (eds.), *Traditsii I Perspektivy Dejatelnostnogo Podhoda v Psikhologii. Shkola A. N. Leontieva* [Traditions and Perspectives of the Activity Approach in Psychology: A. N. Leontiev's School], pp. 284–298. Moscow: Smysl. (In Russian.)

Brint, S. 2001. *Gemeinschaft* revisited: A critique and reconstruction of the community concept. *Sociological Theory* 19: 1–23.

Brown, J. S. 1996. Interview with John Seely Brown in *Minneapolis Star Tribune*. Retrieved from http://www.startribune.com/stonline/html/digage/seelybro.htm/ on September 30, 2005.

Brushlinsky, A. 1990. The activity of the subject and psychic activity. In V. Lektorsky and Y. Engeström (eds.), *Activity: The Theory, Methodology, and Problems*, pp. 67–73. Orlando: Paul M. Deutsch.

Brushlinsky, A. 1994. *Problemy psikhologii subjekta* [Problems of the psychology of the subject]. Moscow: Russian Academy of Sciences, The Institute of Psychology. (In Russian.)

Burke, K. 1966. *Language as Symbolic Action: Essays on life, Literature, and Method*. Berkeley: University of California Press.

Büscher, M., P. Mogensen, D. Shapiro, and I. Wagner. 1999. The Manufaktur: Supporting work practice in (landscape) architecture. In *Proceedings of the 6th European Conference on Computer Supported Cooperative Work*, pp. 21–40. Copenhagen, Denmark, September 12–16.

Button, G., J. Coulter, and W. Sharrock. 1995. *Computers, Minds, and Conduct*. Cambridge: Polity Press.

Button, G., and P. Dourish. 1996. Technomethodology: Paradoxes and possibilities. In *Proceedings of the 1996 ACM Conference on Human Factors in Computing Systems*, pp. 19–26. Vancouver, British Columbia, Canada, April 13–18.

Callon, M. 1986. Some elements of a sociology of translations: Domestication of the scallops and the fishermen of St. Brieuc Bay. In J. Law (ed.), *Power, Action, and Belief*, pp. 196–233. London: Routledge and Kegan Paul.

Callon, M., and B. Latour. 1981. Unscrewing the big Leviathan: How actors macro-structure reality and how sociologists help them do so. In A. Cicourel and K. Knorr Cetina (eds.), *Advances in Social Theory and Methodology: Towards an Integration of Micro- and Macro-sociologies*, pp. 277–303. Boston: Routledge and Kegan Paul.

Callon, M., J. Law, and A. Rip. 1986. *Mapping the Dynamics of Science and Technology: Sociology of Science in the Real World*. London: Palgrave Macmillan.

Card, S., T. Moran, and A. Newell. 1983. *The Psychology of Human–Computer Interaction*. Hillsdale, N.J.: Lawrence Erlbaum.

Carmien, S., M. Dawe, G. Fischer, A. Gorman, A. Kintsch, and J. Sullivan. 2005. Socio-technical environments supporting people with cognitive disabilities using public transportation. *ACM Transactions on Computer–Human Interaction* 12: 233–262.

Carmien, S., R. dePaula, A. Gorman, and A. Kintsch. 2004. Increasing workplace independence for people with cognitive disabilities by leveraging distributed cognition among caregivers and clients. *Computer Supported Cooperative Work: The Journal of Collaborative Computing* 13: 443–470.

Carroll, J. (ed.). 1987. *Interfacing Thought.* Cambridge, Mass.: MIT Press.

Carroll, J. (ed.). 1991. *Designing Interaction: Psychology at the Human–Computer Interface.* Cambridge: Cambridge University Press.

Carroll, J. (ed.). 1995. *Scenario-based Design: Envisioning Work and Technology in System Development.* New York: Wiley.

Carroll, J. (ed.). 2003. *HCI Models, Theories, and Frameworks: Toward a Multidisciplinary Science.* San Francisco: Morgan Kauffman.

Caspar, M. 1994. Reframing and grounding nonhuman agency. *American Behavioral Scientist* 37: 839–856.

Center for Activity Theory and Developmental Work Research. N.d. Retrieved from http://www.edu.helsinki.fi/activity/pages/chatanddwr/chat/ on July 29,2005.

Cerrato Pargman, T. 2003. Collaborating with writing tools: An instrumental perspective on the problem of computer-supported collaborative writing. *Interacting with Computers* 15: 737–757.

Cheyne, J., and D. Tarulli. 1999. Dialogue, difference, and the "third voice" in the zone of proximal development. *Theory and Psychology* 9: 5–28.

Christensen, H., and J. Bardram. 2002. Supporting human activities—Exploring activity-centered computing. In G. Borriello, G. and L.-E. Holmquist (eds.), *Proceedings of the 4th International Conference: UbiComp 2002*, pp. 107–116. Lecture Notes in Computer Science 2498. Berlin: Springer.

Christiansen, E. 1996. Tamed by a rose: Computers as tools in human activity. In B. Nardi (ed.), *Context and Consciousness: Activity Theory and Human–computer Interaction*, pp. 175–198. Cambridge, Mass.: MIT Press.

Clark, A. 1997. *Being There.* Cambridge, Mass.: MIT Press.

Clases, C., and T. Wehner. 2002. Steps across the border: Cooperation, knowledge production, and systems design. *Computer Supported Cooperative Work: The Journal of Collaborative Computing* 11: 39–54.

Cole, M. 1985. The zone of proximal development: Where culture and cognition create each other. In J. Wertsch (ed.), *Culture, Communication, and Cognition: Vygotskian Perspectives*, pp. 146–161. Cambridge: Cambridge University Press.

Cole, M. 1996. *Cultural Psychology: A Once and Future Discipline.* Cambridge, Mass.: The Belknap Press of Harvard University Press.

Cole, M., and Y. Engeström. 1993. A cultural-historical approach to distributed cognition. In G. Salomon (ed.), *Distributed Cognitions: Psychological and Educational Considerations*, pp. 1–46. New York: Cambridge University Press.

Cole, M., and S. Scribner (eds.). 1974. *Culture and Thought: A Psychological Introduction.* New York: Wiley.

Collins, H., and S. Yearley. 1992. Epistemological chicken. In A. Pickering (ed.), *Science as Practice and Culture*, pp. 301–326. Chicago: University of Chicago Press.

Collins, P., S. Shukla, and D. Redmiles. 2002. Activity theory and system design: A view from the trenches. *Computer Supported Cooperative Work: The Journal of Collaborative Computing* 11: 55–80.

Cooper, G., and J. Bowers. 1995. Representing the user: Notes on the disciplinary rhetoric of human–computer interaction. In P. Thomas (ed.), *The Social and Interactional Dimensions of Human–Computer Interfaces*, pp. 48–66. New York: Cambridge University Press.

Crick, F. 1993. *The Astonishing Hypothesis: The Scientific Search for the Soul.* New York: Touchstone.

Csikszentmihaly, M. 1996. *Creativity: Flow and the Psychology of Discovery and Invention.* New York: Harper Collins.

Cypher, A. 1986. The structure of users' activities. In D. Norman and S. Draper (eds.), *User Centered System Design, New Perspectives on Human–Computer Interaction*, pp. 243–264. Hillsdale, N.J.: Lawrence Erlbaum.

Czerwinski, M., E. Horvitz, and S. Wilhite. 2004. A diary study of task switching and interruptions. In *Proceedings of the 2004 ACM Conference on Human Factors in Computing Systems*, pp. 175–182. Vienna, Austria, April 19–24.

Davydov, V. 1990a. On the place of the category of activity in modern theoretical psychology. In V. Lektorsky and Y. Engeström (eds.), *Activity: The Theory, Methodology, and Problems*, pp. 75–81. Orlando: Paul M. Deutsch.

Davydov, V. 1990b. *Types of Generalisation in Instruction: Logical and Psychological Problems in the Structuring of School Curricula.* Soviet Studies in Mathematics Education, vol. 2, J. Kilpatrick (ed.), J. Teller (trans.). Reston, Virginia: NCTM.

Davydov, V., V. Zinchenko, and N. Talyzina. 1982. Problema dejatelnosti v rabotakh A. N. Leontieva [The problem of activity in A. N. Leontiev's works]. *Voprosy Psikhologii* 1982 (4): 61–66. (In Russian.)

de Certeau, M. 2002. *The Practice of Everyday Life.* Berkeley: University of California Press.

DeCortis, F., A. Rizzo, and B. Saudelli. 2003. Mediating effects of active and distributed instruments on narrative activities. *Interacting with Computers* 15: 801–830.

dePaula, R. 2004. The construction of usefulness: How users and context create meaning with a social networking system. Ph.D. dissertation, Boulder, University of Colorado.

de Souza, C. D. 2005. *The Semiotic Engineering of Human–Computer Interaction.* Cambridge, Mass.: MIT Press.

de Souza, C. D., and D. Redmiles. 2003. Opportunities for extending activity theory for studying collaborative software development. Workshop on Applying Activity Theory to CSCW Research and Practice, 8th European Conference of Computer-Supported Cooperative Work (ECSCW 2003, Helsinki, Finland), September 2003.

Donald, M. 1991. *Origins of the Modern Mind.* Cambridge, Mass.: Harvard University Press.

Dourish, P. 2001a. *Where the Action Is: The Foundations of Embodied Interaction.* Cambridge, Mass.: MIT Press.

Dourish, P. 2001b. Seeking a foundation for context-aware computing. *Human–Computer Interaction* 16: 229–241.

Dourish, P., W. Edwards, A. LaMarca, and M. Salisbury. 1999. Presto: An experimental architecture for fluid interactive document spaces. *ACM Transactions on Computer–Human Interaction* 6: 133–161.

Draper, S. 1993. Activity theory: The new direction for HCI? *International Journal of Man–Machine Studies* 37: 812–821.

Ducheneaut, N., and V. Bellotti. 2001. E-mail as habitat: An exploration of embedded personal information management. *interactions* 8: 30–38.

Edelman, G. 1992. *Bright Air, Brilliant Fire.* New York: Basic Books.

Ehn, P. 1988. *Work-Oriented Design of Computer Artifacts.* Stockholm: Arbetslivscentrum.

Ehn, P., and D. Sjögren. 1991. From system descriptions to scripts for action. In J. Greenbaum and M. Kyng (eds.), *Design at Work: Cooperative Design of Computer Systems*, pp. 241–268. Hillsdale, N.J.: Lawrence Erlbaum.

El'konin, D. 1977. Toward the problem of stages in the mental development of the child. In M. Cole (ed.), *Soviet Developmental Psychology*, pp. 538–563. White Plains, N.Y.: Sharpe.

Ellul, J. 1964. *The Technological Society.* New York: Vintage. (First published in French in 1950.)

Emirbayer, M., and A. Mische. 1998. What is agency? *American Journal of Sociology* 103: 962–1023.

Engeström, Y. 1987. *Learning by Expanding: An Activity-Theoretical Approach to Developmental Research.* Helsinki: Orienta-Konsultit Oy.

Engeström, Y. 1990. *Learning, Working, and Imagining: Twelve Studies in Activity Theory.* Helsinki: Orienta-Konsultit Oy.

Engeström, Y. 1995. Objects, contradictions, and collaboration in medical cognition: An activity-theoretical perspective. *Artificial Intelligence in Medicine* 7: 395–412.

Engeström, Y. 1999a. Introduction. In Y. Engeström, R. Miettinen, and R.-L. Punamäki (eds.), *Perspectives on Activity Theory*, pp. 1–16. Cambridge: Cambridge University Press.

Engeström, Y. 1999b. Activity theory and individual and social transformation. In Y. Engeström, R. Miettinen, and R. Punamäki (eds.), *Perspectives on Activity Theory*, pp. 19–38. Cambridge: Cambridge University Press.

Engeström, Y. 2005. Development, movement, and agency: Breaking away into mycorrhizae activities. Paper presented at the International Symposium on

Artefacts and Collectives: Situated Action and Activity Theory (ARTCO). Lyon, France, July 4–6.

Engeström, Y., K. Brown, L. Christopher, and J. Gregory. 1987. Coordination, cooperation, and communication in the courts. In: M. Cole, Y. Engeström, and O. Vasques (eds.), *Mind, Culture, and Activity*, pp. 369–385. Cambridge: Cambridge University Press.

Engeström, Y., and V. Escalante. 1996. Mundane tool or object of affection? The rise and fall of the Postal Buddy. In B. Nardi (ed.), *Context and Consciousness: Activity Theory and Human–Computer Interaction*, pp. 325–373. Cambridge, Mass.: MIT Press.

Engeström, Y., R. Miettinen, and R. Punamäki (eds.). 1999. *Perspectives on Activity Theory*. Cambridge: Cambridge University Press.

Erickson, T. 1996. The design and long-term use of a personal electronic notebook: A reflective analysis, pp. 11–18. In *Proceedings of the 1996 ACM Conference on Human Factors in Computing Systems*. Vancouver, British Columbia, Canada, April 13–18.

Fertig, S., E. Freeman, and D. Gelernter. 1996a. "Finding and Reminding" reconsidered. *ACM SIGCHI Bulletin* 28: 66–69.

Fertig, S., E. Freeman, and D. Gelernter. 1996b. Lifestreams: An alternative to the Desktop metaphor. In *Conference Companion of the 1996 ACM Conference on Human Factors in Computing Systems*, pp. 410–411. Vancouver, British Columbia, Canada, April 13–18.

Fichtner, B. 1984. Co-ordination, co-operation, and communication in the formation of theoretical concepts in instruction. In M. Hedegaard, P. Hakkarainen, and Y. Engeström (eds.), *Learning and Teaching on a Scientific Basis*, pp. 207–228. Aarhus: Aarhus University, Psikologisk Institut.

Fischer, G. 2004. Social creativity: Turning barriers into opportunities for collaborative design. In *Proceedings of the Participatory Design Conference (PDC'04)*, pp. 152–160. Palo Alto: CPSR.

Fisher, D., and B. Nardi. In press. Soylent and ContactMap: Tools for constructing the social workscape. In M. Czerwinski and V. Kaptelinin (eds.), *Beyond the Desktop Metaphor: Designing Integrated Digital Workspaces*. Cambridge, Mass.: MIT Press.

Fjeld, M., N. Ironmonger, S. Guttormsen Schär, and H. Krueger. 2001. Design and evaluation of four AR navigation tools using scene and viewpoint handling. In *Proceedings of the Eighth IFIP TC.13 Conference on Human–Computer Interaction. INTERACT 2001*, pp. 214–223. Tokyo, Japan, July 9–13.

Fjeld, M., K. Lauche, M. Bichsel, F. Voorhorst, H. Krueger, and M. Rauterberg. 2002. Physical and virtual tools: Activity theory applied to the design of groupware. *Computer Supported Cooperative Work: The Journal of Collaborative Computing* 11: 153–180.

Fjeld, M., M. Morf, and H. Krueger. 2004. Activity theory and the practice of design: Evaluation of a collaborative tangible user interface. *International Journal of Human Resources Development and Management* 4: 94–116.

Fleck, L. 1979. *Genesis and Development of a Scientific Fact*. Chicago: University of Chicago Press. (Originally published in German in 1935.)

Fogg, B. J. 2000. Persuasive technologies and Netsmart devices. In E. Bergman (ed.), *Information Appliances and Beyond: Interaction Design for Consumer Products*, pp. 335–360. San Francisco: Morgan Kaufmann.

Folcher, V. 2003. Appropriating artifacts as instruments: When design-for-use meets design-in-use. *Interacting with Computers* 15: 647–664.

Foot, K. 2001. Cultural-historical activity theory as practical theory: Illuminating the development of a conflict monitoring network. *Communication Theory* 11: 56–83.

Foot, K. 2002a. *Object: Constructed or apprehended?* Paper presented at the Fifth Congress of the International Society for Cultural Research and Activity Theory (ISCRAT 2002), Amsterdam, the Netherlands, June 18–22.

Foot, K. 2002b. Pursuing an evolving object: Object formation and identification in a conflict monitoring network. *Mind, Culture and Activity: An International Journal* 9: 132–149.

Foot, K. 2006. Corporate e-cruiting: The construction of work in Fortune 500 recruiting web sites. Forthcoming in *Journal of Computer-mediated Communication*.

Foot, K., S. Schneider, M. Dougherty, M. Xenos, and E. Larsen. 2003. Analyzing linking practices: Candidate sites in the 2002 US Electoral Web Sphere. *Journal of Computer-Mediated Communication* 8, July.

Foucault, M. 1984. *The Foucault Reader*. New York: Pantheon.

Friedman, B. 1997. *Human Values and the Design of Computer Technology*. Cambridge: Cambridge University Press.

Fujimura, J. 1987. Constructing doable problems in cancer research: Articulating alignment. *Social Studies of Science* 17: 257–293.

Fussell, S., S. Kiesler, L. Setlock, P. Scupelli, and S. Weisband. 2004. Effects of instant messaging on the management of multiple project trajectories. In *Proceedings of the 2004 ACM Conference on Human Factors in Computing Systems*, pp. 191–198. Vienna, Austria, April 24–29.

Galison, P. 1985. Bubble chambers and the experimental workplace. In P. Achinstein and O. Hannaway (eds.), *Observations, Experiments, and Hypotheses in Modern Science*, pp. 309–373. Cambridge, Mass.: MIT Press.

Gallie, D., M. White, C. Yuan, and M. Tomlinson. 1998. *Restructuring the Employment Relationship*. Oxford: Clarendon.

Galperin, P. 1976. *Vvedenie v Psikhologiju* [Introduction to Psychology]. Moscow: Izdatelstvo MGU. (In Russian.)

Galperin, P. 1992. Stage-by-stage formation as a method of psychological investigation. *Journal of Russian and East European Psychology* 30: 60–80.

Galperin, P., and S. Kabylnitskaya. 1974. *Eksperimentalnoe Formirovanie Vnimanija* [Experimental Formation of Attention]. Moscow: Izdatelstvo MGU. (In Russian.)

Gantt, M., and B. Nardi. 1992. Gardeners and gurus: Patterns of collaboration among CAD users. In *Proceedings of the 1992 ACM Conference on Human Factors in Computing Systems*, pp. 107–117. Monterey, California, May 3–7.

Garfinkel, H. 1967. *Studies in Ethnomethodology*. New York: Prentice Hall.

Garfinkel, H., and H. Sacks. 1970. On formal structures of practical actions. In J. McKinney and E. Tiryakian (eds.), *Theoretical Sociology: Perspectives and Developments*, pp. 337–366. New York: Appleton-Century-Crofts.

Gaver, B., T. Dunne, and E. Pacenti. 1999. Cultural probes. *interactions* 6: 21–29.

Gaver, W., J. Beaver, and S. Benford. 2003. Ambiguity as a resource for design. In *Proceedings of the ACM Conference on Human Factors in Computing Systems*, pp. 233–240. New York: ACM Press.

Gay, G., and H. Hembrooke. 2004. *Activity-Centered Design: An Ecological Approach to Designing Smart Tools and Usable Systems*. Cambridge, Mass.: MIT Press.

Geisler, C. 2003. When management becomes personal: An activity-theoretic analysis of Palm technologies. In C. Bazerman and D. Russell (eds.), *Writing Selves/Writing Societies: Research from Activity Perspectives*. Perspectives on Writing. Fort Collins, Colorado: The WAC Clearinghouse and Mind, Culture, and Activity. Retrieved from http://wac.colostate.edu/books/selves_societies/ on September 5, 2005.

Geyer, W. V. J., L. Cheng, and M. Muller. 2003. Supporting activity-centric collaboration through peer-to-peer shared objects. In *Proceedings of the 2003 Interrnational ACM SIGGROUP Conference on Supporting Group Work*, pp. 115–124. New York: ACM Press.

Gherardi, S., and D. Nicolini. 2000. To transfer is to transform: The circulation of safety knowledge. *Organization* 7: 329–348.

Gibson, J. J. 1979. *The Ecological Approach to Visual Perception*. Boston: Houghton Mifflin.

Gifford, B., and N. Enyedy. 1999. Activity centered design: Towards a theoretical framework for CSCL. In *Proceedings of the1999 Conference on Computer Support for Collaborative Learning*, pp. 189–196. Stanford, California, December.

González, V., and G. Mark. 2004. "Constant, constant, multi-tasking craziness": Managing multiple working spheres. In *Proceedings of the 2004 ACM Conference on Human Factors in Computing Systems*, pp. 113–120. Vienna, Austria, April 24–29.

González, V., and G. Mark. 2005. Managing currents of work: Multi-tasking among multiple collaborations. In *Proceedings of the Ninth European Conference on Computer Supported Cooperative Work*. Paris, France, September 18–22.

González, V., and B. Nardi. 2005. Engagements: Understanding the instantiation of activities. In preparation, University of California, Irvine.

Goodall, J. 1964. Tool-using and aimed throwing in a community of free-living chimpanzees. *Nature* 201: 1264–1266.

Goodwin, C. 1994. Professional vision. *American Anthropologist* 96: 606–633.

Goodwin, C. 2003. The body in action. In J. Coupland and R. Gwyn (eds.), *Discourse, the Body, and Identity*, pp. 19–42. New York: Palgrave-MacMillan.

Gould, E. 1998. Psychological information systems frameworks: A contrast between cognitive science and activity theory. In H. Hasan, E. Gould, and P. Hyland (eds.), *Information Systems and Activity Theory: Tools in Context*, pp. 39–58. Wollongong: University of Wollongong Press.

Greif, S. 1991. The role of German work psychology in the design of artifacts. In J. Carroll (ed.), *Designing Interaction: Psychology at the Human Computer Interface*, pp. 203–226. New York: Cambridge University Press.

Grudin, J. 1990. The computer reaches out: the historical continuity of interface design. In *Proceedings of the 1990 ACM Conference on Human Factors in Computing Systems*, pp. 261–268. Seattle, Washington, April 1–5.

Hackos, J., and J. Redish. 1998. *User and Task Analysis for Interface Design*. New York: John Wiley.

Halloran, J., Y. Rogers, and M. Scaife. 2002. Taking the "no" out of Lotus Notes: Activity theory, groupware, and student groupwork. In *Proceedings of the 2002 Conference on Computer Support for Collaborative Learning*, pp. 169–178. Boulder, Colorado, January.

Halverson, C. 1993. *Distributed Cognition as a Theoretical Framework for HCI*. COGSCI Tech Report 94-03. University of California, San Diego.

Halverson, C. 2002. Activity theory and distributed cognition, or, What does CSCW need to do with theories? *Computer Supported Cooperative Work: The Journal of Collaborative Computing* 11: 243–267.

Halverson, C., and M. Ackerman. 2003. "Yeah, the rush ain't here yet—take a break": Creation and use of an artifact as organizational memory. In *Proceedings of the 36th Hawaii International Conference on System Sciences*, pp. 113–126. Hawaii, January 6–9.

Hanseth, O., and Lundberg. 2001. Designing work oriented infrastructures. *Computer Supported Cooperative Work: The Journal of Collaborative Computing* 10: 347–372.

Haraway, D. 1991. *Simians, Cyborgs, and Women: The Reinvention of Nature*. New York: Routledge.

Harrison, B. 2004. An activity-centric approach to context-sensitive time management. Paper presented at CHI 2004, Workshop on Temporal Aspects of Work, Vienna.

Hasan, H. 1998. Activity theory: A basis for the contextual study of information systems in organizations. In H. Hasan, E. Gould, and P. Hyland (eds.), *Information Systems and Activity Theory: Tools in Context*, pp. 19–38. Wollongong: University of Wollongong Press.

Hasan, H., E. Gould, and P. Hyland (eds.). 1998. *Information Systems and Activity Theory: Tools in Context*. Wollongong: University of Wollongong Press.

Haythornwaite, C. 2002. Building social networks via computer networks: Creating and sustaining distributed learning communities. In A. Renninger and W. Shuman (eds.), *Building Virtual Communities*, pp. 159–190. Cambridge: Cambridge University Press.

Heath, C., and P. Luff. 1992. Collaboration and control: Crisis management and multimedia technology in London underground line control rooms. *Computer Supported Cooperative Work: The Journal of Collaborative Computing* 1: 69–94.

Hedegaard, M. 1999. Activity theory and history teaching. In Y. Engeström, R. Miettinen, and R. Punamaki (eds.), *Perspectives on Activity Theory*, pp. 282–297. Cambridge: Cambridge University Press.

Hedestig, U., and V. Kaptelinin. 2002. Re-contextualization of teaching and learning in videoconference-based environments. In *Proceedings of the 2002 Conference on Computer Support for Collaborative Learning: Foundations for a CSCL Community*, pp. 179–188. Boulder, Colorado, January 7–11.

Hedestig, U., and V. Kaptelinin. 2005. Facilitator's roles in a videoconference learning environment. *Information Systems Frontiers* 7: 71–83.

Heidegger, M. 1962. *Being and Time*. English translation. New York: Harper and Row. (First published in 1927.)

Helle, M. 2000. Disturbances and contradictions as tools for understanding work in the newsroom. *Scandinavian Journal of Information Systems* 12: 81–114.

Henderson, A., and S. Card. 1986. Rooms: The use of virtual workspaces to reduce space contention in a window-based graphical user interface. *ACM Transactions on Graphics* 5: 211–243.

Herzberg, F. 1959. *The Motivation to Work*. New York: John Wiley. (Republished in 1993 by Transactions Press.)

Hill, W., and L. Terveen. 1994. New uses and abuses of interaction history: Help form the research agenda. In *Conference Companion of the 1994 ACM Conference on Human Factors in Computing Systems*, p. 472. Boston, Massachusetts, April 24–28.

Hollan, J., and E. Hutchins. 2003. Position paper for the CHI'03 Panel on Post-cognitivist HCI: Second wave theories. ACM Conference on Human Factors in Computing Systems. Ft. Lauderdale, Florida, April 5–10.

Hollan, J., E. Hutchins, and D. Kirsch. 2000. Distributed cognition: Toward a new foundation for human–computer interaction research. *ACM Transactions on Computer–Human Interaction* 7: 174–196.

Holland, D., and J. Reeves. 1996. Activity theory and the view from somewhere: Team perspectives on the intellectual work of programming. In B. Nardi (ed.), *Context and Consciousness: Activity Theory and Human–Computer Interaction*, pp. 257–282. Cambridge, Mass.: MIT Press.

Holmström, J. 2005. Theorizing in IS research: What came before and what comes next? *Scandinavian Journal of Information Systems* 17: 167–174.

Holmström, J., and F. Stalder. 2001. Drifting technologies and multi-purpose networks: The case of the Swedish cashcard. *Information and Organisation* 11: 187–206.

Holtzblatt, K., and H. Beyer. 1993. Making customer-centered design work for teams. *Communications of the ACM* 36: 93–103.

Hutchins, E. 1995. *Cognition in the Wild*. Cambridge, Mass.: MIT Press.

Hutchins, E., J. Hollan, and D. Norman. 1986. Direct manipulation interfaces. In *User Centered System Design, New Perspectives on Human–Computer Interaction*, pp. 87–124. Hillsdale, N.J.: Lawrence Erlbaum.

Hyland, P. 1998. Exploring some problems in information retrieval: An activity-theory approach. In H. Hasan, E. Gould, and P. Hyland (eds.), *Information Systems and Activity Theory: Tools in Context*, pp. 93–108. Wollongong: University of Wollongong Press.

Hyysalo, S. 2005. Objects and motives in a product design process. *Mind, Culture, and Activity: An International Journal* 12: 19–36.

Iacucci, G., K. Kuutti, and M. Ranta. 2000. On the move with a magic thing: Role playing in concept design of mobile services and devices. In *Proceedings of the 2000 ACM Conference on Design of Interactive Systems*, pp. 193–202. New York, August 24–26.

Illich, I. 1980. *Tools for Conviviality*. New York: Harper.

Ilyenkov, E. 1977. *Dialectical Logic: Essays on Its History and Theory*. Moscow: Progress Publishers.

Ilyenkov, E. 1982. *Dialectics of the Abstract and the Concrete in Marx's* Capital. Moscow: Progress Publishers. (First published in Russian in 1960.)

Imaz, M., and D. Benyon. 1996. Cognition in the workplace: Integrating experientialism into activity theory. In *Proceedings of the 8th European Conference on Cognitive Ergonomics*. Granada, Spain, September 9–13.

James, W. 1890. *The Principles of Psychology*, volumes I and II. New York: H. Holt.

Johnson, J., T. Roberts, W. Verplank, D. Smith, C. Irby, M. Beard, and K. Mackey. 1989. The Xerox Star: A Retrospective. *IEEE Computer* (September): 11–29.

Jonassen, D., and L. Rohrer-Murphy. 1999. Activity theory as a framework for designing constructivist learning environments. *Educational Technology, Research, and Development* 47: 61–79.

Jordan, B., and A. Henderson. 1995. Interaction analysis: Foundations and practice. *Journal of the Learning Sciences* 4: 39–103.

Kaptelinin, V. 1991. Skill automatization and user interface transparency. In *Proceedings of the First Moscow International Workshop on Human–Computer Interaction*, pp. 280–283. Moscow, USSR, August 5–9. (In Russian; English abstract.)

Kaptelinin, V. 1992. Human computer interaction in context: The activity theory perspective. In *Proceedings of the 1992 East-West International Conference. EWHCI'92*, pp. 7–13. St. Petersburg, Russia, August 4–8.

Kaptelinin, V. 1993. Item recognition in menu selection: The effect of practice. In *Conference Companion of the 1993 ACM Conference on Human Factors in Computing Systems, INTERCHI'93*, pp. 183–184. Amsterdam, the Netherlands, April 24–29.

Kaptelinin, V. 1996a. Activity theory: Implications for human computer interaction. In B. Nardi (ed.), *Context and Consciousness: Activity Theory and Human–Computer Interactio*, pp. 103–116. Cambridge, Mass.: MIT Press.

Kaptelinin, V. 1996b. Distribution of cognition between minds and artifacts: Augmentation or mediation? *AI and Society* 10: 15–25.

Kaptelinin, V. 1996c. Computer-mediated activity: Functional organs in social and developmental contexts. In B. Nardi (ed.), *Context and Consciousness: Activity Theory and Human–Computer Interaction*, pp. 45–68. Cambridge, Mass.: MIT Press.

Kaptelinin, V. 1996d. Creating computer-based work environments: An empirical study of Macintosh users. In *Proceedings of the 1996 ACM SIGCPR/ SIGMIS Conference*, pp. 360–366. Denver, Colorado, April 11–13.

Kaptelinin, V. 2002. Making use of social thinking: The challenge of bridging activity systems. In Y. Dittrich, C. Floyd, and R. Klischewski (eds.), *Social Thinking—Software Practice*, pp. 45–68. Cambridge, Mass.: MIT Press.

Kaptelinin, V. 2003. UMEA: Translating interaction histories into project contexts. In *Proceedings of the 2003 ACM Conference on Human Factors in Computing Systems*, pp. 353–360. Ft. Lauderdale, Florida, April 5–10.

Kaptelinin, V. 2005. The object of activity: Making sense of the sense-maker. *Mind, Culture, and Activity: An International Journal* 12: 4–18.

Kaptelinin, V., and M. Cole. 2002. Individual and collective activities in educational computer game playing. In T. Koschmann, R. Hall, and N. Miyake (eds.), *CSCL 2: Carrying Forward the Conversation*, pp. 303–316. Mahwah, N.J.: Lawrence Erlbaum.

Kaptelinin, V., K. Kuutti, and L. Bannon. 1995. Activity theory: Basic concepts and applications. In B. Blumenthal, J. Gornostaev, and C. Unger (eds.), *Selected*

Papers from the 5th International Conference on Human–Computer Interaction. EWHCI'95, pp. 189–201. Lecture Notes in Computer Science 1015. London: Springer.

Kaptelinin, V., and B. Nardi. 1997. *Activity Theory: Basic Concepts and Applications*. Tutorial notes for the 1997 ACM Conference on Human Factors in Computing Systems. Atlanta, Georgia, March 1997. Retrieved from http://www.acm.org/sigchi/chi97/proceedings/tutorial/bn.htm/ on September 5, 2002.

Kaptelinin, V., B. Nardi, and C. Macaulay. 1999. The Activity Checklist: A tool for representing the "space" of context. *interactions* 6: 27–39.

Kensing, F. 2003. *Methods and Practices in Participatory Design*. Copenhagen: ITU Press.

Kidd, A. 1994. The marks are on the knowledge worker. In *Proceedings of the 1994 ACM Conference on Human Factors in Computing Systems*, pp. 186–191. Boston, Massachusetts, April 24–28.

Kirsh, D. 1995. The intelligent use of space. *Artificial Intelligence* 73: 31–68.

Kirsh, D. 2001. The context of work. *Human–Computer Interaction* 16: 305–322.

Kirsh, D. 2004. Metacognition, distributed cognition, and visual design. In P. Gärdenfors and P. Johansson (eds.), *Cognition, Education, and Communication Technology*. Mahwah, N.J.: Lawrence Erlbaum.

Kling, R., G. McKim, and A. King, A. 2003. A bit more to it: Scholarly communication forums as socio-technical information networks. *Journal of the American Society for Information Science and Technology* 54: 47–67.

Knorr Cetina, K. 1997. Sociality with objects: Social relations in postsocial knowledge societies. *Theory, Culture, and Society* 14: 1–30.

Koffka, K. 1924. *The Growth of the Mind*. Trans. R. M. Ogden. London: Routledge and Kegan Paul. (Original work published 1921.)

Köhler, W. 1925. *Mentality of Apes*. Trans. E. Winter. London: Routledge and Kegan Paul. (Original work published 1917.)

Korpela, M., A. Mursu, H. Soriyan, and A. Eerola. 2002. Information systems research and information systems practice in a network of activities. In Y. Dittrich, C. Floyd, and R. Klischewski (eds.), *Social Thinking—Software Practice*, pp. 287–308. Cambridge, Mass.: MIT Press.

Koschmann, T. (ed.). 1996a. *CSCL: Theory and Practice of an Emerging Paradigm*. Mahwah, N.J.: Lawrence Erlbaum.

Koschmann, T. 1996b. Paradigm shifts and instructional technology. In T. Koschmann (ed.), *CSCL Theory and Practice of an Emerging Paradigm*, pp. 1–23. Mahwah, N.J.: Lawrence Erlbaum.

Koschmann, T., K. Kuutti, and L. Hickmann. 1998. The concept of breakdown in Heidegger, Leont'ev, and Dewey and its implications for education. *Mind, Culture, and Activity: An International Journal* 5: 25–41.

Kuutti, K. 1991. Activity theory and its applications to information systems research and development. In H.-E. Nissen, H. K. Klein, and R. Hirschheim (eds.), *Information Systems Research Arena of the 90's*, pp. 525–549. Amsterdam: North Holland.

Kuutti, K. 1992. HCI research debate and activity theory position. In *Proceedings of the 1992 East-West International Conference on Human–Computer Interaction*, pp. 13–22. EWHCI'92. St. Petersburg, Russia, August 4–8.

Kuttii, K. 1996. Activity theory as a potential framework for human–computer interaction research. In B. Nardi (ed.), *Context and Consciousness: Activity Theory and Human–Computer Interaction*, pp. 17–44. Cambridge, Mass.: MIT Press.

Kuutti, K. 1998. Making the object of a work activity accessible. In *Proceedings of the Workshop on Understanding Work and Designing Artefacts*, pp. 1–12. York, UK, September.

Kuutti, K. 1999. Activity theory, transformation of work, and information systems design. In Y. Engeström, R. Miettinen, and R.-L. Punamäki (eds.), *Perspectives on Activity Theory*, pp. 360–376. Cambridge: Cambridge University Press.

Kuutti, K., and T. Arvonen. 1992. Identifying CSCW applications by means of activity theory concepts: A case example. In *Proceedings of the 1998 ACM Conference on Computer-Supported Collaborative Work*, pp. 233–240. Toronto, Ontario, Canada, November 1–4.

Kuutti, K., and L. Bannon. 1993. Searching for unity among diversity: Exploring the "interface" concept. In *Proceedings of the 1993 ACM Conference on Human Factors in Computing Systems: INTERCHI'93*, pp. 263–268. Amsterdam, the Netherlands, April 24–29.

Kuutti, K., G. Iacucci, and C. Iacucci. 2002. Acting to know: Improving creativity in the design of mobile services by using performances. In *Proceedings of the Fourth Conference on Creativity and Cognition*, pp. 95–102. Loughborough, UK, October 13–16.

Lamb, R., and E. Davidson. 2005. Information and communication technology challenges to scientific professional identity. *Information Society* 21: 1–24.

Lancaster University and Manchester University. 1994. *Field Studies and CSCW. COMIC Esprit Basic Research Project 6225. Deliverable 2.2.* Available at ftp:// ftp.comp.lancs.ac.uk/pub/comic/ on September 5, 2005.

Larson, E. 2003. *The Devil in the White City*. New York: Crown.

Latour, B. 1988. The Prince for machines as well as machinations. In B. Elliott (ed.), *Technology and Social Processes*, pp. 20–43. Edinburgh: Edinburgh University Press.

Latour, B. 1992. One turn after the social turn. In E. McMullin (ed.), *The Social Dimensions of Science*, pp. 272–294. Notre Dame, Ind.: Notre Dame Press.

Latour, B. 1993. Ethnography of a "High-Tech" Case: About Aramis. In P. Lemannier (ed.), *Technological Choices: Transformations in Material Culture since the Neolithic*, pp. 372–398. London: Routledge and Kegan Paul.

Latour, B. 1994. On technical mediation: Philosophy, genealogy, and sociology. *Common Knowledge* 3: 29–64.

Latour, B. 1996a. *Aramis, or The Love of Technology*. Cambridge, Mass.: Harvard University Press.

Latour, B. 1996b. On interobjectivity. *Mind, Culture, and Activity: An International Journal* 3: 264–270.

Lave, J., M. Murtaugh, and O. de la Rocha. 1984. The dialectic of arithmetic in grocery shopping. In B. Rogoff and J. Lave (eds.), *Everyday Cognition: Its Development in Social Context*, pp. 67–94. London: Harvard University Press.

Lave, J., and E. Wenger. 1991. *Situated Learning: Legitimate Peripheral Participation*. Cambridge: Cambridge University Press.

Law, J., and M. Callon. 1992. The life and death of an aircraft. In W. Bijker and J. Law (eds.), *Shaping Technology/Building Society*, pp. 20–52. Cambridge, Mass.: MIT Press.

Leontiev, A. 1929. Retsenzija na knigu: Basov M. Ya. "Obschie Osnovy Pedologii" [Book review: *General Foundations of Pedology* by M. Ya. Basov]. *Estestvoznanie i Marxizm* 1929 (2): 211–213. (In Russian.)

Leontiev, A. 1931. *Razvitie Pamjati* [Development of Memory]. Moscow: Uchpedgiz. (In Russian.)

Leontiev, A. 1974. The problem of activity in psychology. *Soviet Psychology* 13: 4–33.

Leontiev, A. 1975. *Dejatelnost. Soznanie. Lichnost* [Activity. Consciousness. Personality]. Moscow: Politizdat. (In Russian.)

Leontiev, A. 1977. Activity and Consciousness. In *Philosophy in the USSR, Problems of Dialectical Materialism*. Moscow: Progress Publishers. Available at http:// www.marxists.org/archive/leontev/works/1977/leon1977.htm/.

Leontiev, A. 1978. *Activity, Consciousness, and Personality*. Englewood Cliffs, N.J.: Prentice-Hall. (Original work published in Russian in 1975.)

Leontiev, A. 1981. *Problemy Razvitija Psihiki* [Problems of the Development of Mind, fourth edition]. Moscow: Izdatelstvo MGU. (In Russian; original work published 1959. English edition: Leontiev, A. [1981], *Problems in the Development of the Mind*. Moscow: Progress Publishers.)

Leontiev, D. 1993. Systemno-smyslovaya priroda I funktsii motiva [Sense-system nature and functions of the motive]. *Vestnik MGU. Serija 14. Psikhologija* 1993 (2): 73–81. (In Russian.)

Lewin, K. 1936. *Principles of Topological Psychology*. New York: McGraw-Hill.

Licoppe, C. 2004. "Connected" presence: The emergence of a new repertoire for managing social relationships in a changing communication technoscape. *Environment and Planning: Society and Space* 22: 135–156.

Licoppe, C. 2005. Processing distress calls, from telephone to email: A distributed collective practice? Paper presented at ARTCO, Artefacts and Collectivities 2005. Lyon, France.

Lieberman, H. 2000. *Your Wish Is My Command: Giving Users the Power to Instruct Their Software.* San Francisco: Morgan Kaufmann.

Linard, M., and R. Zeiliger. 1995. Designing navigational support for educational software. In B. Blumenthal, J. Gornostaev, and C. Unger (eds.), *Selected Papers from the 5th International Conference on Human–Computer Interaction, EWHCI'95,* pp. 63–78. Lecture Notes in Computer Science 1015. London: Springer.

Logvinenko, A. 1988. Introduction. In J. J. Gibson, *Ekologicheskij Podhod k Zritelnomu Vosprijatiju* [The Ecological Approach to Visual Perception], pp. 5–20. Moscow: Progress. (In Russian.)

Logvinenko, A., and V. Stolin. 1982. Vosprijatie prostransrvennyh svoistv predmetov [Perception of spatial properties of objects]. In A. V. Zaporozhets, B. F. Lomov, and V. P. Zinchenko (eds.), *Poznavatelnye Protsessy: Oschuschenija, Vosprijatie* [Cognitive Processes: Sensations and Perception], pp. 246–277. Moscow: Pedagogika. (In Russian.)

Lomov, B. 1981. K probleme dejatelnosti v psikhologii [On the problem of activity in psychology]. *Psikhologicheskij Zhurnal* 2: 3–23. (In Russian.)

Löwgren, J., and E. Stolterman. 2004. *Thoughtful Interaction Design: A Design Perspective on Information Technology.* Cambridge, Mass.: MIT Press.

Luria, A. 1972. *The Man with the Shattered World.* New York: Basic Books.

Lynch, M. 1999. Silence in context: Ethnomethodology and social theory. *Human Studies* 22: 211–233.

Macaulay, C. 1999. The checklist in the field. *interactions* 6: 30–31.

Macaulay, C., D. Benyon, and A. Crerar. 2000. Ethnography, theory, and systems design: From intuition to insight. *International Journal of Human–Computer Studies* 53: 35–60.

MacIntyre, B., E. Mynatt, S. Voida, K. Hansen, J. Tullio, and G. Corso. 2001. Support for multitasking and background awareness using interactive peripheral displays. In *Proceedings of the 14th Annual ACM Symposium on User Interface Software and Technology,* pp. 41–50. Orlando, Florida, November 11–14.

Mackay, W. 1990. Patterns of sharing customizable software. In *Proceedings of ACM Conference on Computer-Supported Cooperative Work,* pp. 209–221. Los Angeles, October 7–10.

Mahring, M., J. Holmström, M. Keil, and R. Montealegre. 2004. Trojan actor-networks and swift translation: Bringing actor-network theory to project escalation studies. *Information Technology and People* 17: 210–238.

Malinowski, B. 1922. *Argonauts of the Western Pacific.* New York: E. P. Dutton.

Malone, T. 1983. How do people organize their desks? Implications for the design of office information systems. *ACM Transactions on Office Information Systems* 1: 99–112.

Mannheim, K. 1936. *Ideology and Utopia: An Introduction to Sociology of Knowledge.* New York: Harvest/Harcourt, Brace, Jovanovich.

Mark, G., V. González, and J. Harris. 2005. No task left behind? Examining the nature of fragmented work. In *Proceedings of the 2005 ACM Conference on Human Factors in Computing Systems*, pp. 321–330. Portland, Oregon, April 2–7.

Marx, K., and F. Engels. 1976. *The German Ideology*. Moscow: Progress Publishers. (Originally published in 1846.)

Maslow, A. 1968. *Toward a Psychology of Being*. New York: Wiley.

Maslow, A. 1970. *Motivation and Personality*. New York: Harper and Row.

Mayer, R. 1988. From novice to expert III. Individual differences and training. In M. Helander (ed.), *Handbook of Human–Computer Interaction*, pp. 569–580. New York: North Holland.

McCarthy, J., and P. Wright. 2004. *Technology as Experience*. Cambridge, Mass.: MIT Press.

McClelland, D. 1988. *Human Motivation*. Cambridge: Cambridge University Press.

McGrenere, J., and W. Ho. 2000. Affordances: Clarifying and evolving a concept. In *Proceedings of Graphic Interface 2000*, pp. 179–186. Montreal, Canada, May.

Mercader, J., M. Panger, and C. Boesch. 2002. Excavation of a chimpanzee stone tool site in the African rainforest. *Science* 296: 1452–1455.

Merlin, V. S. 1975. Psychological views of M. Ya. Basov. In M. Ya. Basov, *Izbrannye Psikhologicheskie Proizvedenija* [Selected Psychological Works], pp. 5–25. Moscow: Pedagogika. (In Russian.)

Middle-Length Discourses of the Buddha. 1995. Boston: Wisdon Publications.

Middleton, D., and S. Brown. 2002. The baby as a virtual object: Agency and stability in a neonatal care unt. *Athenea Digital* 1 (spring): 1–23.

Miettinen, R. 1998. Object construction and networks in research work. *Social Studies of Science* 28: 423–463.

Miettinen, R. 1999. The riddle of things: Activity theory and actor-network theory as approaches to studying innovation. *Mind, Culture, and Activity: An International Journal* 6: 170–195.

Miettinen, R. 2002. Trajectories of artifact creation and the object of activity. Paper presented at the Fifth Congress of the International Society for Cultural Research and Activity Theory (ISCRAT 2002). Amsterdam, The Netherlands, June 18–22.

Millen, D., M. Muller, W. Geyer, E. Wilcox, and B. Brownholtz. 2005. Media choices in an activity-centric collaborative environment. In *Proceedings of the 2005 ACM Conference on Human Factors in Computing Systems*, pp. 270–277. New York: ACM Press.

Moran, T. 2003. Activity: Analysis, design, and management. Paper given at the Symposium on the Foundations of Interaction Design, Interaction Design Institute, Ivrea, Italy. Available at http://www.interaction-ivrea.it/en/news/education/2003-04/symposium/programme/moran/index.asp/.

Mortensen, M., and P. Hinds. 2001. Fuzzy teams: Boundary disagreement in distributed and collocated teams. In P. Hinds and S. Kiesler, *Distributed Work*, pp. 283–308. Cambridge, Mass.: MIT Press.

Morteo, R., V. Gonzalez, J. Favela, and G. Mark. 2004. Sphere Juggler: Fast context retrieval in support of working spheres. In *Proceedings of ENC (Encuentro Internacional de Ciencias de la Computacion) 2004: Fifth Mexican International Conference on Computer Science*, pp. 361–367. Los Alamitos, Calif.: IEEE Press.

Muller, M. 1999. Invisible work of telephone operators: An ethnocritical analysis. *Computer Supported Cooperative Work: The Journal of Collaborative Computing* 8: 31–61.

Muller, M., E. Christiansen, B. Nardi, and S. Dray. 2001. Spiritual life and information technology. *Communications of the ACM* 4: 82–84.

Muller, M., W. Geyer, B. Brownholtz, E. Wilcox, and D. Millen. 2004. One hundred days in an activity-centric collaboration environment based on shared objects. In *Proceedings of the 2004 ACM Conference on Human Factors in Computing Systems*, pp. 375–382. Vienna, Austria, April 24–19.

Mumford, L. 1934. *Technics and Civilization*. New York: Harcourt, Brace, and World.

Munipov, V. 1983. Vklad A. N. Leontjeva v razvitie inzhenernoj psikhologii i ergonomiki [Leont'ev's contribution to engineering psychology and ergonomics]. In A. Zaporozhets, V. Zinchenko, O. Ovchinnikova, and O. Tikhomirov (eds.), *A. N. Leontiev i sovremennaja psikhologija* [A. N. Leontiev and Contemporary Psychology], pp. 88–96. Moscow: Izdatelstvo MGU 1983. (In Russian.)

Mwanza, D. 2000. *Mind the Gap: Activity Theory and Design*. KMi Technical Reports (KMI-TR-95).

Mwanza, D. 2002a. Conceptualising work activity for CAL systems design. *Journal of Computer Assisted Learning* 18: 84–92.

Mwanza, D. 2002b. Towards an Activity-Oriented Design Method for HCI Research and Practice. Ph.D. dissertation, The Open University, UK.

Nardi, B. 1992. Studying context: A comparison of activity theory, situated action models, and distributed cognition. In *Proceedings of the 1992 East-West International HCI Conference*, pp. 352–359. EWHCI'92. St. Petersburg, Russia, August 4–8.

Nardi, B. 1993. *A Small Matter of Programming*. Cambridge, Mass.: MIT Press.

Nardi, B. 1994. Studying task-specificity; or, How we could have done it right the first time with activity theory. In *Proceedings East-West International Conference on Human–computer Interaction*, pp. 1–6. St. Petersburg, Russia, August 2–6.

Nardi, B. (ed.). 1996a. *Context and Consciousness: Activity Theory and Human–Computer Interaction*. Cambridge, Mass.: MIT Press.

Nardi, B. 1996b. Some reflections on the application of activity theory. In B. Nardi (ed.), *Context and Consciousness: Activity Theory and Human–Computer Interaction*, pp. 235–246. Cambridge, Mass.: MIT Press.

Nardi, B. 1996c. Studying context: A comparison of activity theory, situated action models, and distributed cognition. In B. Nardi (ed.), *Context and Consciousness: Activity Theory and Human–Computer Interaction*, pp. 69–102. Cambridge, Mass.: MIT Press.

Nardi, B. 1998. Concepts of cognition and consciousness: Four Voices. *ACM Journal of Computer Documentation* 22: 31–48.

Nardi, B. 2005. Objects of desire: Power and passion in collaborative activity. *Mind, Culture, and Activity: An International Journal* 12: 37–51.

Nardi, B., K. Anderson, and T. Erickson. 1995. Filing and finding computer files. In *Proceedings East-West Conference on Human Computer Interaction*, pp. 162–179. Moscow, Russia, July 4–8.

Nardi, B., J. Miller, and D. Wright. 1998. Collaborative, programmable intelligent agents. *Communications of the ACM* 41: 96–104.

Nardi, B., and V. O'Day. 1999. *Information Ecologies: Using Technology with Heart*. Cambridge, Mass.: MIT Press.

Nardi, B., H. Schwarz, A. Kuchinsky, R. Leichner, S. Whittaker, and R. Sclabassi. 1993. Turning away from talking heads: Video-as-data in neurosurgery. In *Proceedings InterCHI 93*, pp. 327–334. New York: ACM.

Nardi, B., S. Whittaker, E. Isaacs, M. Creech, J. Johnson, and J. Hainsworth. 2002. Integrating communication and information through ContactMap. *Communications of the ACM* 45: 89–95.

Nardi, B., S. Whittaker, and H. Schwarz. 2002. NetWORKers and their activity in intensional networks. *Computer Supported Cooperative Work: The Journal of Collaborative Computing* 11: 205–242.

Newell, A., P. Rosenbloom, and J. Laird. 1989. Symbolic architectures for cognition. In M. Posner (ed.), *Foundations of Cognitive Science*, pp. 93–131. Cambridge, Mass.: MIT Press.

Nicolini, D., S. Gherardi, and D. Yanow. 2003. Introduction: Toward a practice-based view of knowing and learning in organizations. In D. Nicolini, S. Gherardi, and D. Yanow (eds.), *Knowing in Organizations: A Practice-Based Approach*, pp. 3–31. Armonk, N.Y.: Sharpe.

Nielsen, J. 1986. A virtual protocol model for computer–human interaction. *International Journal of Man–Machine Studies* 24: 301–312.

Norman, D. 1988. *The Psychology of Everyday Things*. New York: Basic Books.

Norman, D. 1991. Cognitive artifacts. In J. Carroll (ed.), *Designing Interaction: Psychology at the Human–Computer Interface*, pp. 17–38. Cambridge: Cambridge University Press.

Norman, D. 1993. *Things That Make Us Smart: Defending Human Attributes in the Age of the Machine*. Reading, Mass.: Addison-Wesley.

Norman, D. 1998. *The Invisible Computer: Why Good Products Can Fail, the Personal Computer Is So Complex, and Information Appliances Are the Solution.* Cambridge, Mass.: MIT Press.

Norman, D. 1999. Affordance, conventions, and design. *interactions* 6: 38–42.

Norman, D. 2004. *Emotional Design: Why We Love (Or Hate) Everyday Things.* New York: Basic Books.

Norman, D., and S. Draper (eds.). 1986. *User-Centered System Design: New Perspectives on Human–Computer Interaction.* Hillsdale, N.J.: Lawrence Erlbaum.

O'Malley, C. (ed.). 1995. *Computer-Supported Collaborative Learning.* Berlin: Springer.

Orlikowski, W. 1992. Learning from Notes: Organizational issues in groupware implementation. In *Proceedings of the 1998 ACM Conference on Computer-Supported Collaborative Work*, pp. 362–369. Toronto, Ontario, Canada, November 1–4.

Orlikowski, W., and M. Tyre. 1994. Windows of opportunity: Temporal patterns of technological adaptation in organizations. *Organization Science* 5: 98–118.

Ozhegov, S. 1982. *Slovar Russkogo Yazyka, 14-e izdanie* [Dictionary of the Russian Language, 14th edition]. Moscow: Russky Yazyk. (In Russian.)

Pea, R. 1993. Practices of distributed intelligence and designs for education. In G. Salomon (ed.), *Distributed Cognition: Psychological and Educational Considerations*, pp. 47–87. New York: Cambridge University Press.

Pea, R. 1999. New media communication forums for improving education research and practice. In E. Lagemann and L. Shulman (eds.), *Issues in Education Research: Problems and Possibilities*, pp. 336–370. San Francisco: Jossey Bass.

Pederson, T. 2001. Magic Touch: A simple object location tracking system enabling the development of physical-virtual artefacts in office environments. *Journal of Personal and Ubiquitous Computing* 5: 54–57.

Perkins, D. 1993. Person plus: A distributed view of thinking and learning. In G. Salomon (ed.), *Distributed Cognitions: Psychological and Educational Considerations*, pp. 88–110. New York: Cambridge University Press.

Petrovsky, A. 1975. K psikhologii aktivnosti lichnosti [On the psychology of the activity of personality]. *Voprosy Psikhologii* 1975 (3): 26–38. (In Russian.)

Petrovsky A., and V. Petrovsky. 1983. Lichnost I ee razvitie v svete idej A. N. Leontieva [Personality and its activity in the light of A. N. Leontiev's ideas]. In A. Zaporozhets, V. Zinchenko, O. Ovchinnikova, and O. Tikhomirov (eds.), *A. N. Leontiev i Sovremennaja Psikhologija* [A. N. Leontiev and Contemporary Psychology], pp. 231–239. Moscow: Izdatelstvo MGU. (In Russian.)

Piaget, J. 1952. *The Origins of Intelligence in Children.* New York: W. W. Norton.

Picard, R. 1997. *Affective Computing.* Cambridge, Mass.: MIT Press.

Pickering, A. 1993. The mangle of practice: Agency and emergence in the sociology of science. *American Journal of Sociology* 99: 559–589.

Pickering, A. 1995. *The Mangle of Practice: Time, Agency, and Science.* Chicago: University of Chicago Press.

Pirhonen, A., H. Isomäki, C. Roast, and P. Saariluoma (eds.). 2005. *Future Interaction Design.* London: Springer-Verlag.

Pollner, M. 1991. Left of ethnomethodology. *American Sociological Review* 56: 370–380.

Postman, N. 1993. *Technopoly: The Surrender of Culture to Technology.* New York: Vintage Books.

Preece, J., Y. Rogers, and H. Sharp. 2002. *Interaction Design: Beyond Human–Computer Interaction.* New York: John Wiley and Sons.

Quek, A., and H. Shah. 2004. A comparative survey of activity-based methods for information systems development. In *Proceedings of the 6th International Conference on Enterprise Information Systems (ICEIS)*, pp. 221–232. Porto, Portugal, April 14–17.

Rabardel, P., and G. Bourmaud. 2003. From computer to instrument system: A developmental perspective. *Interacting with Computers* 15: 665–691.

Radzikhovsky, L. 1983. Dejatelnost: Struktura, genez, edinitsy analiza [Activity: Structure, genesis, and units of analysis]. *Voprosy Psikhologii* 1983 (6): 121–127. (In Russian.)

Rae, J. 1994. Social fax: Repair mechanisms and intersubjectivity. *American Behavioral Scientist* 37: 824–838.

Raeithel, A. 1992. Activity theory as a foundation for design. In C. Floyd, H. Zullighoven, R. Budde, and R. Keil-Slawik (eds.), *Software Development and Reality Construction*, pp. 391–415. Berlin: Springer.

Raeithel, A. 1996. From coordinatedness to coordination via cooperation and co-construction. Paper presented at the Workshop on Work and Learning in Transition. San Diego, Calif., January.

Ravasio, P., S. Guttormsen-Schär, and H. Krueger. 2004. In pursuit of desktop evolution: User problems and practices with modern desktop systems. *ACM Transactions on Human Computer Interaction* 11: 156–180.

Reynolds, C. 1987. Flocks, herds, and schools: A distributed behavioral model. *Computer Graphics* 21: 25–34.

Rich, C., and C. Sidner. 1997. Segmented interaction history in a collaborative interface agent planning based approaches. In *Proceedings of the Second International Conference on Intelligent User Interfaces*, pp. 23–30. Orlando, Florida, January 6–9.

Robertson, G., M. van Dantzich, D. Robbins, M. Czerwinski, K. Hinckly, K. Risden, D. Thiel, and V. Gorokhovsky. 2000. The task gallery: A 3D window manager. In *Proceedings of the 2000 ACM Conference on Human Factors in Computing Systems*, pp. 494–501. The Hague, the Netherlands, April 1–6.

Robertson, S. 2005. A contextual, voter-centered approach to the design of electronic ballot systems. *ACM Transactions on Computer–Human Interaction* 12: 263–292.

Robinson, M. 1980. *Housekeeping.* New York: Farrar, Straus, and Giroux.

Rogers, Y., and J. Ellis. 1994. Distributed cognition: An alternative framework for analysing and explaining collaborative working. *Journal of Information Technology* 9: 119–128.

Rorty, R. 1991. *Objectivity, Relativism, and Truth: Philosophical Papers,* vol. 1. Cambridge: Cambridge University Press.

Roschelle, J., and R. Pea. 2002. A walk on the WILD side: How wireless handhelds may change CSCL. In *Proceedings of the 2002 Conference on Computer Support for Collaborative Learning: Foundations for a CSCL Community,* pp. 51–60. Boulder, Colorado, January 7–11.

Rose, J., M. Jones, and D. Truex. 2005. Socio-theoretic accounts of IS: The problem of agency. *Scandinavian Journal of Information Systems* 17: 133–152.

Roth, W.-M. 2004. Activity theory and education: An introduction. *Mind, Culture, and Activity: An International Journal* 11: 1–8.

Roth, W.-M. 2006. Motive, emotion, and identity at work: A contribution to third-generation cultural historical activity theory. *Mind, Culture, and Activity* 13(3).

Roth, W.-M. In press. Mathematical modeling "in the wild": A case of hot cognition. In R. Lesh, J. Kaput, E. Hamilton, and J. Zawojewski (eds.), *Users of Mathematics: Foundations for the Future.* Mahwah, N.J.: Lawrence Erlbaum.

Rubinshtein, S. L. 1946. *Osnovy Obschej Psikhologii, 2-e izdanie* [Foundations of General Psychology, second edition]. Moscow: Uchpedgiz. (In Russian; originally published 1940).

Russell, D., N. Streitz, and T. Winograd. 2005. Building disappearing computers. *Communications of the ACM* 48: 42–48.

Saari, E. 2003. The pulse of change in research work: A study of learning and development in a research group. Ph.D. dissertation, University of Helsinki, Department of Education.

Saari, E., and R. Miettinen. 2001. Dynamics of change in research work: Constructing a new research area in a research group. *Science, Technology, and Human Values* 26: 300–321.

Sachs, P. 1995. Transforming work: Collaboration, learning, and design. *Communications of the ACM* 38: 36–44.

Salomon, G. (ed.). 1993. *Distributed Cognition: Psychological and Educational Considerations.* Cambridge: Cambridge University Press.

Salomon, G., and D. Perkins. 1998. Individual and social aspects of learning. *Review of Research in Education* 23. Available at http://construct.haifa.ac.il/~gsalomon/indsoc.htm/.

Sandberg, J., and R. Wielinga. 1993. Situated cognition: A paradigm shift? *Journal of Artificial Intelligence in Education* 3: 129–138.

Schatzki, T., K. Knorr Cetina, and E. von Savigny (eds.). 2001. *The Practice Turn in Contemporary Theory*. London, Routledge.

Schegloff, E., G. Jefferson, and H. Sacks. 1977. The preference for self-correction in the organization of repair in conversation. *Language* 53: 361–382.

Sclove, R. 1995. *Democracy and Technology*. New York: Guilford Press.

Scribner, S., and P. Sachs. 1990. On the job-training. IEE Document no. B-9, August.

Searle, J. 1995. The mystery of consciousness. *New York Review of Books* (November 2 and 16): 22–31.

Seitz, J. 2003. A communitarian approach to creativity. *Mind, Culture, and Activity: An International Journal* 11: 245–249.

Shaffer, D., and K. Clinton. In press. Toolforthoughts: Reexamining thinking in the digital age. Forthcoming in *Mind, Culture, and Activity: An International Journal*.

Shapiro, D. 2000. Technologies for self-organization. In Y. Dittrich, C. Floyd, N. Jayaratna, F. Kensing, and R. Klischewski (eds.), *Social Thinking—Software Practice*, pp. 76–79. Dagstuhl Seminar Report 250. Schloss Dagstuhl, Germany: IBFI.

Sharples, M. 2000. The design of personal mobile technologies for lifelong learning. *Computers and Education* 34: 177–193.

Shneiderman, B. 1983. Direct manipulation: A step beyond programming languages. *IEEE Computer* 16: 57–69.

Shneiderman, B. 1998. *Designing the User Interface: Strategies for Effective Human–Computer Interaction*, 3rd ed. Boston, Mass.: Addison-Wesley.

Shneiderman, B. 1999. *The Future of History*. Available at http://www.cs.umd.edu/hcil/about/events/history-workshop/slides/Shneiderman/index.htm/.

Shneiderman, B. 2002. *Leonardo's Laptop*. Cambridge, Mass.: MIT Press.

Simon, H. 1945. *Administrative Behavior*. New York: Free Press.

Simon, H., and C. Kaplan. 1989. Foundations of cognitive science. In M. Posner (ed.), *Foundations of Cognitive Science*, pp. 1–47. Cambridge, Mass.: MIT Press.

Smith, A. 2003 (1776). *An Inquiry into the Nature and Causes of the Wealth of Nations*. New York: Bantam Classics.

Smith, D., C. Irby, R. Kimball, W. Verplank, and E. Harslem. 1982. Designing the Star user interface. *Byte* 7: 242–282.

Spinuzzi, C. 2003. *Tracing Genres through Organizations: A Sociocultural Approach to Information Design*. Cambridge, Mass.: MIT Press.

Stahl, G. 2006. *Group Cognition: Computer Support for Building Collaborative Knowledge*. Cambridge, Mass.: MIT Press.

Stetsenko, A. 1995. The role of the principle of object-relatedness in the theory of activity. *Journal of Russian and East European Psychology* 33: 54–69.

Stetsenko, A. 2005. Activity as object-related: Resolving the dichotomy of individual and collective planes of activity. *Mind, Culture, and Activity: An International Journal* 12: 70–88.

Stetsenko, A., and I. Arievitch. 1997. Constructing and deconstructing the self: Comparing post-Vygotskian and discourse-based versions of social constructivism. *Mind, Culture, and Activity: An International Journal* 4: 160–173.

Suchman, L. 1987. *Plans and Situated Actions*. Cambridge: Cambridge University Press.

Suchman, L. 2000. Embodied practices of engineering work. *Mind, Culture, and Activity: An International Journal* 7: 4–18.

Suchman, L., and R. Trigg. 1992. Understanding practice: Video as a medium for reflection and design. In J. Greenbaum and M. Kyng (eds.), *Design at Work: Cooperative Design of Computer Systems*, pp. 65–89. Hillsdale, N.J.: Lawrence Erlbaum.

Sutter, B. 2002a. Instructional artifacts. In G. Stahl (ed.), *Computer Support for Cooperative Learning: Foundations for a CSCL Community, Proceedings of CSCL 2002*, pp. 33–42. Boulder, Colorado, January 7–11. Mahwah, N.J.: Lawrence Erlbaum.

Sutter, B. 2002b. Design at heart: Activity-theoretical studies of learning and development in coronary clinical work. Ph.D. dissertation, Department of Human Work Science and Media Technology, Blekinge Institute of Technology, Sweden.

Sutter, B. 2002c. The guiding function of the object of work. Paper presented at the Fifth Congress of the International Society for Cultural Research and Activity Theory (ISCRAT 2002). Amsterdam, the Netherlands, June 18–22.

Taylor, C. 1985. What is human agency? In his *Philosophical Papers*, vol. 1, pp. 15–44. Cambridge: Cambridge University Press.

Tenner, E. 1997. *Why Things Bite Back: Technology and the Revenge of Unintended Consequences*. New York: Vintage Books.

Tetzlaff, L., and R. Mack. 1991. Discussion: Perspectives on methodology in HCI research and practice. In J. Carroll (ed.), *Designing Interaction: Psychology at the Human–Computer Interface*, pp. 286–314. Cambridge: Cambridge University Press.

Thomas, J., and W. Kellogg. 1989. Minimizing ecological gaps in user interface design. *IEEE Software* 14: 78–86.

Tomlinson, B. 2005. Social characters for computer games. *International Journal of Interactive Technology and Smart Education* 2: 101–115.

Torenvliet, G. 2003. We can't afford it! The devaluation of a usability term. *interactions* 10: 12–17.

Toulmin, S. 1978. The Mozart of psychology. *New York Review of Books* 25: 51–57.

Turner, P., S. Turner, and J. Horton. 1999. From description to requirements: An activity theoretic perspective. In *Proceedings of the 1999 International ACM SIGGROUP Conference on Supporting Group Work*, pp. 286–295. Phoenix, Arizona, November 14–17.

Uden, L., and N. Willis. 2001. Designing user interfaces using activity theory. In *Proceedings of the 34th Hawaii International Conference on System Sciences (HICSS 43)*, v. 5, p. 5031. Full text available at http://csdl2.computer.org/persagen/DLPublication.jsp?pubtype=p&acronym=hicss/.

Ukhtomsky, A. 1978. *Izbrannye trudy* [Selected works]. Leningrad: Nanka. (In Russian.)

Velichkovsky, B. 1982. Funktsionalnaja struktura perteptivnyh protsessov [The functional structure of perceptual processes]. In A. V. Zaporozhets, B. F. Lomov, and V. P. Zinchenko (eds.), *Poznavatelnye pprotsessy: Oschuschenija, Vosprijatie* [Cognitive Processes: Sensations and Perception], pp. 219–246. Moscow: Pedagogika. (In Russian.)

Verenikina, I., and E. Gould. 1998. Cultural-historical psychology and activity theory. In H. Hasan, E. Gould, and P. Hyland (eds.), *Information Systems and Activity Theory: Tools in Context*, pp. 7–18. Wollongong: University of Wollongong Press.

Vergnaud, G., and M. Récopé. 2000. *De Renault d'Allonnes à une théorie du schème aujourd'hui. Psychologie Française* 45: 35–50.

Vitousek, P., A. Mooney, J. Lubchenco, and J. Melillo. 1997. Human domination of Earth's ecosystems. *Science* 277: 494–499.

Voida, S., E. Mynatt, B. MacIntyre, and G. Corso. 2002. Integrating virtual and physical context to support knowledge workers. *IEEE Pervasive Computing* 1: 73–79.

von Goethe, J. W. 1808. *Faust*. Translated by G. M. Priest. Retrieved from http://pinkmonkey.com/dl/library1/faust.pdf/ on September 6, 2005.

Vygotsky, L. 1978. *Mind in Society: The Development of Higher Psychological Processes*. Cambridge, Mass.: Harvard University Press.

Vygotsky, L. 1982a. Instrumentalnyj metod v psikhologii [Instrumental method in psychology]. In A. Luria and M. Yaroshevsky (eds.), L. S. Vygotsky, *Sobranie Sochinanij*, t. 1 [L. S. Vygotsky, *Collected Works*, vol. 1], pp. 103–109. Moscow: Pedagogika. (In Russian.)

Vygotsky, L. 1982b. Myshlenie i rech [Thinking and speech]. In V. Davydov (ed.), L. S. Vygotsky, *Sobranie Sochinanij*, t. 2 [L. S. Vygotsky, *Collected Works*, vol. 2], pp. 5–361. Moscow: Pedagogika. (In Russian.)

Vygotsky, L. 1983. Istorija razvitija vysshyh psikhicheskih funktsij [The history of the development of higher psychological functions]. In A. Matyushkin (ed.), L. S. Vygotsky, *Sobranie Sochinanij*, t. 3 [L. S. Vygotsky, *Collected Works*, vol. 3], pp. 5–328. Moscow: Pedagogika. (In Russian.)

Vygotsky, L. 1986. *Thought and Language*. Cambridge, Mass.: MIT Press.

Want, R., and A. Hopper. 1992. The active badge locator system. *ACM Transactions on Office Information Systems* 10: 91–102.

Wartofsky, M. 1979. *Models*. Dordrecht: D. Reidel.

Waste in the Wireless World: The Challenges of Cell Phones. INFORM, Inc. 2002. 120 Wall St. 16th Floor, NY, NY. 10005. Http://www.informinc.org/wirelesswaste.php/.

Watson, J. 1913. Psychology as a behaviorist views it. *Psychological Review* 23: 150–177.

Weber, M. 1947. *The Theory of Social and Economic Organization*. London: William Hodge.

Wellman, B. 2001. Computer networks as social networks. *Science* 293: 2031–2034.

Wells, G. 2000. From action to writing: Modes of representing and knowing. In J. Astington (ed.), *Minds in the Making*. Oxford: Blackwell.

Wertheimer, M. 1961. *Productive Thinking*. London: Tavistock.

Wertsch, J. 1981. The concept of activity in Soviet psychology: An introduction. In J. Wertsch (ed.), *The Concept of Activity in Soviet Psychology*, pp. 3–36. Armonk, N.Y.: M. E. Sharpe.

Wertsch, J. (ed.). 1985. *Culture, Communication, and Cognition: Vygotskian Perspectives*. Cambridge: Cambridge University Press.

Wertsch, J. 1998. *Mind as Action*. New York: Oxford University Press.

Wexelblat, A., and P. Maes. 1999. Footprints: History-rich tools for information foraging. In *Proceedings of the 1999 ACM Conference on Human Factors in Computing Systems*, pp. 270–277. Pittsburgh, Pennsylvania, May 15–20.

Whang, L., and J. Kim. 2005. The comparison of online game experiences by players in games of Lineage & EverQuest: Role play vs. consumption. In *Proceedings Digital Games Research Association Conference*. Burnaby, Canada.

Whittaker, S., L. Terveen, and B. Nardi. 2000. Let's stop pushing the envelope and start addressing it: A reference task agenda for HCI. *Human Computer Interaction* 15: 75–106.

Wiberg, M. 2000. Bridging physical and virtual group meetings with a PC and multiple hand-held devices. In *Extended Abstracts of the 2000 ACM Conference on Human Factors in Computing Systems*, pp. 367–358. The Hague, the Netherlands, April 1–6.

Wilson, E. O. 1975. *Sociobiology: The New Synthesis*. Cambridge, Mass.: Belknap Press.

Window Managers for X: The Basics. N.d. Retrieved from http://xwinman.org/basics.php/ on September 6, 2005.

Winner, L. 1977. *Autonomous Technology: Technic Out of Control as a Theme in Political Thought*. Cambridge, Mass.: MIT Press.

Winner, L. 1986. *The Whale and the Reactor: A Search for Limits in an Age of High Technology.* Chicago: University of Chicago Press.

Winner, L. 2003. *Langdon Winner's Testimony to the Committee on Science of the U.S. House of Representatives on the Societal Implications of Nanotechnology.* Retrieved from http://www.rpi.edu/%7Ewinner/testimony.htm/ on September 3, 2005.

Winograd, T. (ed.). 1996. *Bringing Design to Software.* New York: Addison-Wesley.

Winograd, T., and F. Flores. 1986. *Understanding Computers and Cognition.* Norwood, N.J.: Ablex.

Wiredu, G. 2005. Mobile computing in work-integrated learning: Problems of remotely-distributed activities and technology use. Ph.D. dissertation, Department of Information Systems, London School of Economics and Political Science, University of London.

Wroblewski, D. 1991. The construction of human–computer interfaces considered as a craft. In J. Karat (ed.), *Taking Software Design Seriously,* pp. 1–19. Boston: Academic Press.

Yaroshevsky, M. 1993. *L. S. Vygosky: V Poiskah Novoj Psikhologii* [L. S. Vygotsky: In Search for the New Psychology]. St. Petersburg: Publishing House of the International Foundation for History of Science. (In Russian.)

Yaroshevsky, M. 1996. *Nauka o Povedenii: Russkij Put. Izbrannye Psikhologicheskie Trudy* [Behavioral Science: The Russian Way. Selected Psychological Works]. Moscow: Academy of Educational and Social Pedagogical Sciences. (In Russian.)

Yaroshevsky, M., I. Sirotkina, and N. Danilicheva. 1993. Pioner dejatelnostnogo podhoda (K 100-letiju so dnja rozhdenija M. Ya. Basova) [A pioneer of the activity approach (On 100th anniversary of M. Ya. Basov's birthday)]. *Psikhologicheskij Zhurnal* 14 (1): 156–169. (In Russian.)

Yee, N. 2002. Befriending ogres and wood-elves: Understanding relationship formation in MMORPGs. Http://www.nickyee.com/hub/relationships/home.html/.

Zager, D. 2002. Collaboration as an activity: Coordinating with pseudo-collective objects. *Computer Supported Cooperative Work: The Journal of Collaborative Computing* 11: 181–204.

Zimmerman, A. 2003. Data sharing and secondary use of scientific data: Experiences of ecologists. Ph.D. dissertation, Information and Library Studies, University of Michigan, Ann Arbor.

Zinchenko, V. 1971. Produktivnoe vosprijatie [Productive perception]. *Voprosy Psikhologii* 1971 (6): 27–42. (In Russian.)

Zinchenko, V. 1993. Kulturno-istoricheskaya psikhologija i psikhologicheskaja teotija dejatelnosti: Zhivye protivorechija i tochki rosta [Cultural-historical psychology and psychological activity theory: Living contradictions and points of growth]. *Vestnik MGU. Serija 14. Psikhologija* 1993 (2): 41–50. (In Russian.)

Zinchenko, V. 1996. Developing activity theory: The zone of proximal development and beyond. In B. Nardi (ed.), *Context and Consciousness: Activity Theory and Human–Computer Interaction*, pp. 283–324. Cambridge, Mass.: MIT Press.

Zinchenko, V., and V. Gordon. 1976. Metodologicheskie problemy psikhologicheskogo analiza dejatelnosti [Methodological problems of psychological analysis of activity]. *Sistemnye issledovanija. Ezhegodnik*. 1975 [Systems Studies. Annual Review 1975] 16: 129–150. (In Russian.)

Zinchenko, V., A. Leontiev, and D. Panov. 1964. Problemy inzhenernoj psikhologii [Problems of engineering psychology]. In *Inzhenernaja Psikhologija* [Engineering Psychology], pp. 5–23. Moscow: Izdatelstvo MGU. (In Russian.)

Zinchenko, V., and V. Munipov. 1979. *Osnovy Ergonomiki* [Foundations of ergonomics]. Moscow: Izdatelstvo MGU. (In Russian.)

Index